D0896331

TEEMU
SELANNE

TEEMU SELANNE

My Life

Teemu Selanne with Ari Mennander

HarperCollins*Publishers*Ltd

My Life
Copyright © 2019 by Ari Mennander and Teemu Selanne
All rights reserved.

Published by HarperCollins Publishers Ltd, by arrangement with Triumph Books.

First published in Canada by HarperCollins Publishers Ltd in a hardcover edition: 2019
This trade paperback edition: 2020

No part of this book may be used or reproduced in any manner whatsoever without the prior
written permission of the publisher, except in the case of brief quotations embodied in reviews.

HarperCollins books may be purchased for educational, business or
sales promotional use through our Special Markets Department.

HarperCollins Publishers Ltd
Bay Adelaide Centre, East Tower
22 Adelaide Street West, 41st Floor
Toronto, Ontario, Canada
M5H 4E3

www.harpercollins.ca

Library and Archives Canada Cataloguing in Publication
Title: My life / Teemu Selanne with Ari Mennander.
Other titles: Teemu Selanne : my life
Names: Selanne, Teemu, 1970- author. | Mennander, Ari, 1965- author.
Identifiers: Canadiana 20200183303 | ISBN 9781443460194 (softcover)
Subjects: LCSH: Selanne, Teemu, 1970- | LCSH: Hockey players—Finland—Biography. |
LCGFT: Autobiographies. | Classification: LCC GV848.5.S45 A3 2020 | DDC 796.962092—dc23

Translation and additional reporting by: Risto Pakarinen, Alan Adams,
Arthur Pincus, and Joe Pascucci.

Design by Nord Compo

Photos courtesy of Teemu Selanne unless otherwise indicated.

Printed and bound in the United States of America
LSC/C 9 8 7 6 5 4 3 2 1

To Mom and Dad,
without whom none of this would have been possible.

CONTENTS

Part Three

Part Four

INTRODUCTION

I **WAS BORN INTO A FAMILY THAT BELIEVED IN DREAMS** and hard work. My family had nothing in excess. We lived within our means, and we never felt we needed anything more than we had.

My mother's upbringing helped me throughout my life. She taught me I may not like every person I meet, but I can get along with almost everybody. She taught me to respect others and to treat people as I would want them to treat me. Mom gave me warmth and love.

Dad taught me the importance of ambition and that what goes around comes around. He once told me that loving what you do is one of the best things that could ever happen to you. I remember him telling me that even if you're not good at something, even if you struggle doing it, if you really love what you are doing, no matter what it is—whether you're a plumber or a physician—then it's what you should do. His credo was if you are passionate about something, and you work hard at it and you are willing to make sacrifices, then the sky is the limit.

My parents gave me the keys to my dream when I was 12 years old. They saw how much I loved hockey—how much I loved lacing up my skates, putting on the gear, and stepping onto the ice, stick in hand. And as loving parents, they supported me so I could chase my dream. They also told me if hockey did not work, I could always go back to school. "If you're ready to do your best, we'll do our best to support you. But if you're not fully committed to giving it your all, that's the end," they said.

And that's why if I wasn't in bed by nine in the evening as we had agreed, I had to take the bus and train to practice. Simple as that.

For a few different reasons, the book you're about to read is written in the third person. Part of the reason why is that I wanted to include quotes from my friends, family members, and former teammates, who know me better than anyone. And part of it is that I wanted to make sure my story, translated into English, appeared exactly as I intended it. But I have been deeply involved in the writing and shaping of this book, and I hope you enjoy reading about my life as much as I enjoy living it.

—Teemu Selanne

PART ONE

A DREAM COME TRUE

Coto de Caza, California, June 6, 2007

Southern California was in the middle of a heat wave, with scorching temperatures and humidity turning the area saunalike. Most of the Anaheim Ducks players had spent the previous night at a hotel, but Teemu Selanne woke up at home. Hockey players are creatures of habit, and on the eve of the biggest game of his career to date, Selanne preferred sleeping in his own bed. It might have been the eve of Game 5 of the Stanley Cup Final, but Selanne treated it as just another home game, which meant familiar surroundings rather than a hotel room.

He ached all over. It had been a long season, and that night's pressure-packed game was going to be his 103rd of the season and the 21st in the grinding marathon known as the Stanley Cup playoffs. It would also be the Ducks' first chance to clinch the most desired championship in hockey, the Stanley Cup, the Holy Grail of the coolest game on ice.

"I slept at home before every home game because I slept much better there. Almost everybody else in the Ducks stayed at a hotel throughout the playoffs," Teemu said. "Although that night, I didn't sleep a wink. It was so hard to even sleep.

"Pretty much every night in the Finals I did not sleep that much. I was so tired and beaten up like everybody else at that point. The playoffs are two months of war, mentally and physically. It is so hard. Every shift is so challenging. During the season you can take shifts off but in the playoffs, one shift can change the whole thing.

"I knew what was at stake. Funny thing is, in the playoffs, your body is like a racehorse and is ready to go. I knew we could win the Stanley Cup that night, and I was awake and ready to go."

In 14 seasons with the Winnipeg Jets, the Mighty Ducks of Anaheim, the San Jose Sharks, and the Colorado Avalanche, Selanne had earned the reputation of a marksman, a skilled scorer. He had hands of gold and lightning-fast speed on the ice.

But one prize had escaped his clutches—the Stanley Cup. For players in the world's best professional hockey league, the NHL, nothing else compared and nothing else mattered. The Stanley Cup is the hardest club trophy to win; after a grinding, 82-game regular season, NHL teams have to endure the pressure-packed playoffs.

The closest thing to winning the Cup is winning an Olympic gold medal. Selanne's silver medal from the 2006 Torino Olympic Winter Games was merely a reminder that a championship team wins its last game of the season. You don't mine silver in hockey.

Players often play hurt, but they never play when they are injured, and Selanne's body ached all over. But he was determined not to let a championship slip away again, not when reaching the top was one victory away.

The Stanley Cup is extremely difficult to win: many, possibly most, players go an entire career without even having had the chance to play for it.

Selanne re-signed with the Ducks in 2005 and nobody knew if his wonky knee, which underwent reconstruction the year before, would hold up to the rigors of an 82-game schedule plus a punishing playoff run.

Selanne was a fan favorite during his first tour with Anaheim, and when he reached out to management about returning to the team, he told them he was willing to play "for nothing." "I didn't care about the money," he said. "I believed in the team and I wanted to stay at home."

His goal was to be on the first California-based team to win the Cup. And the Ducks were good; some said it was best Ducks team ever.

The old adage that timing is everything spoke to this point in Selanne's career. An ugly labor dispute between the NHL and the NHL Players' Association had wiped out the entire 2004–05 season. This provided Selanne ample time to recover from reconstructive knee surgery, timing that gave him a chance to heal.

His comeback was one for the ages. The veteran forward led his team in scoring in 2005–06 and in 2006–07 at the age of 35 and 36, respectively.

On the morning of Game 5 of the Stanley Cup Final against the Ottawa Senators, Teemu did what he had done thousands of times before. He woke up, ate a bowl of cereal with berries, had a coffee, and left for the rink.

No words were needed, and no words could have encapsulated the moment.

Family and friends have always meant everything to Selanne, and there was no chance he would not have shared this playoff run with those who meant the most to him. On hand at his sprawling home in Coto de Caza were Teemu's mother and father, Liisa and Ilmari; his twin brother, Paavo, and sister-in-law, Reija; his wife, Sirpa; and his mother-in-law, Terttu.

Ilmari and Liisa were separated by then, and Ilmari's new wife, Kirsi, hadn't been able make the trip for work reasons. Sirpa's father, Erkki, had been stopped from traveling on doctor's orders. Teemu's brother Panu didn't get a new passport in time and had to stay in Finland.

"I don't think many other players are used to having their mother and mother-in-law living with them during the playoffs," Teemu said with a laugh.

It's not like the Selanne household was an oasis of calm to begin with. Teemu and Sirpa had three boys under 12. Eemil was 11, Eetu, 9, and Leevi, 7, and it was constant chaos.

To add to the drama, Teemu and Sirpa were sitting on a secret they had shared only with their parents: Sirpa was pregnant. "We had always considered our family to be complete until I wanted to have another little baby," Sirpa said.

Not just a baby, though: a daughter. Teemu was excited about the idea of being a father to a girl. "I had never even given it a thought before," he said.

A fan had casually given him a copy of the book *How to Choose the Sex of Your Baby* years earlier, and when a family friend claimed to have had success following the book's instructions, Teemu and Sirpa decided to give it a shot.

Well, Sirpa got pregnant in April, during the first round of the Stanley Cup playoffs, in which the Ducks played the Minnesota Wild. Perhaps, Sirpa's pregnancy gave Teemu the distraction he needed off the ice; he believes it gave him an energy boost on the ice.

On the ice, the Ducks were unstoppable.

They beat the Minnesota Wild in five games and then took down the Vancouver Canucks in the second round of the playoffs. That set up a meeting against the powerhouse Detroit Red Wings in the Western Conference Final, and the Ducks were determined not to have history repeat. Anaheim had gone deep in the playoffs the year earlier, only to lose the conference final to the Edmonton Oilers in five games. In 2007, many experts expected them to get to at least the conference final again.

"We had been a big Stanley Cup favorite when the camps opened, and we were very driven from the get-go," Teemu said.

After breakfast, it was business as usual, as if Game 5 were just another day at the office. Teemu drove to the rink for the morning skate while Sirpa took the kids to school. The only slightly unusual thing about the lead-up to the game was that Sirpa and the kids would leave home for the game earlier than normal.

Teemu, meanwhile, went through his game-day routine and rituals without missing a step. He drove his silver Mercedes ML63 to the rink, blasting Finnish pop on the stereo. He parked his car in the Honda Center basement and said hello to the arena staff. He gave his keys to a guard.

"I was very calm and quiet. I did my normal routine. I had a cup of coffee, fixed my equipment, and stepped on the ice, just like before any other game. The locker room was very quiet. I think everyone else felt the same way. It was a good feeling, you could feel it, and everybody knew the situation.

"I remember being in the locker room and it was laser focus, everybody was on the same page. Guys are getting treatments, and there were many more guys than usual because everybody was beat up.

"I always said if I do not win this, it will be sad. I think I deserve this. People have no idea how hard it is to win the Stanley Cup. And even that year, I think back to how lucky you have to be. The breaks have to go your way."

The morning skate was a light one, and afterward Teemu rode the stationary bike before stretching. As his teammates showered and headed to the hotel, Selanne sat in front of his locker. It was the same stall he had had in his first stop in Anaheim after he was traded from Winnipeg in February 1996.

The media stood by, wanting to hear what the most important player in Anaheim's history had on his mind; Teemu had nothing but time for the media members. Teemu was living his dream and now, just a handful of hours before the most important game of his life, the affable Selanne was more than willing to share his thoughts with everybody.

"Teemu is the real thing. He's never disappointed me, and he always gives the most interesting comments," said Helene Elliott, *Los Angeles Times* columnist and the first female journalist to be inducted into the Hockey Hall of Fame.

Once the scrum was over, Selanne joined his teammates at the hotel for the pregame meal, rest, and final preparations. "I usually took a nap at the hotel and went back to the rink, but that day I couldn't sleep at all. I was so pumped for the game," he said.

The Ducks had won the first two games of the Cup Final at home 3–2 and 1–0, but the Senators cut the margin in half by winning their first home game 5–3. The Ducks took Game 4 by a 3–2 margin, leaving them one win short of the ultimate prize, which they now had a chance to win on home ice in front of their devoted fans.

As is customary in the NHL, when a team has a chance to clinch the Stanley Cup, the NHL makes sure the trophy is in the building, all shined up in the event of its being presented after that game.

"Everything had gone exactly according to plan. We had the opportunity to clinch it in our own arena, in front of our fans. We were in the zone in Game 5," Teemu said.

While Teemu was focusing on what would be the biggest game of his career, Sirpa was in charge of getting the rest of the clan to the rink. Her parents took the Selanne children to a luxury box they co-owned with Ducks captain Scott Niedermayer. Sirpa was across the street at a restaurant called JT Schmid's to meet up with Teemu's buddies and some Finnish fans before she joined other players' wives and girlfriends in the VIP area at the arena.

Teemu has always arranged for his friends to have tickets to his games, but the playoffs are unpredictable. A team can win the Cup in four games—or five, or six, or the best-of-seven Finals could go the distance. When Ottawa won Game 3, that meant there would be at least a Game 5 in Anaheim. Teemu started to scramble for the tickets.

Teemu has always been loyal to his family and friends. His hockey posse consisted of about 20 people, including childhood friends, more recent friends from the NHL cities he had played in, and friends of friends.

Teemu was close to a group of friends and family from Finland who faithfully followed his career once he made the jump to the NHL. He had promised to pay for their flights and hotels if the Ducks made it to the Stanley Cup Final, and Teemu's brother Paavo and seven others were on hand for the historic moment. The guys wore orange T-shirts that had Finnish flags and DUCKS and TEEMU featured on them.

Selanne's cheering section of Finnish celebrities included *Die Hard 2* and *The Long Kiss Goodnight* director Renny Harlin. His fans became media favorites as well, often shown on the scoreboard and in broadcasts. Reporters referred to them as "Crazy Finns."

Teemu was a longtime fan favorite in Anaheim, and it was common to see Ducks fans wearing his No. 8 jersey in the stands. In fact, seeing a Ducks jersey without the No. 8 on it was the anomaly.

The Selannes were treated like royalty. When Eemil, Eetu, and Leevi got restless and wanted to leave the private box at the arena, they could walk anywhere in the rink and the doors were opened for them. "The arena was like their second home," Teemu said.

As part of the in-game entertainment for the fans in the stands, facts, figures, and trivia relating to the Stanley Cup were displayed on the scoreboard at the Honda Center, and one popular item about the magical 2007 playoffs was about Teemu.

Of active players in the NHL, only the Vancouver Canucks' Trevor Linden and fellow Finn Teppo Numminen of the Buffalo Sabres had played more regular season games without winning the Stanley Cup than Teemu. Linden had played 1,323 games, Numminen 1,314, and

Teemu 1,041 without hoisting the trophy. Linden had come oh-so-close in 1994, going to Game 7 with the Canucks before losing to the New York Rangers.

The all-time leader in NHL games without winning the Cup is Selanne's former teammate, Phil Housley, who played 1,495 regular season games over 21 seasons.

Game 5, coincidentally, started at 5:00 PM Pacific Time to suit prime time television audiences in the Eastern US and Canada. In Finland, the puck dropped at 3:00 AM, and all major Finnish media had reporters in Anaheim. The Finnish newspapers were making good use of their staff on hand, running story after story on Teemu's big chance to finally win the Cup.

"NOW! TEEMU SELANNE ONE WIN SHY OF A DREAM COME TRUE. TEEMU SELANNE IS THE GREATEST OF ALL-TIME IN FINNISH HOCKEY," screamed *Ilta-Sanomat*, Finland's biggest newspaper.

The No. 2 paper, *Iltalehti*, shouted: "NOW, TEEMU!"

Anaheim took control of the game early on and it seemed that NOW, TEEMU was surely going to take place at the Honda Center. The Ducks scored twice in the first period and never looked back. The Senators fought back, with captain Daniel Alfredsson scoring twice, but Travis Moen netted his second of the night early in the third period for a 5–2 lead for Anaheim. Corey Perry scored the Ducks' sixth goal with 3:00 remaining in the third to put the game well out of reach.

After Perry's goal, Teemu fought back the tears on the bench for the last 3:00 of the game. "You soak everything in. I had goosebumps all over, and [head coach] Randy Carlyle just kept putting me out there and I didn't want to go. I just wanted to watch the fans. When the buzzer went off, you can't describe the feeling. It was, 'Thank God it is over.' And I thought at that time that it was my career, it was over. I thought 100 per cent this is it, and when they brought that Stanley Cup, I could not wait to get my hands on it."

In the stands, Teemu's Crazy Finns took off the orange T-shirts with the Finnish flag to reveal another shirt with the message MISSION STANLEY COMPLETED.

The Ducks won the Cup in their 14th season in the NHL; they were the first California-based Cup-winning team and the first on the West Coast since the league exclusively began competing for the Cup after the Western Hockey League folded in 1926.

Emotions ran high both on the ice and in the stands.

"It was wild," Teemu recalls. "We knew after two periods that we were going to win, which gave me a chance to just enjoy every second of the last period. With no pressure in the third period, I could take it all in in a special way."

After the final buzzer, confetti rained down from the ceiling of the Honda Center and the entire Anaheim bench stormed the ice, piling on goalie Jean-Sebastien Giguere.

Teemu wasn't the only veteran player to win his first Cup. Somewhere in the pile there was Rob Niedermayer, a 14-season veteran who got to win his first championship with his brother Scott, who added a fourth Cup (after three with the New Jersey Devils) onto an impressive resume that already included a World Juniors gold, a World Championship gold, an Olympic gold, a World Cup championship, a Western Hockey League championship, and a Memorial Cup win.

"It's probably the most memorable of my four Cup wins because I was able to win that time with Rob and Teemu," said Scott Niedermayer.

For all the other Ducks, this was their first Stanley Cup. Defenseman Chris Pronger won the Cup for the first time in his 13th season, and goaltender Giguere in his 11th.

After 1,041 regular season games and 86 playoff games, Selanne could say he was a Stanley Cup champion. The guy who told close friend Thomas Steen when he broke into the NHL as a rookie in the 1992–93 season that he would only spend three seasons on this side of the Atlantic Ocean was a veteran of 15 seasons.

Selanne knew how precious this moment was—how lucky he was to be on top and how little things can have a big impact and be the difference between a contender and a pretender: "If you go to a corner with a guy and you know the other guy is way stronger than you, and it is going to hurt. . .if you let that guy go first, you are done. One shift can change the whole thing. You never know. You just have to get into the playoffs."

Years later, during Selanne's last playoff appearance in the NHL, he recalled watching the 2014 playoff series between the Los Angeles Kings and the San Jose Sharks at his home with his son. The Kings trailed 3–0 in the series and were one loss away from elimination. Teemu and his son made a bet.

"I said, 'The Kings are done,' and he said, 'You never know.' I said, 'I know.' It is the Stanley Cup playoffs and not many teams come back. He said, 'What will you give to me if the Kings come back?' I said, 'What do you want?' and he said my Audi."

The Kings became just the fourth team in NHL playoff history (after the 1942 Toronto Maple Leafs, 1975 New York Islanders, and 2010 Philadelphia Flyers) to come back from a 3–0 deficit to win a series 4–3, and they went on to win the Stanley Cup.

Teemu chuckles when he remembers what happened next.

"My son left the room and he came back in 15 minutes with all my stuff in a plastic bag. He handed it to me and said, 'Where is the pink slip?' You never know when the playoffs start what will happen."

The Ducks, originally owned by Disney and called the Mighty Ducks of Anaheim after the 1992 movie *The Mighty Ducks*, had joined the NHL at a time when the Californian hockey audience was mostly interested in fights and a good show.

By 2007, the fans had learned to appreciate great hockey, and when captain Scott Niedermayer hoisted the Cup, the crowd went wild. Niedermayer handed it over to his brother, Rob, who gave it to Pronger, the other alternate captain, before Teemu fulfilled a childhood dream and took his turn raising the Stanley Cup into the air.

"It was a surreal feeling to raise the Cup above my head. It was heavier than I thought," Teemu said.

"There is no feeling like it when you get that above your head. I remember when the New York Rangers won and there was a guy in the stands crying, holding a sign that said 54 YEARS. NOW I CAN DIE IN PEACE. I almost got the same feeling. We had guys who won the Cup in their first year and maybe they thought they were going to win many more. I waited 15 years. We all tried to remind each other, *Guys, there is a 99 percent chance you won't get this chance again.* Do whatever it takes, leave everything out there, and everybody did."

In numerous interviews after the game, Teemu thanked his family, parents, and other important people who had helped him during his career, especially Ismo Syvahuoko, the orthopedic surgeon and friend from Helsinki who had operated on his knee three years earlier and extended his career.

"Without him, I wouldn't be here," Teemu said. "I've been waiting for this moment for so long, dreaming about winning something big. Our loss to the Edmonton Oilers in the conference final last season made everybody on the team work even harder this season. We had to take a step back before we could go all the way, and it was an important lesson.

"Every single player on the team played his part, I'm so proud of everyone. It was wonderful to win the Cup in front of our home crowd.

"After my knee surgery in 2004, I knew there will be a happy ending. I am so thankful head coach Randy Carlyle had confidence in me. He gave me chance to show that I can be great again; he gave me best players to play with. He wanted me to be on the first power play unit. I have always said that you are only as good as your coach wants you to be, and Randy really wanted me to succeed. He knew a healthy and motivated Teemu Selanne would help on the road to Stanley Cup success."

Ask anybody who has played in the pressure-packed NHL playoffs about the toil it takes on your body and everyone will tell a tale of playing hurt. Nobody emerges unscathed by the end of the physically demanding playoffs, and Teemu was no exception. Everybody is willing to do what it takes to win, and Teemu was nursing problems with his back, his groin, his shoulder, and a broken finger, which is why he wore a special glove. He also received injections to be able to play.

"Which finger was it?" reporters asked him.

"Who cares?" he said with a smile.

He had broken his right pinky in the Western Conference Final against the Detroit Red Wings when Henrik Zetterberg slashed him in the faceoff circle. Teams don't usually speak about injuries during the playoffs so that the opposing team can't take advantage of them.

"Of course a broken finger made it a little more difficult to shoot, for example, and I wouldn't have played with that injury during the regular season, but during the playoffs, it was another story. One injection took care of everything. We had a dozen players visiting the team doctor's office before a game," Teemu said.

"I was a wreck. . .but so was everybody else."

The Ducks made their players go through lab tests every week to make sure they were okay.

"When you use such strong painkillers, you have to make sure that the liver and kidneys are fine. The injections aren't good for your health in the long run, but during the Stanley Cup playoffs, everybody's willing to do whatever it takes."

Teemu joined an elite club when he won the Stanley Cup. He became the sixth Finnish Cup champion, following Jari Kurri, Esa Tikkanen, Reijo Ruotsalainen, Jere Lehtinen, and Ville Nieminen.

The Ducks players had no idea what plans were made in the event they clinched the Cup with a victory, and that also extended to their families. And the result was some uncomfortable moments amid the joy for the Selanne party.

When Ducks extended their lead to two goals at the end of the second period, word spread around the family members that they should go downstairs near the bench area before the game ended. That way, they could join in on the celebrations on the ice.

"I was a little surprised at that," Sirpa said, "and wondered how we could go down, but I told Ilmari, Teemu's father, that he should join us downstairs. Ilmari's wife hadn't made the trip, so he was lonely. I didn't say anything to our mothers, because they had each other to keep company. In hindsight, it was a mistake."

As the clock wound down to the final buzzer, Sirpa headed to the ice surface area with the kids. Ilmari decided to stay in the private box high above the ice surface.

"By the time we got to the bench, the players were already celebrating the win. Teemu was wearing the traditional championship cap and was giving an interview when he saw us. We hugged and cried a little. It was an emotional moment and a terrific one," Sirpa said, adding that seeing their parents embrace in tears of happiness left a big impression on the Selanne children. While Teemu and his teammates continued their celebrations on the ice, the Selanne children found some sticks and played a game of their own at the other end of the rink. Then, out of nowhere, Ilmari appeared at the side of the rink. Teemu's father had been walking around the arena when an usher had recognized him and showed him the way to the bench.

"I was doing an interview next to the Ducks bench and stood next to Teemu's father, so I happened to see when Teemu noticed him, nodded, pointed to him, and looked deep into his eyes. His father walked onto the ice and Teemu embraced him," said Brian Hayward, a TV analyst and a former NHL goalie.

"My producer kept telling me to 'get Selanne, get Selanne,' but I couldn't go between those two. It was a fantastic moment between father and son."

The embrace encapsulated a lifetime of gratitude and all the love Teemu felt for his father and his family. Their way of making Teemu believe in his dreams had now brought him the biggest prize in hockey.

"My dad for sure, everything he has done for me in hockey. It would not be possible if it weren't for him. My mom made everything else possible, but he took the time for driving, coaching, and everything in the end," Teemu said.

"It was so emotional. We hugged for about 30 seconds and we just said we did it and thank you. It was one of those moments when you do not need words."

To Hayward, it seemed that time stood still. He said it was the most emotional moment of his broadcast career. "There he was, a player we had followed for years, a true fan favorite. He had finally reached his biggest goal and was sharing his innermost feelings with his dad. I never won the Stanley Cup, but thanks to that one moment, I have an idea of what it feels like."

Sirpa saw Ilmari on the ice and realized that their mothers were nowhere to be seen. She asked Teemu's twin brother Paavo to go get his mother and hers. Paavo rushed up only to hear that his mother, Liisa, refused to go anywhere. She had seen her ex-husband Ilmari on the ice and was upset because she assumed Teemu had asked him— but not her—to go down. She told Paavo she'd only go downstairs if Teemu specifically invited her there.

Meanwhile, Teemu kept on with his celebrations, clueless about the family drama brewing.

"It was my fault, and I should've gone upstairs to fix things. I should've told our mothers clearly to come down after the game," said Sirpa.

Teemu disagrees.

"Mom was just being childish. None of us knew what was going to happen after the game," he said.

On the ice, Sirpa tried to get everybody together for a family photo at that special moment. In the end, in almost all the photos, there are the Selannes, Ilmari, and the Stanley Cup. No mothers, and except for one magazine shot, no seven-year-old Leevi, either. He was busy playing hockey.

"I went looking for our mothers and found them and asked them to join us in the dressing room. I wanted them to feel the atmosphere there, but Liisa said she wouldn't do it."

Emotions were running high even for those not on the ice. Ismo Syvahuoko, Teemu's old friend, was fighting back tears in the box.

"When Teemu hoisted the Cup and turned to us, I cried like a baby. It was just complete happiness," he said. "I didn't think it was appropriate for me to be on the ice, so I stayed in one of the bars to watch the celebration. Paavo came to get me from there and asked me to come down to the dressing room, where the party was getting wilder."

The dressing room was awash in celebrations. The room was packed with players, their friends and families, and reporters. Music was blasting on the speakers, and players were shouting their joy to the world. Reporters wanted to know everything about everything, while champagne showers followed, one after the other.

Teemu was like a kid in a candy store. He showered media members with champagne and as soon as one bottle emptied, another was handed to him. The only Crazy Finn on the Stanley Cup–champion team kept the champagne flowing. The dressing room party kept going as the happy champions danced and sang until the wee hours.

"Paavo had brought a CD into the room and suddenly I stood on the table, in full hockey gear, with a cigar in my mouth, and sang to [Finnish pop star] J. Karjalainen's "Sankarit" ["Heroes"]. The rest of the guys were surprised to see us sing in Finnish. By then, there were lots of Finns in the room. The others seemed to sing along, too, even though they didn't understand a word of the lyrics," Teemu said.

"After that, the next song was Queen's "We Are the Champions." And everybody, it must have been a couple of hundred people, sang it together. Wow. That was another great moment."

Teemu was wearing his hockey equipment all through the night. Others began to shave off their playoff beards. Even Teemu did, eventually.

"I wore a George Parros–style mustache for another day," he said, referring to the team's enforcer, and Teemu's children's favorite player, famous for his mustache and his willingness to protect the team's stars.

When the players left the dressing room, they went to a VIP space outside the arena and continued the celebrations there. A car service picked up each player and ferried him home. The players had agreed to take a couple of days off and to come together at the championship parade.

At the Selanne household, the party never stopped. Hollywood stars who were friends of the Selannes stopped by and were joined by friends and family alike.

Around 6:00 AM, Teemu poured himself one last glass of scotch, lit up a celebratory cigar, and went to the front patio. "That was when I realized what had happened, what we had accomplished. All the pressure I had carried with me fell off my back. I felt light, and great."

Before he headed to bed for some much-needed sleep, Teemu made a couple of phone calls to Finland. His phone was full of text messages. He slept for a few hours, had breakfast, and played some golf with his friends. They had fun, enjoyed the good life.

His mother, Liisa, congratulated him, but she still wasn't her usual self. The misunderstanding at the arena still bothered her. "I told her to cut it out, that I appreciated her support just as much as Dad's and that we should just enjoy the moment," he said.

Liisa passed away in 2018, and to the day she died, she did not want to talk about it. She did enjoy the rest of the championship week when Southern California celebrated the Ducks' win.

"Let bygones be bygones. I'm so proud of Teemu," she said at the time.

The day after the emotional game, Teemu had the Stanley Cup delivered to his house. "I took it to the kids' school, a couple of golf courses, and to a few friends. Then we had a Cup party at our house."

Being a Finn, Selanne fired up the sauna despite the fact it was another scorcher of a day in California. "Of course the Cup had to be taken to a sauna."

Three days after the Ducks won the Cup, the players gathered at the Honda Center for the championship rally with their fans. The Niedermayer brothers arrived at the Honda Center in a helicopter, together with the Stanley Cup, and others came by car.

With an estimated crowd of 15,000 awaiting their heroes, a fire truck escorted the players, who arrived in an open-air double-decker bus.

When Teemu carried the Cup onto the stage, the crowd roared their approval of the veteran holding the coveted trophy. Suddenly, as if on cue, California governor Arnold Schwarzenegger walked onto the stage. It was a great moment for Teemu, who was a big fan of the movie star and had seen almost all of his movies. Schwarzenegger shook the players' hands and gave a speech.

"When I was an actor, I didn't have many lines of dialogue. I had more action scenes instead. This team was just like my characters. After each loss, they said, "I'll be back," and after the last game, they said "Hasta la vista, baby," he said, referring to his famous lines in the Terminator movies.

When the players were interviewed, Teemu received the biggest cheers. When he was asked if he'd return for the following season, Teemu joked, "If I were Arnold, I might say 'I'll be back'."

He promised to make up his mind within the next couple weeks.

The last thing Ducks general manager Brian Burke wanted was to have the celebrations overshadowed by Teemu or Scott Niedermayer making a surprise retirement announcement. Burke recalled the damper put on the Avalanche's Stanley Cup celebrations when Ray Bourque announced he was hanging up his skates.

"If Brian hadn't said anything, I might have announced my retirement," said Teemu, who did not rain on the parade. The party went on.

What surprised and impressed Teemu was how collected everybody was and how well-behaved they were during the celebrations. "Compared to a Finnish team celebrating a championship, everything was scaled back. Nobody was even drunk at any point. It was such a unique situation that nobody wanted to miss anything. It was about taking it all in, enjoying every moment.

"When you win something in Finland, everybody goes crazy with the booze. We just sat on sofas and enjoyed life. It was sweet."

The media-friendly Teemu was in high demand for interviews, and he took every opportunity to thank and praise his teammates and his fans. He also thanked his fans in his homeland and promised them a celebration with the Cup in the summer months.

Unlike the other professional sports leagues in North America, the NHL allows each Cup winner to have the Cup for a 24-hour period for personal use in the summer. It wasn't a centuries-old tradition—barely a decade, having started with the New Jersey Devils in 1995.

"It'll be awesome to take the Cup to Finland. There are so many people I am grateful for," Teemu said.

The Ducks were keen to capitalize on their sudden popularity and made plans to promote the game in the region. Given Teemu's history with the club and his popularity in Southern California, they asked him to remain in California for a couple of weeks to do some promotional appearances, and he agreed.

"I said yes. It was the first time I missed my hockey school back in Finland and had to send the kids a video greeting instead," Teemu said.

Teemu and a couple of his teammates took the Cup to different events and, most importantly to Teemu, to children's hospitals, knowing in the back of his mind that his wife was pregnant.

As the Ducks toured the area, Teemu and Sirpa were getting ready for another exciting event, and their wish was going to come true. "We saw the 3-D ultrasound. Sirpa was expecting a girl," Teemu said.

For Teemu, it was a wild few weeks in which everything he had wanted, he had gotten. Sirpa was happy, the boys were looking forward to getting a little sister, and he was a Stanley Cup champion.

Veera was born on December 5, 2007. "It was the best year of my life," Teemu said. He passed *How to Choose the Sex of Your Baby* on to Chris Pronger (who later became a father to a baby girl).

When the commitments to the Ducks were over, the Selannes traveled to Finland, to their home in Kirkkonummi, 35 minutes outside Helsinki, just in time to celebrate midsummer.

"It was the first time we'd been there for midsummer. Usually we spend it in Vuokatti in northern Finland, where my hockey school is," Teemu said about the late June day that marks the summer solstice.

Selanne had not announced whether he would retire, but others tried to speak for him. Ilmari gave interviews in which he said he believed Teemu was going to retire at the top.

"He's given 30 years of his life to hockey. He's won everything. It may be time to spend time with his family," he said. "Teemu has worked hard for this for a long time, and his success is entirely the result of what he's done. Whatever sacrifices we as parents have made for his career we have gotten back many, many times."

Teemu himself said nothing. He had, however, told the media numerous times that he'd retire if he ever won the Cup.

"The last two years have been the best time in my career. I've played better than ever. I've always dreamt of retiring at the top, and this would be a good opportunity to do that. This is as good as it gets."

While Teemu would not commit to anything, his heart was telling him it was time to go.

"Right then, I was convinced that nothing could be better than that. You can't retire in a better way, and I was sure there was nothing that would motivate me to come back. All my teammates were sure that I was going to retire, and it had also been used as a motivational tool: this is Teemu's last season, let's make it a great one," he said.

The champion was exhausted. Done.

"It took everything out of me, both mentally and physically. It was like going through war," he said.

He did leave the door ajar, though, and he did make up his mind about one thing.

He would not make any decisions before his daughter was born.

STRAIGHT OUTTA ESPOO

—————

TEEMU ILMARI SELANNE AND HIS TWIN BROTHER, Paavo, were born in Turku, Finland, on July 3, 1970, although the birth certificate states Helsinki. Their parents, along with three-year-old Panu, were sailing when they had to seek shelter from a storm.

In Ilmari's 1993 book *Teemu*, he explained what happened next. "The weather changed that night and we slept poorly. A thunderstorm kept us awake and the summer sky was ablaze with lightning, fitting for the birth of the Finnish Flash. I guess it had become crowded inside mummy's tummy, so at four in the morning, she woke me up and told me that her contractions had begun."

The closest place to get help was Turku. Teemu was born at 7:09 PM, Paavo about 20 minutes later.

Ilmari Selanne married Liisa Viitanen in 1964 and Panu was born two years later in Helsinki, where the Selannes lived in an apartment owned by Liisa's employer, a privately owned senior citizens' home. Liisa was the manager.

Ilmari and Liisa had decided that she would stay at home as soon as the couple had children. They had bought a two-bedroom apartment

in the Helsinki neighborhood Lauttasaari, but while it was being renovated, they spent the first month after the birth of the twins at Ilmari's
brother's place in Espoo. Then it was four weeks in Inkeroinen, at Liisa's
parents', before they were able to get under their own roof.

Teemu's first home was in a Helsinki apartment building by the
Baltic Sea.

"For the kids it was like a paradise. We had our own beach," Liisa
said in 2014, when she was interviewed for a Finnish biography on her
son. "Teemu was an active child and as soon as he learned to walk, he
was always up to something. If it wasn't a teddy bear in the oven, Teemu
himself got locked in the bathroom. There was always something."

Ilmari worked days as the service manager at Atoy, a family-
owned company that imports everything related to cars. Then, at night,
he would moonlight as a translator and a freelance writer. He had
also financed his studies as a restaurant musician.

They took a mortgage when they bought the apartment in Helsinki. Liisa quit her job in 1970 when it was time for her to go on a
maternity leave. Having a mortgage meant some lean years for the
family. Liisa worked as a home day care provider to have some income.

"That also had a big effect on how the boys were raised. We didn't
have a lot of money, and we only bought things we really needed. We
picked berries and mushrooms in the forest, and if we saw apples that
had fallen off the tree, we asked to get them," Ilmari said.

The small apartment was full of action. On top of the three Selanne
boys, Liisa also had four other kids in a day care she ran. And then
there were all their friends on top of everything.

"The boys had to learn to be social," she said.

The sea had always been important to Ilmari, and he hoped his
sons would also learn to sail. Lauttasaari was perfect for all kinds of
water activities.

"They went to the beach every day in the summer, and they swam
and played in the water. We had an old wooden sailboat that we used

to get out to the local islands every weekend, and we even made it to Gdansk, Poland, on one summer holiday," Ilmari continued.

The boys weren't interested in sailing, but Teemu enjoyed driving around in uncle Pauli's motorboat. He always liked speed, whether it concerned swings, boating, or all the rides at the Linnanmaki theme park in Helsinki.

When Teemu thinks back to his first home, what comes to his mind first are the beach and the sea.

"We were always on the beach or out sailing. These days you couldn't get me on a sailboat even if you paid me. I don't enjoy fishing, either. I need speedier activities and challenges."

Another important piece of Teemu's childhood were his grandparents, especially his mother's parents and their home.

"My grandfather was the local sales representative for Mallasjuoma, a Finnish brewery and soft drink company, and while we never had any soft drinks or candy at home, when we were there we were allowed to drink as much pop as we wanted. They spoiled us rotten," Teemu said.

The other grandparents' home in Rauma was a sailing destination every summer.

The Selannes' neighborhood, Lauttasaari, had a great reputation for summer sports, but it wasn't great for winter sports. And yet, that's where Teemu was first introduced to hockey, when he and the kids his mother had in her day care went to a local park to "play."

"In the beginning, he mostly just stood on the ice with a plastic stick in his hand, wearing winter overalls, gloves, and a warm hat. As soon as we thought his ankles were strong enough, we bought him skates. He was four," Ilmari said.

The Selannes moved from the Lauttasaari apartment to a house in Espoo, 20 minutes farther west, in 1975. There were two rooms and a kitchen downstairs and two rooms and a hall upstairs. They had water from their own well. The plumbing? There was an outhouse, and the only way to get to the sauna was to go out of the house and back in through another door.

"In the winter, you had to make sure to go to the bathroom before you went to bed so that you wouldn't have to go outside to the outhouse and sit on the cold seat in the middle of the night," Teemu said.

They didn't have any neighbors in sight, and next door, there were horses. The Selannes also bought a dog, another piece in Ilmari's and Liisa's plan to bring up the kids right. Repe, a German shepherd, also made everybody feel safe. Repe is also the reason that Teemu is still an animal lover.

One day, a friend's father told Teemu and Paavo to run a race against one another. Teemu was still clearly smaller and weaker than Paavo, but he compensated by being fast. Ilmari had never thought there was anything special about his sons until the other father, Erkki Auna, pointed out that Teemu was exceptionally fast.

"Teemu had always been faster than Paavo, but nobody had thought there was anything special about it until Erkki realized that since Paavo was a good runner, Teemu had to be super-fast," Ilmari said.

"We had 2,500 square meters to run around, play games, or ride soapbox cars. Soon they had more friends, and Teemu was always the one up to something. He always made Paavo do things, and Paavo always did as his brother said," said Liisa.

Paavo didn't mind being playing goal when he and Teemu were kids, and although he didn't know it at the time, Paavo had a huge impact on Teemu's hockey career. Teemu didn't forget his brother's role in his road to fame and he paid tribute to him when he gave his acceptance speech at the Hockey Hall of Fame 40 years later.

"I am sorry, Paavo, that I shook your self-confidence. You thought you sucked. But by playing goal, you played a role in how I learned how to score, and look where I am now, the Hockey Hall of Fame. I really needed that confidence, so thank you, my brother," Teemu said with a laugh.

"I wouldn't have become a pro hockey player without Paavo. He was my personal goalie all year round," Teemu said.

In 1976, the brothers started preschool and had to leave the security of their home. Their preschool was about a third of a mile away, and the boys usually got themselves there by foot—Teemu running.

"We were told it showed that they were able to spend their early years at home with Mom, because they were so happy and balanced. That felt good," said Liisa.

The parents didn't have a master plan for turning the kids into hockey players or other athletes, even if they had noticed that Teemu was exceptionally speedy.

"The thought didn't even cross our minds," said Ilmari.

Things soon changed, however.

After the 1974 Ice Hockey World championship, hosted by Finland, Veli-Pekka Ketola and Heikki Riihiranta became the first Finnish-born and trained pro players in North America when they signed with the Winnipeg Jets in the World Hockey Association (WHA). It made Finns aware of professional hockey, but in the Selanne family, nobody knew what the NHL was. Even the idea of playing hockey for a living was strange.

In the fall of 1976, Matti Hagman became the first Finnish-born and trained player in the NHL when he signed with the Boston Bruins. Teemu has some memories from that time in his life, but unlike today's children, he had no idea of what the NHL was.

The Selanne boys played all sports. In the winter, they went skiing and to the municipal swimming pool and skated on the nearby outdoor rink. In the summer, they played soccer, ran, and played games.

Ilmari had now been made aware of his son's exceptional speed, but Teemu didn't join organized hockey and soccer teams until two years later.

As the boys grew, their territory expanded, and they started to spend a lot of time on the Kivenlahti schoolyard. Teemu and Paavo weren't really alike, and there was a certain brother fatigue between them. Teemu was fast, Paavo was strong. Teemu was open and wild, Paavo shy and good. Teemu was lazy about school; Paavo even did Teemu's homework if needed.

Teemu and Paavo started first grade in the fall of 1977. They were supposed to start it at the closest school, but the parents thought the road there was too dangerous.

There was another option.

"If you chose Swedish, Finland's second official language, from Grade 3, you went to another school," Paavo said. And that's how the Selanne boys were able to start school at a place they knew well. Their school was next door to their preschool.

Organized sports began in school and continued in the summers in Espoo's sports camps, held in nearby sports fields.

It was hard not to notice the Selanne brothers when they came to the camp in crew cuts, dirty and tanned from their outdoor activities. Teemu was almost hyperactive, and he did everything in his power to beat the others. When the other kids did four to five chin-ups, Teemu did 20 or 30.

When the 1978 edition of the camp ended, Teemu wanted to run in both the 100-meter and the cross-country race, but the program was too tight for him to do that. He asked them to push back the 100-meter so that he could run both distances, and when they didn't accommodate him, Teemu ran the cross-country race so fast that he made it to his 100-meter start on time. He won both races.

Sports were all the Selannes paid any attention to. There were no boy scouts or choir singers in the family.

Espoo is to Helsinki like Anaheim is to Los Angeles. But Espoo was also the destination for a lot of families who wanted to get a house and a yard, like the Selannes. With young families come organized sports, and Espoo had several to choose from.

Teemu joined his first hockey team in Espoo when he was in second grade, and he played a total of six seasons (1978–84) in the city before he moved to one of the big Helsinki clubs, Jokerit, at 14.

His first team, EPS (Espoon Palloseura), played its games on local outdoor rinks that didn't have artificial ice. Teemu and Paavo, who really wasn't interested in hockey but tagged along for fun, played only one season for EPS because a second Espoo team, EJK (Espoon Jaaklubi), was moving into a new indoor arena.

"We were able to play inside. We were so pumped," said Teemu.

Switching to the team with an indoor ice surface also affected the boys' parents. Ilmari and Liisa also had to get more involved in their sons' activities, because someone had to drive the boys to practices. By then, Liisa was also working outside the home, as manager of home day care for the City of Espoo.

To keep the family afloat, Ilmari was holding down three jobs, but when Teemu turned 10, life changed. Ilmari started to focus more of his attention on bringing discipline into the picture to develop Teemu's promising abilities.

Bedtime was always 9:00 PM. No shower or sauna at night if the boys hadn't gone for a run before it. On their way to the sauna, the twins had to do 10 chin-ups and then 10 more on the way down. It was no coincidence the chin-up bar was on the staircase.

"We weren't given any slack, we had detailed rules for how to behave and live," Teemu said. "When Dad left for work in the morning, he left instructions for each of us. For Paavo and Panu, it usually meant work around the house, and for me, sports.

"It was often annoying to go to school and hear my friends talk about some TV show they'd watched or something else they had done the night before."

But according to Ilmari, the play was fair. "It was always up to Teemu. If he was going to get serious about sports, he was supposed to do his best. On the other hand, Teemu could have just said 'enough' at any point," Ilmari said.

"The twins were 15 years old when they still had to be in bed by 9:00. I'm sure they thought I was being unfair, but the foundation of a good athlete is made of good sleep," Ilmari said.

By this time, the EJK hockey program was one of the best in Finland, and the group that managed the program decided to throw the club's full support behind a team of boys born in 1970.

Ilmari, meanwhile, had developed an interest in coaching. He knew Teemu was talented and he decided to do what many parents would for their children. He did whatever he could to support a potential professional career for his son, and for Ilmari, that meant becoming Teemu's personal coach, trainer, mental coach, and masseuse.

Ilmari became a quick learner and picked up pieces of information on hockey development everywhere. After every practice and game, the father and son had a debriefing in the car on their way home. Teemu liked it so much he always wanted to talk more, until they ended up talking about hockey until it was time to go to bed.

"Teemu always wanted to talk hockey. That gave me an opportunity to use hockey as a way of teaching other things as well, so that if some player had started to smoke, we concluded that 'he didn't take hockey that seriously,'" Ilmari said. "Teemu liked it best when I compared his play to the one I thought had been the best one on the ice in that game or practice."

Ilmari switched careers again to be able to support Teemu even more. His new job as a service manager of another import company in Espoo allowed him more flexibility.

On the home front, life soldiered on, but the family finances were still stretched. The solution was to take on one more job, which the entire family would take care of together.

"Every Wednesday and Sunday, we delivered local papers in our neighborhood, where there were a lot of apartment buildings. Running up and down the stairs with newspapers was good practice for the kids. They sure didn't get their hockey equipment and trips delivered on a silver platter," said Ilmari.

Despite the financial struggles, the boys led a happy life. Every penny had to be carefully spent, but they didn't miss out on anything.

Under the surface, however, trouble was brewing.

Ilmari and Liisa had grown apart. Ilmari spent all his evenings and weekends with the twins at their sports activities, and instead of spending her evenings at home, Liisa, a social person, came up with activities of her own.

In the summer of 1980, when Teemu was 10, the parents decided to lead separate lives but still live under the same roof—for their children's sake. The boys didn't learn about the split until five years later, in 1985, when Liisa moved to Helsinki and Ilmari stayed in their Espoo home with the boys.

The parents hadn't pushed the boys toward any particular sport; they hadn't even really made them pick any sport. All they wanted was for the twins to have something to do in their free time.

Teemu's brother Panu, who's four years older, had a lot more liberties than the twins, and the parents saw the consequences when they moved to Espoo. One night, when everybody was about to visit Liisa's parents, Panu went missing. He stayed missing for three days.

Panu and the twins never developed a close bond. The twins had sports and the older brother had his own activities and his own friends. He was more into music than sports.

As for Paavo, it's easy to imagine it being difficult to be Teemu Selanne's twin brother. But according to Teemu, he never felt Paavo was jealous of him.

"He's always been a loyal brother who's stood up for me ever since we were kids, even if we're not the best of friends. If somebody's mistreated me somehow, Paavo has always been there for me," Teemu said.

Panu is another story.

His disappearance before the family vacation wasn't just a one-off. When he was 13, the police paid a visit to the Selannes, wanting to search the house for drugs.

After that visit, Ilmari's and Panu's relationship deteriorated, and Ilmari didn't even make an effort to patch things up. Teemu's friends don't remember Panu and Ilmari being at home at the same time after the parents' divorce.

Panu was jailed in 1988 just after Ilmari had taken a new job in Africa that had him mostly away from the family for four years. Liisa had moved back to their Espoo house; Teemu was doing his compulsory military service during his first season with Jokerit in the second-tier league in Finland.

Over the years, Panu has been able to talk about the trouble he got into. "I was carrying quite a lot of drugs, and they took me straight from the car to the jail. I was sentenced to two years in prison, and I was let out of the Helsinki prison after 18 months," Panu said.

There was nothing the family could do; Panu had become an addict. Panu's life has been a roller coaster, and he's been back to prison again. The drugs took a toll on his friends, some of whom have overdosed, including his girlfriend.

Panu has gone through rehabilitation and now uses medication daily that helps him to stay clean.

Decades later, Teemu said his parents' split had no impact on him.

"I was so focused on hockey. People around me said they saw something change, but I don't think it affected me at all. Everything else was on the side. If it would have happened earlier, it would have been way tougher. The hardest thing was my older brother, all the drugs involved in his life. It was hard to see, to watch him struggle, and that is why I have never touched any types of drugs.

"And everything was happening so quickly. When I was 17, I was playing my first national team game and then I was drafted. It was a roller-coaster drive. Nothing was bothering me.

"It wasn't a big deal, but I have to hand it to them, they put on a great show for us. I guess it would have been more traumatic had they divorced five years earlier, that probably would have scarred me," he said.

According to Paavo, the divorce must have been tough for Teemu, as well, but he dealt with it the way he deals with everything in life. He's never—not even as an adult—stopped to reflect.

"Back then, Teemu could block his emotions and inner thoughts because he was always training so hard. He just switched them off and went full steam ahead. He's the same way even today; he'll never stop and speak about his feelings."

When Teemu picked up hockey in the late 1970s, Espoo was a minor hockey powerhouse in Finland. For players born in 1970, the Espoo team that made waves was EJK. They had all the best players, the entire organization was behind the team, they played in an indoor arena, and they had top coaches and more than sufficient practice time.

The team was coached by Jorma Ikonen, whose son Juha was one of the 1970-born players management was high on. By the time Teemu arrived, Juha had already spent a season on a team with kids a year older than he was.

Teemu was at a bit of a disadvantage, because he learned to play on natural ice. And as odd as it seems, the difference between natural ice and artificial ice is night and day. Artificial ice is faster.

Juha Ikonen was the centerman on the first line, while Teemu played center on the second line, with Jukka Nieminen and Antti Tormanen on the wings. Tormanen would play 50 games in the NHL and was on the team that won Finland's first world championship in 1995.

Jorma Ikonen was the head coach, and that turned out to be a stroke of luck for the kids. When he wasn't working with his young players, Jorma was at an arena somewhere, watching a practice. Jorma was out to make winners out of the boys and the kids who didn't want to take hockey seriously found their place on EJK's second team, the B team.

Ikonen was a demanding coach and—according to Teemu—the kids were a little afraid of him. "He was really strict and demanding. . .especially toward his son Juha."

Antti Tormanen lived in another part of Espoo but often made the trip to Selanne's neighborhood rink in Kivenlahti because the ice there was so good. It didn't take long for Tormanen to figure out that Teemu had loads of talent.

"Juha [Ikonen] was the star, he could pick up the puck from behind our net and go coast-to-coast. He did whatever he wanted. Teemu's game was more mature, maybe, but whenever he got a good pass, he took off like a shot out of a cannon. When we played soccer, he was so fast that whenever he got the ball as a striker, he was almost always alone with the goalie," he said.

Two years after he joined the EJK team, Selanne played in the unofficial under-12 Finnish championship in 1982. The four-team final tournament was played at Helsinki's main arena, and Selanne led the tournament with three goals.

"We were the best team in our age group in the country. At one point we went 18 months without losing a game," Teemu recalls. "We were also an elite team in that we had the coolest uniforms, and we looked better than the rest. It was a lot of fun to be a part of a team like that."

That same year, the EJK team made the trip across the Atlantic Ocean to play in a tournament called the Esso Cup in Toronto. It was during a stopover in the New York area that the 12-year-old Selanne saw his first NHL game, the Philadelphia Flyers against the New Jersey Devils. The Flyers had Finnish forward Ilkka Sinisalo in the lineup. New Jersey's top defenseman was also a Finn, Tapio Levo. The Flyers won the game 3–1.

According to Tormanen, EJK gave Teemu the best opportunity to become an elite player.

"First of all, if you could play on that team, you could play anywhere. Secondly, Juha [Ikonen] was just enough ahead of everybody else to push Teemu to become a better player. Competition makes players develop," said Tormanen.

When he wasn't on the ice, the soccer pitch, or the track, you could find Teemu in the pool or on a tennis court.

Ilmari—always the coach—saw right away that tennis was good practice for someone shooting from the right. "In addition to being good for his leg muscles and foot speed, tennis made his right hand stronger," he said.

In the winter, Teemu and his teammates played bandy to get more ice time and practice skating.

Teemu had great success in every sport he participated.

In soccer, his team finished second at the 1981 Finnish championships and the 11-year-old Teemu led the tournament in scoring. The following season, he played 60 matches and scored 57 goals (and added 22 assists).

On the track he was unique because he had both speed and endurance.

In 1980, he won the Helsinki district championship in both 60 and 1,000 meters. His 3:17.8 for 1 kilometer is still the record for 10-year-olds with the Espoo organization. On the same day he set the 1,000-meter record, he ran his personal best in 60 meters, 8.8 seconds. His 100-meter record, 13.9, is still among the best in the club's all-time records. He ran that as a 12-year-old in a Helsinki meet where he also jumped his long-jump record, 4.44 meters (14 feet, 7 inches).

"My career in track and field ended just like that," Teemu said, snapping his fingers. "It was starting to be too much. There were days when I had a track meet in the morning, and competed in three disciplines, say 60 meters, 1,000 meters, and the long jump. And then I'd go straight to a hockey tournament."

At 17, Teemu held his own test day to gauge his times. He ran 3,560 meters (2.2 miles) in 12 minutes. He then ran 100 meters in 11.3 seconds and jumped 6.60 meters in the long jump (21 feet, 8 inches).

On the bandy field, Teemu was a right winger and Paavo stood in goal when their team won the Finnish championship on home ice in Espoo in 1982. The year after that, they won the Finnish title in the next age group. Teemu also won an individual award when he won the skills competition.

Teemu was always practicing, either on his own or with his friends. Ilmari constructed a plastic board for the boys to use for shooting pucks at the garage door.

"Teemu used to practice for hours each day, and his wrists were so sore that we had to tell him to not shoot for a while," Ilmari said.

The future NHL sniper wanted to shoot only slap shots, like most kids do, but again, coach Ilmari stepped in and told him to practice his wrist shots and backhands every day. "I told him that when he gets the puck in front of the net, he's not going to have time to settle the puck but that he'll have to shoot it as quickly as possible."

To improve his wrist shot, Teemu needed to get stronger arms. At first, he worked on that by doing chin-ups, until Ilmari made him a special tool. They filled an old paint can with nails and attached it to a foot-long piece of a hockey stick with a rope.

"Then we had to rotate the stick until the rope was rolled all the way around the stick, with our arms straight out. Then we'd take it down the same way, and up again," Teemu said.

Jorma Ikonen focused on the players' skating skills. That turned into a real passion for Teemu, to the point that his father thought it was sometimes more fun for him to just skate fast and carry the puck to the net than it was to score a goal. No surprise, then, Teemu always wanted to practice scoring, and during every break at practice, he challenged his friends to a penalty shootout.

According to Ilmari, a good shot is hard, accurate, and unexpected. It's not always the hardest shot that goes in; it has to surprise the goalie.

Ilmari had no hockey background, never played the game, but he studied it. And most importantly, he used common sense. Parents can't produce world-class athletes; the child must have the passion for the sport inside him or her. With no passion, no help from the parents will work, but with Teemu, Ilmari pushed him forward.

The results speak for themselves: Teemu became one of the greatest goal scorers in the history of hockey.

But the Selanne kids' lives weren't only about sports.

Friends became increasingly important for them, especially Teemu, who, to this day, remains close with two of his old childhood friends, Mikko Vaahtoranta and Harri Ylonen.

Teemu wasn't the most skilled soccer player in their world, but he may have been the fastest. "He couldn't really control the ball, but speed was his weapon. If he could keep the ball in his feet when he ran, he'd score a goal. It was the same thing in hockey when he was a kid," said Vaahtoranta.

The three were friends first and fierce competitors second: "Every match was for keeps. None of us was ready to give an inch," said Ylonen.

Vaahtoranta is a year older than Teemu, and his first contact with him was, let's call it, "business-related." When they were barely in school, the kids collected empty bottles and cans and financed their candy purchases with the money they got at the store for them.

"I met him at the Kivenlahti beach, and we decided to become business partners," Vaahtoranta said. "I basically lived summers at the Selanne house."

Vaahtoranta never played on the same club team as Teemu, but he has played against him many, many times. "It was my job to keep him off the score sheet. I couldn't do it."

He remembers how seriously Teemu took his training when he joined the Helsinki Jokerit organization. When the other Espoo kids started to hang out in the park with a bag of beer, Teemu sometimes joined later, but only after workout sessions.

"He was proud of what he was doing, and he's always liked to work hard. I don't think I saw him with a beer many times; he simply didn't want that kind of life.

"We others drank beer and looked up to Teemu. He was such a fun guy to be around that we didn't need alcohol to have fun. And we always had fun," he said.

Teemu was 15 when he got drunk for the first time.

"[Vaahtoranta] and I drank mint chocolate liqueur on the beach and slept in their house, which was pretty close," Teemu said.

As the boys grew older, their business dealings got some shades of gray into them. In other words, they either pulled off a scam or they stole bottles. Back in the 1970s, empty bottles were simply left at a counter in the back of the store.

"We always rattled the plastic bags to make it sound like there were lots of bottles in them. When the owner asked us how many bottles we had found that day, we always rounded the amounts up, and didn't differentiate between the big and the small bottles. They never checked them," Teemu said with a laugh.

"The Cajander store in our neighborhood always had a window open right behind the candy shelves. If the register was unattended, we could always throw a couple of candy bars to a buddy waiting outside," Vaahtoranta said.

And even the candy they did pay for was sometimes paid for with money they had stolen.

"Teemu took money from his parents every day, whatever he could find on tabletops or in their pockets. It was great being his friend because he always shared his candy with everybody. He always wanted the best for everyone, except the ones he liked to fool. Like Paavo," Vaahtoranta added.

Some things never change, and Teemu is still a lot like that 15-year-old kid in Espoo. He remains close to his friends, sometimes to the detriment of his relationship with family.

"Buddies have always been important for him, sometimes even more important than the rest of his family. He barely ever calls me, and when he does, it's about something work-related. It's not easy to get a hold of him, and he doesn't always pick up our parents' calls, either. But he does talk to his buddies every day," said Paavo.

The older the kids got, the more they began to get curious about Ilmari's role in Teemu's career.

"It was nuts, really, to focus only on one child like that. When I slept over at their house, and we watched TV, Ilmari would massage Teemu. Not every father would have done that, and I often wondered what Paavo thought about that. Had I done something like that to just one of my kids, they would have rioted," said Juha Ikonen.

Ilmari's hard line had its soft sides. Once when Teemu's team was returning home from a long road trip, Ilmari let Teemu sleep in his lap on the bus and was criticized for it by Jorma Ikonen and a few other parents. He disagreed, but the incident bothered him often later on, when Teemu was older. Had the other parents been right? Was he being a helicopter parent? Was he too protective?

––––––––––––

When Teemu was 12, there was trouble, and it wasn't family-related. His legs were an issue. Playing soccer made his legs and heels ache. Nobody knew what caused the pain, and the Selannes tried everything. The only thing that helped with his leg pains was simply to run less. The off-ice training for hockey became more difficult. In the evenings, when the pain was at its worst, only a massage helped ease the discomfort, and Ilmari massaged Teemu's legs until the boy fell asleep.

Finally, Ilmari consulted a doctor and Teemu was diagnosed with Osgood-Schlatter disease. According to the Mayo Clinic, "Osgood-Schlatter disease can cause a painful lump below the kneecap in children and adolescents experiencing growth spurts during puberty.

Osgood-Schlatter disease occurs most often in children who participate in sports that involve running, jumping, and swift changes of
direction—such as soccer, basketball, figure skating, and ballet."

Teemu quit soccer to focus on hockey. The pain persisted, and
doctors suggested he give up sports altogether, but Ilmari didn't want
to give up.

He always found a doctor who cleared Teemu to play, although
the ailment took its toll. Teemu couldn't shake his opponents like he
used to, and he slid down his team's lineup. But Teemu did not give
up, and he and his father decided to work on other skills rather than
just his blazing speed.

"We decided that Teemu should put all his energy into becoming a better passer. He couldn't really skate at that point, but he tried
to keep up by using his hockey sense and positioning," Ilmari said.

"The leg pains were a blessing in disguise. I had always gone full
out all the time, but when I had to play a slower-paced game, my
hockey sense improved. I learned to pass well," said Teemu.

Teemu's team didn't fare as well as previous years, and people
attributed the decline to Teemu's scoring drought. At his peak, he
had scored about a third of the team's goals.

There comes a point in every athlete's career when he realizes
that talent isn't enough. For Teemu, it came at 13, and that's when
he decided to put more effort into hockey.

Ilmari, meanwhile, was on a collision course with Coach Ikonen.
Ilmari thought the coach didn't take Teemu's pains seriously, and that
instead of at least trying to use Teemu in another way, the coach had
just benched him.

"Teemu was going through some tough times with his leg pains, so
I think the coach was being unfair. I had had enough, so we decided
to look elsewhere," Ilmari said.

Elsewhere wound up being Helsinki Jokerit, and Ilmari realized
at that time that he should step back as Teemu's coach.

THE JOKERS

I N THE MID-1980s, Espoo was famous for its excellent junior hockey program, but the city did not have a team in Finland's top league. When Teemu was mulling over a move, one of the options was IFK, the Helsinki-based team that was once described as the Montreal Canadiens of Finland. It seemed that a move to IFK would give Teemu a better chance to get ahead in his career, but Teemu and Ilmari listened to their hearts more than their heads.

He picked IFK rival Jokerit.

"Teemu and I decided to choose a team that had good coaching and that would be fun to play for," Ilmari said. "Also, Jokerit was definitely an underdog, and Teemu liked that. That's why he liked the Rocky movies, too. Their lesson was that if you try hard, work hard, and don't give up, anything is possible."

The head of Jokerit's junior system and legendary founder of the club, Aimo Makinen, wanted to sign Leo Aikas as the head coach of Jokerit's under-15 team. It may have been the biggest signing of his career, and Makinen had signed some big Finnish hockey stars—such as Veli-Pekka Ketola and Lauri Mononen—over the years.

Jokerit's top men's team was in decline, and the only way to dig itself out of the hole was to retool the roster. Aikas joined Jokerit and brought with him Petri Aaltonen and Keijo Sailynoja from TJV.

Ilmari Selanne liked Aikas' reputation as a coach who knew how to develop young talent. He wanted Teemu to play for him, and Teemu attended the Jokerit tryouts with about 40 other players. He was one of the last players to make the team.

"I was given new skates right away, and we were given new sticks from the Jokerit major junior team. It felt great. Up until that point we had had to buy everything ourselves," Teemu said.

Teemu's first connection with Jokerit can be traced back to school, where his gym teacher, Olli Hietanen, was the head coach of Jokerit in the Finnish League. He also coached Finland to back-to-back silver medals at the World Juniors.

More importantly for Teemu, though, Hietanen often gave the kids tickets to Jokerit games.

The school's biggest Jokerit star was Teppo Kivela, three years older than Teemu, who often played with other kids in the Kivenlahti rink, and whose games even the Selannes would drive to Helsinki for. Kivela would later win the Finnish League scoring title with another team. And when he played for Finland in the 1991 World Championship in Turku, one of his teammates was Teemu.

Teemu was on a mission to become the best player he could possibly be, and Jokerit offered him the best opportunity to achieve his goals.

His first season did not work out the way he had hoped, but things improved in his second season, highlighted by being named to the U16 national team. The turning point came in the summer of 1984, and it was the start of an eight-year period during which Aikas coached Teemu, both at Jokerit and at the national team level. Aikas nurtured the player who would become the biggest star in Finnish hockey. Their journey would come to a glorious finish in 1992, when Jokerit won the Finnish league championship.

"I could tell Teemu was a future star because he had the burning desire to work hard even though his pains were at their worst," Aikas said.

Teemu's legs continued to bother him. The pain brought him to tears several times during the season. Teemu kept his illness secret from his teammates and friends.

"It was a subpar season for Teemu, for natural reasons. We seriously considered that he take a sabbatical. The pain didn't subside until the following season," Aikas said.

When the team held its off-ice practices, Teemu was given a pass from the running exercises due to his leg problems. Instead, he often took his bicycle for a 50-kilometer spin, and he swam a lot.

During his second season with Jokerit, the other players voted Teemu to be the team captain. The season ended with the Finnish championship playoffs, and IFK beat Jokerit 2–1 in the best-of-three semifinal. "That stung. We hated them because they played dirty, just like their men's team in the Finnish league," Teemu said.

Teemu's offensive production had picked up, catching the attention of officials, who named him to Finland's U16 team. The decision was unpopular; some thought too many players from Jokerit were named to the squad. Aikas, who was the U16 assistant coach, defended the decision, saying he expected Selanne to take his game to another level.

In 1986, Leo Aikas was offered the job as head coach of Jokerit's top junior team and as tempting as the offer was, he told officials he would only do it on one condition: that he could bring three players with him, including Selanne.

At the end of the 1986–87 season, the Jokerit organization suffered a setback when the men's senior team was relegated from Finland's top league. It was uncertain if the organization would survive, but a new generation of stars—including Selanne—played a key role in returning

Jokerit to the top league, and he was a key player when Jokerit won the league title in 1992.

Ilmari, meanwhile, had taken a step back as Teemu's personal coach, but he still played a role in his son's development. The Jokerit practice rink was at least a 40-minute drive from the Selanne home, giving the father plenty of time to talk to his son.

"When he was playing well, I gave him praise. When he wasn't playing well, I told him so. I reminded him constantly about how hard he had to work," Ilmari said.

He also taught Teemu to be self-critical and analyze his own game, regardless of what other people said. And as long as Teemu's leg pains persisted, Ilmari eased them with his massages.

One of Aikas' principles was that his players had to work just as hard at school as in the rink, but Teemu's parents had told their son he could get out of school in 1986 after Grade 9, when compulsory school obligation ends in Finland.

"I never enjoyed school. I only went there to see friends and girls. My grade averages were between 6.7 and 7.3 [on a scale from 4 to 10], and even in some classes I just wrote down names of the top players in the scoring race and worked on my autograph," said Selanne. "I figured you have to play hockey when you're young, and that you can always go back to school later."

"He was very committed to it, and everybody kept telling me he was really good at it," said Liisa. "To me, the most important thing was to see my child lead a life he loves. I believe in lifelong learning, and I always thought he could go back to school later."

By the summer of 1986, the Osgood-Schlatter disease was no longer an issue and Teemu grew about five inches. He still had the passion for hockey and a burning desire to succeed.

When the Selanne twins were in their early teens, one of their goals was to have mopeds. They talked about mopeds daily, and Panu had had one when he had been their age. Ilmari said he would make the purchase if the twins each had grade point averages of 8.0 or better at the end of Grade 8.

Paavo did—Teemu didn't—but Teemu found another way to get his moped. He bought one off a teammate. "With my own savings," he said proudly.

The 15-year-old had had his first summer job at a construction site in Helsinki, and he used the money for the moped, which he rode an hour to practices. Aikas remembers one time Teemu arrived late, covered in mud.

"All you could see were his eyes and teeth. He told me the chains had fallen off a couple of times during his journey. I didn't really like that he rode his moped to practices even late in the fall. It was a long drive, and a little dangerous, and he caught a cold more than once," Aikas said.

Teemu's transportation woes became a much-talked-about subject with his teammates. Sometimes Teemu arrived on time, and other times late. Sometimes Ilmari drove him; other times, he rode his bicycle, hitched a ride with a teammate, or came by himself by moped, later a motorbike.

Ilmari worked long hours and couldn't always make it to the rink in time to pick up Teemu and Waltteri Immonen, who often got a ride home.

Teemu was working for the City of Espoo's land-surveying department in the summer of 1986, and he used his savings to buy a motorcycle, a Honda MBX 125F. His best friend at the time, Kai Eklund, also had a motorcycle.

Teemu's life now had two constants, hockey and motorcycles.

The summer of motorcycles may have been the most dangerous year of Teemu's life. He liked going fast on two wheels and he took considerable risks in traffic. Ilmari tried to reason with him, reminding his son he had to take other people into consideration.

"He was fast and furious. His confidence in himself, his bike, and his skills could not have been better, and he completely ignored everybody else," Ilmari said.

Aikas shared the concerns for Teemu's safety.

"I was very worried for him. I saw how he showed his teammates all kinds of tricks. He'd be doing wheelies in the parking lot. I had never seen anyone do things like that," he said.

"It's a miracle that nothing serious happened, he must have had all kinds of guardian angels watching over him, and the stars aligning just perfectly," he said.

Teemu also kept on riding his bike late into the fall when the weather got freezing cold, and the cold air even slightly paralyzed his face once.

"He had to do some facial exercises, and the muscles did get their elasticity back, but that's the secret of Teemu's crooked smile," Ilmari said.

———————

Teemu found love for the first time when he was almost 17. After Jokerit lost the junior final in overtime to Karhu-Kissat, the team took the ferry to Stockholm for a season-ending trip. During the trip, he met Anu Saari, who was on her way to a swim meet in Stockholm.

"I knew he was an interesting person, and we talked a lot. He was upset with the final they had lost, and I remember how he cried when he talked about it. He took it really hard," Anu said.

Teemu fell in love, and it wasn't long before he asked Ilmari if he could borrow 300 Finnish markka, about $50. He would not say what the money was for, and Ilmari found out a week later.

"Teemu was engaged to Anu, and he needed the money to buy her a ring," he said.

It happened quickly. They met in March and were engaged on June 1.

"Maybe it was partly in jest," Teemu says now, but according to Anu, they were serious.

"We were so much in love, and we acted like we knew everything about everything. That was it, you know, we were going to get married and start a family," she said. "It just felt right, we were so happy and we had similar sense of humor and outlook on life."

Teemu and Anu spent the summer of 1987 together sailing, visiting her parents, and touring on his motorcycle. "Teemu was so charismatic, so different from all other boys. He was outgoing and warm, funny, and genuine. He was very polite with my parents and grandparents."

Their relationship was put to the test five months later when Anu left for Seattle on a student exchange program. "We both cried our eyes out at the airport. It was horrible," Anu said.

When Anu returned home in June 1988, Teemu was doing his compulsory army duty and was unable to meet his bride-to-be at the airport. Teemu was also getting ready for his first season with Jokerit's senior men's team, which had been relegated to Division 1 the season before.

Once he was discharged from the army, hockey took up more and more of Teemu's time. He spent Christmas in Alaska at the World Junior Championships and started to garner more media attention—which was fun for him, but not for Anu.

They went their separate ways in January 1989. Anu had fallen in love with an unknown teenage hockey player but broke up with a star.

"If I have to come up with something that's not just positive I'd say that he knows how to use his popularity to his advantage. I'm not sure that's always great for people close to him. He is everybody's Teemu, and it was difficult to find time alone with him, except in the beginning," she said.

Four months later, Teemu met someone at Paavo's high school graduation party. Her name was Sirpa Vuorinen, and she would become Teemu's wife.

It's difficult to understand how a man who had put all his effort, time, and money into his son's hockey career could leave at such a crucial moment, but that's exactly what happened when Ilmari and his new wife, Kirsi, left for Africa in the spring of 1988 on a four-year work assignment.

Ilmari didn't see any of Teemu's games during that time. He didn't see Jokerit earn promotion to Finland's top league. He didn't see Teemu play in the 1991 World Championship in Turku and he missed Jokerit's Finnish championship. He didn't watch the 1991 Canada Cup or the 1992 Olympics in Albertville, France, on television.

"I lost my job in 1987, and our financial situation worsened. I was still doing translations, and one day when I was at the office delivering one of them, a colleague told me he'd been offered a job in Africa. He said he wasn't going to take it, but he suggested that I should go for it," Ilmari said.

Finland had donated a railway crane to Africa and Ilmari found a job as a crane instructor. He trained workers in Tanzania, Zambia, Zimbabwe, and Botswana on how to use and service the machine.

When he left for Africa, he wasn't sure how Teemu's career would turn out. "I didn't think he'd become an NHL star."

But the opposite happened.

The NHL's Winnipeg Jets drafted Teemu in 1988, just prior to his 18th birthday. Ilmari was in Africa, and when he returned to Finland in April 1992, he was 55 and his son was about to embark on an NHL career.

MAKING OF A STAR

THE FINNISH ICE HOCKEY ASSOCIATION annually invites about 100 of the top under-15 players for a development camp at the Vierumaki Arena Center 130 kilometers northeast of Helsinki.

Teemu was 15 when he was asked to go in 1985, but he was still struggling with Osgood-Schlatter disease. His leg pains were at their worst, and he could barely skate.

His woes continued when he was not named to the extended roster for Finland's U16 team, along with being left off the roster for the national soccer team for his age group.

But he used the rejections as motivation, and his efforts paid off. He was invited to a second camp for the U16 team and played his first national team games for his age group in Denmark in December 1985. That's when he was introduced to team doctor Ismo Syvahuoko, a man who wound up having a profound impact on his career.

Syvahuoko was a former captain of Jokerit's top junior team who became a doctor after a short career in the Finnish top league. He has worked for the three professional teams in the Helsinki area—Jokerit, IFK, and Espoo Blues—and was a staff member on the national junior teams in the 1980s and men's national team in World Championship 2004 and World Cup 2004.

"We got along great from the get-go, even though I was [14 years] younger, and just a kid. It was easy to hang out with him, and we had mutual interests, such as cars, tennis, and girls. Oh, that's right, he was married back then, so scratch girls off the list," Teemu recalled, laughing.

Even though the camp schedule was busy, it wasn't busy enough for Teemu. His schedule looked a little different from the others: breakfast, morning skate, tennis, lunch, tennis, practice, and tennis. When the camp ended, the unlikely duo exchanged phone numbers.

Syvahuoko was not the only person Teemu connected with at the development camp. There was also Erkki Haapanen—whom everybody in Finland knows simply as "Neka." Haapanen gained fame for two reasons. One is that he worked the door at legendary Helsinki restaurant Kosmos, which was a favorite haunt of filmmakers, painters, philosophers, and actors. He also achieved notoriety as the equipment manager for the Finnish Ice Hockey Association in 1982. Three years later, he met Teemu for the first time when he gave him a ride home after the junior national team's camp in Vierumaki.

"He was a small kid, snot running down his nose," Haapanen, who passed away in 2018, said in 2014 when he was interviewed for a Finnish biography on Teemu.

Teemu was 15, Haapanen 41. Their paths crossed at tournaments and camps until finally Haapanen became Teemu's official skate sharpener.

"We started to spend more time together and Neka became a second father figure to me. He taught me how to sharpen my skates until I didn't trust my skates with anyone else. Mostly though, he taught me things about life," Teemu said.

During his first season with Jokerit's Division 1 team, Teemu didn't let the team's equipment managers sharpen his skates. He took his skates to Haapanen's home.

"I fixed his skates for every practice before a game. Sometimes Ismo Syvahuoko would call me at Kosmos and tell me Teemu had lost an edge. I got somebody to cover for me at the door and took a cab to the rink to sharpen his skates in the middle of the game," Haapanen said.

"When Teemu left for Winnipeg [for Jets training camp], I fixed 10 sets of blades for him to take with him. The guys in Winnipeg knew how to sharpen his skates, but they didn't know how to profile them for Teemu. With the profiling already done, Teemu could just have the blades changed every once in a while."

Teemu eventually bought a sharpening machine so that he could do the profiling himself, and, according to Haapanen, he's a pro at that, too. "Many of his teammates wanted Teemu, not their equipment managers, to sharpen their skates," he said.

Skates were not the only item that caught Haapanen's attention. Hockey sticks were another passion.

"As for the sticks, we noticed during the 1991 Canada Cup that the ice surface wasn't always great in the North American rinks, so Teemu added 4–5 millimeters to the width of his blade to make sure the puck wouldn't get out of control," Haapanen said.

Teemu used a wooden—of course—stick, a Titan TPM 2020 TS4.

"It wasn't too stiff because Teemu wanted an accurate shot," said Haapanen.

In February 1986, Teemu was back in the junior national team at tournament in Seinajoki, Finland. At that time, he was about 5-foot-7 and weighed 137 pounds. The shortest and lightest player on the team wasn't the best player on the team—far from it. But he had decided to "never give up."

Teemu was always a student of the game, very curious about everything in hockey. He looked for answers, and he posed questions to coaches, trainers, massage therapists, doctors, everybody. He was never afraid to ask questions.

"Even as a kid, I wanted to know everything about everything, how stiff the shafts were supposed to be, how to sharpen skates. I even taught myself to sharpen my skates with my dad's machine," he said.

Since he was short and light, he had a hard time getting the edges of his skates sharp enough, which meant that he often fell on the ice. He blamed the skates. Naturally, a challenge like that piqued Ilmari's curiosity.

Teemu had been 12 when he got his first pair of good skates. It was the secondhand pair of Bauers his parents bought in Canada. Before that he had been skating with hand-me-downs from friends and relatives, often old and too big.

"I always thought that the equipment didn't make the player. Teemu's first pants were homemade, too. We tried to get everything with as little money as possible," Ilmari said. "It wasn't until he was 14 and got invited to the district camp and then the junior national team that we bought him the gear he wanted."

Before that, Teemu was ashamed of his equipment. He knew exactly which were the cool skates and gloves and which were not. His were not.

"Teemu was shocked to see some of the equipment that the Eastern Bloc players used. The Soviet Union's Pavel Bure wore plastic skates that even Teemu would have refused to wear, for sure, and Bure also wore old motorcycle gloves as hockey gloves," Ilmari said.

———————

Selanne had his coming-out party during his second season with Jokerit's major junior team in 1987–88. He also played for Finland's national men's team late in 1987, which remains a highlight of his year. "I could barely sleep. It was such a big deal to wear the Team Finland jersey for the first time."

He was catching the eye of NHL scouts, the bloodhounds who scour leagues across the planet for prospects.

Teemu then had a great showing at a four nations tournament in Finland in February 1988.

"For some reason, hearing the national anthem before the first game got us fired up. It sent chills up my spine. We beat Sweden 8–3," said Teemu, who had two goals and three assists.

In the second game, Finland rallied back from a 3–1 deficit against Czechoslovakia and won the game 9–3. Teemu scored two and picked up two assists. In the third game, the Soviets beat Finland 8–3. Teemu scored one of Finland's goals and assisted another one.

He had scored five goals and 11 points in three games. That was Teemu's breakthrough tournament. The NHL scouts and general managers present at the tournament made note of the Finnish sniper.

"Jari Kurri's father, Ville, who was always in the stands at Jokerit's major junior team's games, congratulated me after the game against Czechoslovakia and said that Teemu's about to become quite a player, which was nice," said Ilmari.

Teemu's success continued in the Finnish junior league. Jokerit finished second in the regular season, and Teemu's 43 goals in 33 games and 66 points led the league in scoring. It was quite a feat by the 17-year-old, who played against players as many as three years older than he was.

Teemu followed up in April with another stellar effort at the U18 European championships in Olomouc, Czechoslovakia.

Almost overnight, Teemu became one of the top prospects for the NHL draft in June.

"He still wasn't exceptionally skilled, and his shot was average, but somehow he was still one-of-a-kind," said Aikas. "He had a nose for goals. He had the goal scorer's instinct and timing, and that, combined with his fantastic acceleration, meant he was in the right scoring areas all the time, and got the scoring chances."

Teemu was on top of the world. He was in love. He became a fan favorite. You could sense something special was in the air.

Little did he know dark clouds were on the horizon.

The Jokerit men's team was about to go bankrupt, and no one was interested in investing in the team. Management had already decided to shutter everything if no new investors were found, although the rumor mill was speculating on how a group led by Kalervo Kummola, vice president and future president of the Finnish Ice Hockey Association, was interested in putting together a bid.

While the men's team struggled, Jokerit's top junior team was gunning for the Finnish championship. They beat Tampere Ilves in the semifinal and advanced to face Tampere Tappara in the final.

Jokerit won the first game of the best-of-three series in Helsinki 7–5 and the second 7–4 to clinch the crown. Aikas is convinced the junior championship saved Jokerit. "Had we not won the title, the franchise would have folded. Of course, all the junior teams would have continued their work somehow, but the players would have found themselves standing on a trap door, with no future prospects within the system."

Selanne led the league in playoff scoring with four goals and seven points in five games.

Teemu had played five games with the men's team that season, and like other junior players who were called up from Aikas' disciplined and professional coaching, he was shocked to see the men's team's lackadaisical attitude compared with the junior program.

"It was a joke," said Teemu. "Aikas was a modern coach who thought deeply about the game. He also knew who was hot on a particular night."

What made Teemu really appreciate the coach was his genuine presence.

"Every time he made a speech to the team, his lip was twitching because he was so passionate about the game. Nobody could ever question his authority," he said.

Teemu and his teammates were enjoying the championship celebrations in the dressing room when Kummola suddenly appeared in the room. He wanted to congratulate Aikas personally.

"That's when I knew something was definitely going down," Aikas said.

"We rescued Jokerit from a certain bankruptcy and made it the first for-profit, incorporated hockey club in Finland," Kummola said.

Teemu's celebrations were cut short when he was invited to play for Finland in the under-18 European Championship. It was the most important tournament for their age group, as it was their NHL draft year. All NHL teams had their scouts in Czechoslovakia.

Finnish hockey was on its way up.

The country had won its first World Juniors gold medal the year before, and Finland's decades-long medal drought had ended in Calgary when it won silver at the 1988 Olympics.

Meanwhile, Jari Kurri and Esa Tikkanen were winning Stanley Cups with the Edmonton Oilers, playing on the same line with Wayne Gretzky, "The Great One."

The "small lions"—as Finns refer to the junior national teams—were also in the middle of a medal hunt at the U18 tournament.

The team was focused and well coached, they played for each other, and team doctor Ismo Syvahuoko had even taken the players to a tanning salon to have them look stronger and healthier in the eyes of the opponents.

Czechoslovakia was about to break free from communism, and the young Finns were enjoying themselves by making good deals on the exchange rates, using Western currency to get Czech korunas.

"We spent our days off by riding a taxi around town. None of us could afford it in Finland, but over there we were like kings. We just told them drive fast," Teemu said.

Finland won its games in the group stage, beating Switzerland 11–1, Romania 18–0, and Sweden 7–3. In the medal round, they beat Norway 7–1, but lost to Czechoslovakia, led by future NHLer Robert Reichel, 5–3. It all came down to their last game against the Soviet Union.

"There was no massage therapist on the team, so 'Keke' [Saily-noja] and I used some cooking oil from the kitchen to massage each other," Teemu said.

The Czechoslovak crowd was strongly behind Finland, booing the Soviets. They were cheering for Finland partly out of built-in animosity toward the Soviets, and partly because a Finnish victory would have sealed the hosts' gold medals.

Tommy Wide scored Finland's first goal and Teemu its second, but the Soviets managed to tie it both times. The second period was scoreless. With 7:00 remaining in the game, Finland was handed a penalty. Teemu was about to jump onto the ice when coach Lasse Valiaho stopped him.

"He told me to stay on the bench, rest, and then go out and score the game-winner," Teemu said.

After Finland had killed off the penalty, Teemu jumped on the ice, received a pass from a teammate, skated around an opposing defense-man, deked a second one by putting the puck between his legs, and then deked a third one with a fake stop to put himself in position to score.

"[Future NHLer] Sergei Zubov tripped me, but as I was falling down, I took a shot and the puck went in through the five-hole," Teemu said. Finland won the game 3–2, sealing Czechoslovakia's gold and winning silver.

Watching from the stands was Mike Smith, general manager of the Winnipeg Jets. He said it was Teemu's solo show that finally made him want to draft the Finnish teenager in the first round of the NHL draft.

"I admired the European style and especially the Soviets' skilled play, and when I found out here was a Finn who was even more talented than the Soviets, I was sold," Smith said.

Teemu led the U18 tournament in scoring with seven goals and 16 points in six games. Teemu was the hottest name in his age group, not just in Finland, but in all of Europe.

The tournament also marked the beginning of Teemu's relationship with Don Baizley, another person who had a profound impact on his life. Baizley was a highly respected player agent who at one point represented all Finnish NHLers.

"I knew that Don was Kurri's agent and Edmonton Oilers scout Matti Vaisanen was his friend, so when he called me for the first time, I told him that if I ever needed an agent, I would sign with him," Teemu said.

There had been some articles about Teemu in the big newspapers in Finland, but after the European championship tournament, he became a celebrity. Finland's leading morning paper, *Helsingin Sanomat*, wrote, "Selanne is one of the most talked about newcomers in Finnish hockey."

At the Finnish league's annual year-end gala, Teemu took his place with Finnish league superstars Jarmo Myllys, Teppo Numminen, and Janne Ojanen, along with Aikas, to be interviewed on the country's top sports news show.

He was the hottest teenage player in Finland, and several teams from the men's league were hoping he would sign with them for the upcoming season.

Waltteri Immonen, Keijo Sailynoja, and Teemu had agreed to stick together with Jokerit, but they had also agreed to keep all options open until they knew how Jokerit's future would turn out.

After the U18 tournament, Teemu and Sailynoja sat at Ismo Syvahuoko's apartment in Lauttasaari, close to downtown Helsinki. They sat in the sauna, swam, and drank vodka until the wee hours.

"I woke up to Syvahuoko's daughters—Jenna, 3, and Sara, 5—squirting water on my face with a water pistol. Syvahuoko's wife, Anne, had already left for work. Then the phone rang," Teemu said.

At the other end of the line was IFK's CEO Frank Moberg, who wanted to speak with his team doctor about Teemu and Sailynoja leaving Jokerit and joining the only top league team in Helsinki.

"We had talked about it earlier, but when Frank called me then, I just told him that the guys were with me and handed the phone to Teemu," Syvahuoko said.

Teemu told Moberg that he'd listen to offers, but his friends would also have to be included in any deal. Moberg invited all three, separately, to meet with him at the IFK office.

Teemu didn't have an agent to help him negotiate a contract. Ilmari didn't feel that he could be of any help in contract negotiations, and he was also getting ready to move to Africa. Baizley, on the other hand, would deal with NHL clubs, but not with Moberg.

"I trusted that Teemu had so many contacts in the business that he'd find somebody to assist him. He had always found knowledge-able help in the past," Ilmari said.

Teemu met with Moberg by himself. "Frank seemed like a nice guy, although he was all business. We made some small talk while waiting for IFK head coach Pentti Matikainen. Then assistant coach Heikki Riihiranta joined us, and they asked me what my plans were. I told them that I was going to do my military service," Teemu said.

Matikainen scoffed at the plans.

"He told me to forget about the army, go study somewhere, and join IFK instead. He said that doing the military service a couple of years later would be easier, I'd get more leaves and so on," Teemu said.

Then Moberg handed him the envelope with the IFK offer.

"Dad and I opened the envelope in the car. They offered me 10,000 markka for the first season and 15,000 for the second, and 50 markka for each practice. Dad laughed and said that I wasn't a very expensive player," Teemu said.

That 10,000 markka equaled about $1,700, and 15,000 about $2,500. The 50? Probably about $8.

"I didn't really understand just how poor the offer was, but fortunately, Matti Vaisanen, the Edmonton Oilers' Finnish scout and a friend of Jari Kurri, had heard rumors about IFK being after me," Teemu said.

Vaisanen called him up and the two met at a gas station's cafeteria in downtown Helsinki.

"He told me that IFK was famous for being pretty ruthless with young players and he asked me about the offer. I showed it to him and he told me it was outrageously insulting. Then he said he'd help me," Teemu said.

Vaisanen called Moberg and asked him how he had the gall to lowball Teemu like that.

"I told him that Teemu would make more money by delivering the morning paper," Vaisanen said.

Moberg offered to make a new offer, but Teemu had already made up his mind.

"Coming up through the juniors, we had always hated IFK. And now this. Had I received a real offer I would have at least considered it, but that made me promise myself that I'd never play for them," Teemu said.

Today, Moberg says lowballing Teemu was one of the biggest mistakes of his long career. "In hindsight, it's easy to see that it was a huge blunder."

Instead, Vaisanen went to Jokerit and negotiated Teemu's first contract. "I got 80,000 markka ($13,500) and a car, which is about half of what I would have gotten elsewhere, but money wasn't everything," Teemu said.

Another important thing that tipped the scale in Jokerit's advantage was the fact that Aikas had taken the step to the men's team as assistant coach.

"I listened to my heart. Also, I really wanted to do my military service," Teemu said.

The 1988 NHL Entry Draft was held in the historic Montreal Forum on June 11, just weeks before Teemu Selanne's 18th birthday. The Edmonton Oilers and Winnipeg Jets had Teemu high on their wish lists and were ready to do almost anything to claim the speedy Finn. He had not attracted the same attention from the other 19 teams.

Since the North American–dominated NHL started reaching overseas for players, 73 Finns had been drafted heading into the '88 lottery. The first was Tommi Salmelainen, who was drafted by St. Louis in 1969. Matti Hagman had been the first Finnish-trained player to play in the NHL in the 1976–77 season.

Ville Siren and Jukka Seppo had been the highest picked of all Finns, No. 23 overall; Siren by the Hartford Whalers in 1983 and Seppo by the Philadelphia Flyers in 1986. But neither was a first-rounder. Hall of Famer Jari Kurri had been chosen in the fourth round, No. 69 overall, by the Oilers in 1980, and Teppo Numminen No. 29 overall in 1986 by Winnipeg.

"I didn't know anything about the draft. Don Baizley called me and asked me if I wanted to go to Montreal. I told him that I was going to the army," Teemu said.

The Edmonton Oilers had become the favorite NHL team for most Finns, thanks to Jari Kurri, who had won four Stanley Cups with them between 1984 and 1988. Kurri played with the best player in the world, Wayne Gretzky, while the other winger was often another Finn, Esa Tikkanen. In addition, Reijo Ruotsalainen had won the Stanley Cup with the Oilers in 1987. The Oilers were eager to add another Finn to the lineup.

"We worked hard to get Teemu," said Vaisanen, who had been reporting to the Oilers about Teemu's most prominent characteristic, explosiveness, for a year. "When going one-on-one, he could create a scoring chance for himself or a teammate every time, which made him exceptional."

Winnipeg didn't have the Oilers' tradition of winning the Stanley Cup, but it had a history of signing Finns.

"Edmonton had been my favorite team, but it didn't matter who was going to draft me. The NHL seemed so distant," Teemu said.

The first pick had gone to the Minnesota North Stars, the last-place team in the standings, and they chose Mike Modano, who was born in the United States and played junior hockey in Canada.

NHL drafts are known for behind-the-scenes wheeling and dealing, and the Oilers were busy trying to move up past Winnipeg, which had the 10th overall pick, to get Teemu.

The Oilers finished third overall in the 1987–88 regular season and had the 19th pick. Edmonton brass knew the Jets would take Teemu with the 10th pick, and they made a play for the St. Louis Blues' pick at No. 9 overall. The Blues were willing to make the trade, but they placed a condition on the possible changes. The Blues coveted Rod Brind'Amour, and if he was still available when the ninth overall pick was to be announced, the deal was off.

Brind'Amour went to the Blues, much to the elation of the Jets, who picked Teemu at No. 10 overall.

"I've never been as nervous. We really wanted to draft him," said Jets general manager John Ferguson, who died in 2007.

Of European players, only Sweden's Bjorn Johansson (No. 5 in 1976), Czechoslovakia's Peter Svoboda (No. 5 in 1984), and Sweden's Ulf Dahlen (No. 7, 1985) had been drafted higher than Teemu. Sweden's Mats Sundin became the first European No. 1 overall pick, going to the Quebec Nordiques in 1989.

Teemu was oblivious to what was happening at the draft in Montreal. Baizley had tried to call him, but couldn't get a hold of him. He didn't have a cell phone.

Truth be known, Teemu was with Kai Eklund and had forgotten about the draft. He spent the night at another friend's house, and in the morning—two days after the Jets gave him the nod—his friend's mother showed him a report in the morning newspaper that he had been selected in the first round.

"I asked her where to, and she told me Winnipeg. I said okay, and went back to sleep. The next day, I started my military service," Teemu said.

Before he left for the military, Selanne wrote to his father in Africa about the draft.

"The draft was yesterday in Montreal! The Winnipeg Jets drafted me in the first round!" he wrote. "That's great but I have to remember that this is where it begins. Getting drafted is nothing, it doesn't change anything. But it is a step closer to the NHL, right?"

The Jets invited Selanne to their training camp the following September to get a closer look at their top prospect.

If Teemu Selanne hadn't been a household name in Finnish hockey circles before the draft, he certainly became one after it. Expectations were sky high and for Jokerit, it was a good deal since the club got the media attention it so badly needed. The 18-year-old who found himself in the middle of it all had many new things to deal with.

He was in the middle of his military service at the Army Sports Academy, and had to drive from Espoo to Lahti—an hour's drive— almost daily after his basic training was over for his obligations with Jokerit.

"I was able to get leaves to go to practices and games, but I had to report back at seven in the morning, and after some road games, we didn't get back home until 4:00 AM. I had to be back in Lahti just three hours later.

"Once, I did fall asleep at the wheel, but fortunately it was in the winter and I woke up safe and sound when the car hit a snowbank," Teemu said.

The 1988–89 season was one of the busiest ever for Selanne. He wound up wearing the jerseys of six teams—the Jokerit men's team, Jokerit juniors, Army Sports Academy (they played in the major junior league), and the national men's B and A teams—and he played about 70 games.

Selanne missed his father, and he wrote him letters regularly to keep him updated on his career. Anu, then still his fiancée, had returned to Finland, and Teemu wanted to find time for her, too. And on top of everything, Panu was sentenced to prison. And as if all that hadn't been enough, Selanne also traveled the world more than ever.

"I played at the World Juniors in Alaska, attended the Jets' camp in Canada in the fall, and was on another Canadian tour with the B national team. I was also in Sweden with the under-20 national team, and in Switzerland with Team Finland [the men's A team] in November," Selanne said.

On top of all this, he began his 11-month military service in mid-June with 21 other hockey players, including three of his Jokerit teammates.

"The first 50 privates got a leave at midsummer, 10 days after we had begun our training," he said. "It was based on a written test. I wasn't one of those 50. It bummed me out to see Kai [Eklund] and others when they paid me a visit on their way to midsummer festivities."

Anu had been in Finland for weeks, but Teemu had only seen her at the army canteen.

"When I didn't get a leave in July, either, I pretended that I had misunderstood things and just left the barracks with the others," said Teemu, who even called back the next day and asked the duty officer, who was his friend, if the mistake had been noticed.

It hadn't.

"I would have made it back okay, but on Sunday, a senior citizen had gone missing in the Lahti region and the army was called in to help. That's when they noticed I had gone AWOL," he said.

He returned at midnight to hear that he wouldn't be allowed to leave the barracks for 10 days.

"They also added a day to my service. When the others were released in May 1989, I had to stay there for another night," he said.

After his two-month-long basic training ended, Selanne spent only 15 nights in the barracks and only one night on a field exercise. He was playing hockey the rest of the time, but the early mornings made it a physically demanding season.

The recently purchased Jokerit organization had a new CEO in Unto Wiitala, the former men's national team goalie who had participated in the Olympic Winter Games both as a player and a referee.

When Selanne was in the military, Wiitala was on good terms with the army brass, and that was a big help in Selanne's ability to serve his country and play for his club team at the same time.

"Even though I didn't have any problems with getting leaves, whenever there was an issue that needed to be sorted out, I called Wiitala right away. All my friends started to ask me about this man, 'Unski' as he was called, and he became a legend in the army, too," he said.

Selanne recalled an incident one a Friday morning in the fall of 1988. He drove back to Lahti after a few hours' sleep at Anu's place, and when he arrived there, the place was buzzing, getting ready for a big military exercise.

"I was told to pack my full combat gear because it was going to be a tough trip. I told everybody right away that I couldn't go on any trips because I had a game on Saturday. I was so certain that I'd get to play the game that I only put two pillows in my backpack," Teemu said.

But this time the officers meant business, and they told Selanne the exercise was such a big deal that even Teemu Selanne would have to participate.

"I joined the others where we were supposed to go, and that evening, when it got cold and dark, I started to lose faith. Maybe they weren't going to let me take a leave. I didn't even have a sweater with me and just before the trucks were supposed to pick us up, I asked our drill sergeant for permission to visit the canteen."

When given permission, Selanne ran as fast as he could to the closest phone.

"I called Wiitala, but he didn't answer, so I left him a message that I desperately needed his help, that I was in trouble. Then I ran to the canteen to buy some donuts because I figured that I could trade them with my buddies for sweaters and other things I might need. It was going to be a really cold night."

As soon as Selanne got back to his buddies, they asked him if he had been in touch with Wiitala.

"I told them I hadn't, and we were told to get on the vehicles. I started to make deals with the donuts. I was really disappointed when the tarps came down on the trucks," he said.

His friends couldn't have been happier. For once, Selanne did not get his way. They enjoyed seeing him in the truck, with two pillows in his backpack.

The last laugh, however, was on them.

"Just as we were about to drive through the gate, they stopped our vehicle. An officer showed up and told me that I was supposed to go on a leave. I couldn't believe my ears. Wiitala had heard my message and had fixed everything once again. I tossed the donuts to my buddies and jumped down from the truck," he said.

Two months after the draft, shock waves were sent through the hockey world when the unthinkable happened: the Edmonton Oilers traded Wayne Gretzky, The Great One and the unquestionable best player in the world, to the Los Angeles Kings on August 9, 1988.

Trading Gretzky signaled that nothing was sacred anymore and nobody was safe. Business was taking a firmer grip on the sport.

"I remember the trade, but I didn't understand that it would have any effect on my career," he said.

It most certainly would, and in many ways.

The trade changed the way the American sports fan looked at hockey.

Instead of the best player being in what was considered by many hockey's hinterland in Edmonton, Gretzky was taking Los Angeles by storm. He would now play in the entertainment capital of the world, and many people took notice. The Gretzky trade signaled hockey's arrival in the USA's Sun Belt. It was no coincidence Disney produced the successful hockey movie *The Mighty Ducks* in the coming years.

Gretzky's impact was massive for hockey, particularly the NHL, in the United States.

California soon went from having one team—Los Angeles—to adding two more, the Anaheim Mighty Ducks and the San Jose Sharks. Expansion also took the NHL to other unconventional hockey markets with the addition of the Dallas Stars and the Phoenix Coyotes.

In December 1992, the league added two expansion franchises, the Florida Panthers and the Mighty Ducks of Anaheim (owned by Disney, of course), and they were to begin play the following season.

Change was happening and happening fast. And along with the additional teams, player salaries skyrocketed.

The Gretzky trade led to so many changes, it would be hard to keep count. And Selanne was one of the people who wound up being greatly helped by the transaction.

In the 1987–88 season, 12 Finns played in the NHL, and the season after that, the number had risen to 18.

Selanne's 1988–89 season started with the junior national team's first camp in August. The head coach was Olli Hietanen, a man Teemu knew as a gym teacher from Espoo. His assistant was future Finland men's team head coach Erkka Westerlund.

"You could tell right away that Westerlund knew a lot about the game, but Hietanen handled the players with a looser touch," Teemu said.

Finland played against the French men's national team twice before participating in a four nations tournament in Sweden. They lost four of their five games in August, getting just one tie. In December, they played two games against Poland's men's team—without Teemu—and lost one, tied the other one. In other words, the Finnish team that was preparing for its main event—the World Junior Championship—hadn't won a single game that season.

"It was chaos until Erkka became the head coach," recalls Teemu.

The problem, it turned out, was that Hietanen had a problem with alcohol, and it had progressed to a point where the federation fired him. Westerlund took the reins on the eve of World Juniors.

"Our main goal was actually the next year's tournament. Almost everybody on the team was a 1970 birthdate, and it was a tournament for the 1969 year," said Teemu.

He flew to Canada in September to attend the Jets' training camp and to meet people in the organization. "I had said yes mostly because it got me a two-week leave from the army, but it turned out to be a great trip in the end."

That year the Jets held their training camp in Moncton, New Brunswick—the home of their American Hockey League farm team, which is a long way from Winnipeg (over 1,900 miles). This was in early September, and before departing the Manitoba capital for Moncton, a press conference was held at the Winnipeg Arena where Teemu, along with fellow Finns Teppo Numminen and Markku Kyllonen, were introduced to the local media.

Numminen was the Jets' first round pick in 1987, and Kyllonen was selected in the eighth round of the same draft. Teppo, who was Teemu's roommate during the first week of camp, received most of the attention from the media that day, as he had played in both the Canada Cup and the Calgary Winter Olympic Games. Expectations were high that he would be a part of their NHL team that season.

Hannu Jarvenpaa was another Finn at training camp, having played 61 games for the Jets in the previous two seasons.

The second week, Teemu roomed with a different player, one who was a few years older and who proved to be an adventurous fellow. Teemu couldn't sleep because his roommate had several guests in the room all through the night just about every night.

"That gave me a glimpse of what life in the NHL must have been like in the 1980s. In a word: wild," said Teemu, who added that things have calmed down since then.

The 60 players in the camp were divided into four teams. Teemu played five training camp games on a line with Dale Hawerchuk and Brent Ashton. Hawerchuk, the first overall pick of the 1981 NHL Draft, had finished fourth in NHL scoring the year before, behind only Mario Lemieux, Wayne Gretzky, and Denis Savard.

Selanne had a goal and eight points in his audition.

A Jets defenseman named Dave Ellett remembers the young Finn well. "We called him 'Holy Shit' because he didn't speak a lot of English and when he did, he used that expression a lot, often in very odd situations," said Ellett.

Following one of the scrimmages, head coach Dan Maloney spoke glowingly about what he had seen from Selanne's play, telling reporters, "he has poise for a young player. He didn't seem to be a bit nervous. He scored a good goal; he can get into the holes when he has to. Certainly he's got good speed and good hands."

Hawerchuk's nickname was "Ducky" because of his skating style and he said at that camp he dreamed of riding shotgun with Selanne. "I learned at a young age that you get the puck to the fastest guy and [Teemu] was fast," said Hawerchuk. "I was shocked when Fergie [team executive John Ferguson] told me he was going back to Finland for army duty."

Whenever Hawerchuk travels back to New Brunswick, the 2001 Hockey Hall of Fame inductee fondly recalls to the crowd that Moncton was where he played with Teemu Selanne for the first time. Pausing, he then adds, "Little did I know it would also be the last time."

What surprised Teemu most was the poor shape of the players. To him, the other players looked overweight and slow. He couldn't believe that was the best league in the world.

Back then, NHLers didn't prioritize off-season training, and one of the reasons the teams had a training camp was to get them into a good enough shape before the regular season opener.

"We skated for three hours every day, the first hour and a half doing drill and the second hour and a half scrimmaging. And then we had a 30-minute skate in which we skated from one end of the rink to the other, defensemen against each other and forwards against each other.

"I had been on the ice since July and had played games that fall so I did all right."

Teemu was so fast that he had to be told to take it easy.

"The others couldn't keep up with me, which surprised me. One coach came to tell me not to go all out, because the veteran players didn't appreciate seeing me 10 meters in front of them," he said.

Even though the players may have been physically rusty, there was nothing wrong with their attitude. Everybody gave everything they got, especially during the scrimmages.

And once he got started, he was fine with speaking English as well.

"The guys were great, and they encouraged me to speak. I guess I had learned enough at school."

The highlight of the trip was a game against the Minnesota North Stars. Selanne wore No. 17 and hit the post once, but he was left off the score sheet.

"When we came back from Moncton, we were playing Minnesota at home and saw my name on the game roster. I said I don't want to play; I am not prepared to play here. But I had to play, and I was so scared. The game was good, and I have never been that nervous in my life. There were a lot of fights, a lot of ugly stuff, and I was thinking, this is terrible."

"But what changed my whole mind-set was the following year I broke my tibia and I missed the whole year. Winnipeg wanted me to fly to the playoffs to check it out and see a few games. I always remember when I saw them play the Oilers, and I saw those two NHL games, the intensity, how rough they were, it was a war. I was shaking after the game. This is scary.

"So I went back home after that and I told my dad I did not know if I could play in the league. You have no idea, these guys are so tough. They are so rough. It is violent. I have to be ready. And at that time, my focus changed. I even took fighting lessons so I could protect myself. My whole mind-set totally changed."

In a letter to his father from training camp, he wrote: "The game's pretty different, they slash and hook all the time. It's tough to get to the front of the net, they crosscheck you in the head and all that, but I had no problem keeping up with the speed of the game. It's pretty nice to play in front of 12,500 people, you know!"

Jets general manager John Ferguson, who would be fired that fall, was pleased with what he saw.

"He walked into the dressing room after the game against the North Stars with a cigar in his mouth, and he told me that he wanted me to stay. I was nervous and told him I couldn't because I had to go back to the army," he said.

Baizley joined the conversation, and they agreed to revisit the question in a year.

"I didn't want to play in the NHL then, and I really respect players like Aki Berg and Patrik Laine, who left for the NHL as 18-year-olds. That couldn't have been easy," he said.

"I figured I'd be ready for the NHL after the World Championship on home ice in 1991."

Truth be known, Teemu never dreamed that an NHL career was in the cards for him. "I did not know how far I could go. My goal was to make the Finnish league, and I think the national team was a dream and the NHL was a fantasy. I had no idea how to get there."

He relied very much on advice from Baizley, Jari Kurri, and Matti Vaisanen about joining the NHL only when you think you are ready.

"Don't come over before you are ready and 100 percent mentally know how to do it. I don't know how they come now at 18. I could not have done that. That is what I did. I said I wanted to play in the Olympic Games and the World Championship. We won the Finnish national title, and after that I said the only thing I want to do was go to the NHL."

As strange as it sounds, one of the most common rookie initiation rites, and possibly the most embarrassing one, used to be the shaving of the freshman's private parts in front of others in the dressing room.

When veteran players started to sing a certain song, it usually meant that a rookie was going to get shaved.

"It's happened to me once, during my rookie year in Jokerit," Teemu said.

He had another close encounter.

"It was during my first training camp in Moncton. We had a defenseman, Mario Marois, who was known as the team's shaving king. He shaved Numminen, for example. When I arrived at the camp, he was yelling at me all the time how he couldn't wait to shave me. I just told him 'no no, no, not me, not me, I'll only be here for a couple of weeks,'" Teemu said.

They went back and forth like that until they came back to Winnipeg.

"Marois told me not to stay on the ice after a pregame skate because he wanted to shave me before he left the rink. I told him again that I was going to fly back to Finland the next day, that I wasn't even supposed to get shaved, that's it's just for players who make the team, but he told me he couldn't wait.

"I was scared shitless. I snuck back into the dressing room and tried to be as quiet as a mouse. Then Marois told me to get in the shower. I went into the sauna and stayed there for at least half an hour, and when I peeked out the sauna window, he signaled to me that I had two minutes to hit the shower."

As soon as Teemu couldn't see Marois anywhere, he made his move.

"I ran to my stall, grabbed my clothes, and ran out of the dressing room naked. I put my clothes on outside and went to the hotel. Marois didn't play in the game, and when I got back to Winnipeg the next time, he wasn't on the team anymore. He was a dark, hairy, scary guy."

If you thought that incident scared him off the whole ritual, you'd be wrong. Once back with Jokerit, he shaved a couple of players in Helsinki. "That tradition lived on at least for as long as I was there," he said.

When Teemu joined the Jets in 1992, general manager Mike Smith put an end to the shaving ritual, and all rookies celebrated. "Veteran players remembered my drama with Marois, and they joked that they'd finish the job, but it was too late. They weren't allowed to do it," he said.

Instead, the new rookie initiation ritual was to take their teammates out to dinner. "We had eight rookies on the team, so my dinner cost me only $550. We were at Bern's Steak House in Tampa. In addition to paying for the dinner, we had to sing our national anthem and tell a joke."

Rookies weren't the only ones performing that night, though.

Team captain Troy Murray wanted to show the kids how tough real NHLers can be, so he broke a wineglass and ate it. "Except for the stem and foot," Teemu added.

———————

Teemu returned to Finland with one goal in mind: to do everything he could do to get Jokerit promoted to the Finnish top league from the ranks of Division 1. Nothing else mattered. The new coach, Kari Makinen, made sure conditioning was not an issue.

Teemu wrote to Ilmari: "This week I had 15 practices, 25 hours in total. It's almost pushing it, but we have to! The bar is so high that if you want to become something, you have to work hard. It's a long way to the top but the way down is fast if you start to think too much of yourself. I don't think that'll happen to me. I can't afford it, you know?"

Teemu wasn't the only young gun turning heads in Finland. Kiekko-Espoo's Petro Koivunen was another young star, the second-round pick, No. 39 overall, of the Edmonton Oilers in the '88 draft. He was in Edmonton at the Oilers' training camp at the same time Teemu was making an impression at the Jets' camp. When the Division 1 season opened with a game between Kiekko-Espoo and Jokerit, Finland's biggest paper ran a story with the headline SUPERKIDS SELANNE VS KOIVUNEN.

The other story line in the season opener was the battle between Selanne's line and Koivunen's line. Teemu stole the show by scoring two goals and adding two assists. He scored Jokerit's fifth and sixth goals in the 6–5 win.

Afterward, Selanne complained about being tired. The driving from Espoo coupled with the rigors of attending Jets training camp had taken its toll. And he didn't help himself by playing in the first game of the season for Jokerit's major junior team. Jokerit beat Kiekko-Espoo 13–4. Selanne scored five goals and collected eight points.

But if Selanne expected to find sympathy with Makinen, forget it. A couple weeks later, the coach delivered some tough love and constructive criticism. "He played lazy and didn't take a stride to help the defense."

Selanne took the criticism to heart and after six games was second in Division 1 scoring with eight goals and 17 points.

For his first two seasons, Selanne wore jersey No. 11 because a veteran player, Markku Tiinus, had No. 8. Coincidentally, 11 had been Jari Kurri's number when he played for Jokerit.

"It was the only number that I liked that was available. I switched to No. 8 in my second season in the Finnish league in 1990."

In his first national team games he wore No. 20, with both 8 and 11 taken by veteran players. In 1989, No. 11 became available, and Teemu took it. He was finally given No. 8 in 1990.

Since then, No. 8 has been synonymous with Teemu.

"The street number of our house in Espoo was 8. I joined my first team when I was 8 years old. That first motorcycle of mine had 8 in the license plate. I was drafted into the NHL in 1988. And, in the book my father wrote, the story of No. 8 is told on page 88," he said.

Finland was scheduled to play in the Nissan Cup in Berne, Switzerland, together with Sweden and Switzerland. The tournament was held in mid-November and it marked the beginning of the preparation period toward the 1989 World Championship in Sweden.

The media loved the fact that Teemu had been invited to the camp. Having an 18-year-old make his debut was exciting in itself, but that he'd make it before ever having played a game in Finland's top league was unheard of.

Nine players on the team had NHL experience, including Reijo Ruotsalainen, who was a Stanley Cup winner with the Oilers. In the fall of 1988, he was playing in Switzerland.

Finland lost to Switzerland 4–3 in a shootout. Selanne was one of Finland's shooters, but he missed. After the game, Finland head coach Pentti Matikainen gave Teemu some constructive criticism. "He's excellent with the puck but has a lot to learn how to play the game without it," he said.

In the second game against Sweden, Finland had better luck in the shootout and won 3–2. That time he wasn't one of the shooters. (A shootout was a fairly new thing in European hockey then, and all goals scored in the shootout were added on to the final score. Officially, Switzerland beat Finland 5–4 and Finland beat Sweden 4–3.)

"This tournament gave Teemu a taste of international hockey which will help him when we play in bigger tournaments. We wanted to invite him to the team now because he won't be playing in Finland for long."

After the tournament, Selanne missed a Jokerit team meeting, and Makinen benched him for two periods in a game against FoPS. Jokerit lost the game 6–4.

"I overslept. I was so tired and I forgot to ask for a wake-up call. I'm very mad at myself," Teemu told reporters.

At the end of November, Jokerit went on an eastern Finland road trip, playing first a game in Joensuu, five hours from Helsinki, and then the next night in Imatra, about three hours from Helsinki. They lost the game in Joensuu 7–1, and when Imatra rallied back from 4–2 to a 5–4 win in the third period, Teemu lost it.

He slammed his stick against the boards and threw the broken stick into the stands. Unfortunately, it hit a local politician, who filed charges against Selanne. "It was such a stupid thing to do, but I learned a lesson and I asked myself whether I had gotten a little too bigheaded."

He apologized to the politician and was suspended for two games. The charges were dropped.

By Christmas, Jokerit was third in the standings and the fans were filling the stands. Their last game before the holiday season break drew almost 4,500 spectators, up from about 1,000 at the end of the previous season and from about 2,000 earlier in the season.

He was still in the army, and by this time he had played games in Sweden, Canada, and Switzerland. He was about to add Alaska to the list. The 1989 World Junior Championship was being held there, and one of his longtime goals was to play in the showcase event.

It turned out to be quite the tournament.

The Soviet Union was still in existence and featured Alexander Mogilny, who had led the tournament in scoring the year before, on a line with Sergei Fedorov and Pavel Bure.

The USA's Jeremy Roenick (eight goals, 16 points) and Mike Modano (15 points) finished 1–2 in scoring, ahead of Bure, who was named the tournament's best forward. The Soviets won the tournament; Sweden finished second and Czechoslovakia third. Finland beat only Norway (9–3) and West Germany (5–3) and tied its first game against the US (5–5).

"It was a disappointment, but we had had a rough fall with the coaching change and everything. It was a learning experience for us. The upside was that we had 15 players who were eligible to play at the World Juniors the year after," Teemu said.

He finished second in team scoring with five goals and 10 points in seven games. "What mattered to me the most was the game against Canada. I wanted to show I could play well against them. We lost 4–3, but I scored two goals and we were the better team."

His good friend Syvahuoko was Finland's doctor in Alaska and remembered how in earlier tournaments Teemu didn't like to change his underwear and could go weeks wearing the same socks and underwear.

"He had packed just one pair of socks with him to Alaska, but I had anticipated it, so I had with me enough clean underwear and socks for Selanne to wear throughout the tournament," Syvahuoko said.

Teemu simply didn't care about clothes. These days, he pays a lot of attention to how he dresses.

"He thought it was stupid to show off your clothes, and he always wore his worn-out track pants. Of course, they didn't have a lot of money back then," said Anu, his then-fiancée.

Syvahuoko and Selanne stuck together and celebrated Christmas Eve at the hotel's restaurant in the top floor.

"The team had a curfew, but Teemu and I snuck into the elevator and ate a great steak dinner," Syvahuoko said.

And just like the year before, he paid a visit to Syvahuoko's hotel room every night. "He needed someone to talk to. We talked about everything and got to know each other even better," Syvahuoko said.

The Hockey News ranked the best juniors in the world after the tournament. Mogilny topped the list, followed by Bure, Roenick, Fedorov, and Rod Brind'Amour. Teemu was sixth on the list.

Back in Finland, Jokerit finished second in Division 1, which moved it closer to the qualification playoffs against the second-to-last team in the top league, Oulu Karpat, in a best-of-five series. The winner would earn promotion to the men's top league the following season.

Selanne scored 36 goals and 69 points in 35 regular season games and finished seventh in the scoring race, 34 points behind scoring leader Mikko Laaksonen.

He did lead Jokerit in scoring but now he had a bigger task ahead of him. Jokerit had to earn a promotion to the Finnish League; otherwise, the team would certainly lose its young, talented core.

Oddly enough, Jokerit even had Helsinki IFK management in its corner. When Jokerit was relegated from the top division, many expected IFK to become the dominant force in Finnish hockey. It was the only team from the capital and the biggest city, but that did not translate into stands full of people.

Karpat had a good team. They had several former Finland national team players, including Kai Suikkanen, whose number Teemu had taken over. Their goaltender was Canadian Daryl Reaugh, who had played seven NHL games with the Edmonton Oilers in the mid-1980s.

The Jokerit goalie, American Cleon Daskalakis, had played 12 NHL games with the Boston Bruins. "Karpat was the favorite, but we played together as a team and we believed in each other. We were desperate to win," Teemu said.

Karpat won the first game 7–3 at home in Oulu, but Jokerit returned the favor in Helsinki and tied the series with a 7–3 win. Karpat won Game 3 at home again (8–4) and Jokerit won its second home game 3–2. Teemu scored seven goals in the first four games, including the game-winner in Game 4.

It all came down to Game 5 in Oulu, but before that, Teemu needed to call Unto Wiitala again. He was supposed to be with his military unit, doing a 20-kilometer skiing trip the day before Game 5. "Wiitala took care of it again. I got a leave instead," Teemu said with a laugh.

Jokerit had averaged 2,549 spectators in the regular seasons, but the two games in the Helsinki Ice Hall had attracted 5,144 and 5,206 spectators. Game 5 in Oulu was played in front of 6,570 spectators, most of them fans of the home team.

"There were a couple hundred Jokerit fans, but they were so loud it felt like it was a Jokerit home game," said his mother, Liisa, who was also there.

Jokerit flew from Helsinki on the morning of the game and checked into a local hotel. "After the pregame lunch, me and Keke [Keijo Sailynoja] put the newspaper clippings on how Karpat just destroyed us on the hotel room walls to remind us that this is our night—just like Rocky in the movies," Teemu said.

After their pregame naps, Teemu and Keke each drank a liter of blueberry soup—as was their habit—and followed with a glass of a vitamin drink. "Just as we were about to leave the hotel, we looked at the clippings one more time, and then we looked at each other. Then we tore the clippings off the wall, threw them in the garbage, and said, 'Here we go,'" Teemu said.

"We came, we saw, and we got promoted to the top league. That was the beginning of Jokerit's Cinderella story," Teemu said.

Like Rocky, Jokerit went for the knockout.

Six minutes after the opening faceoff, the visitors had a 3–0 lead and chased Reaugh from the Karpat net. Reaugh later became a TV personality who has worked on the Dallas Stars' broadcast team and as an analyst on *Hockey Night in Canada*.

"I've reminded him of that game every time I've met him," Teemu said with a laugh.

Karpat rallied back to 3–2, but Jokerit won the game 5–2 and earned the promotion to the top league.

"This is great! The under-18 European championship silver is nothing compared to this. Now the joke is on all those who thought I shouldn't have stayed with Jokerit," Teemu told the media.

He led the qualification series in scoring with seven goals and 10 points in five games. He was named Best Player in Division 1. "It was voted by the players and meant a lot to me. I voted for Mikko Laaksonen.

"We had a fun team. The veteran players saw that us young guys meant business, and they supported us wholeheartedly," Teemu said.

Some of the veterans returned to Jokerit from IFK and had tried to bring with them "tough" IFK traditions—such as not allowing others to wear long underwear—but they didn't stick.

Teemu had just a couple of days to recover before it was time for him to travel to Canada again, now with Finland's national B team. The team was actually the A team, but since it played against Canada's Olympic team, it was classified as a B-team game in Finland.

"It was preparation for the Worlds, but it also gave the coach an opportunity to see what the kids could do. It was a rough trip. We played six games in seven days and traveled to the next city right after a game," Teemu said.

Finland toured Fort St. John, Prince George, Kitimat, Williams Lake, Kamloops, and Kelowna, all in British Columbia. Finland won three of the six games, lost two, and tied one. Teemu scored one goal and added an assist to another. He's listed as having played six games, but he only played in four.

After the trip to Canada, his season continued with Finland's World Championship training camp, during which Finland played twice against the Soviet Union, once in Joensuu and once in Helsinki.

Teemu wrote to Ilmari, "I wouldn't have thought a year ago that I'd be playing against the top players in the world [Sergei Makarov, Igor Larionov, Vladimir Krutov] now, but I don't mind it! Right?"

Teemu didn't play in the first game, which Finland lost 6–0, but he did play in the Helsinki game and earned his first men's national team point when he assisted Jukka Seppo, who scored Finland's lone goal. Finland lost the game 4–1.

The next games were played in Gavle and Timra in Sweden. Finland lost both games to Sweden 3–2 and 5–1. Teemu was left off the score sheet, and the "super junior" had only one assist in his first games with Team Finland.

"But I had no problem with keeping up," Teemu said.

He wound up being the last player cut from the 1989 World Championship team. Teemu believes he was cut because he hadn't signed with IFK, but Pentti Matikainen, who also coached IFK, and Frank Moberg, who doubled as IFK's CEO and Team Finland's manager, won't admit to it.

Selanne didn't sulk about not being on the team, and instead, he and Sailynoja were Finland's biggest fans in the arena when Finland took on Canada in Sodertalje.

"I had won an award sponsored by a bank. It was a trip for two to the Worlds. So Sailynoja and I went there. It was fun.

"I stood behind the Plexiglas and yelled at the guys, 'Hey, I'm here.' Several players have reminded me of that—decades later," Teemu said.

He was also a bit playful in his unaccustomed role as a fan.

"We sat in a group that had a sign that said, MARJO MATIKAINEN'S BUTT = YES!

"Every time we raised it, we sat down behind it. There was a photo of the sign in a paper, but our faces were behind it, fortunately," Teemu said.

Matikainen had won the gold medal in the 5-kilometer cross-country skiing event at the 1988 Calgary Winter Olympic Games.

Finland lost to Canada 6–4. And although Matikainen added Jari Kurri and Esa Tikkanen on to the team in the middle of the tournament, Finland finished fifth.

Teemu returned home to finish his military service and to sign a new contract with Jokerit. His army buddies had been waiting for the last day of their service for one very good reason: it was going to be their time for payback.

Remember, Teemu was handed an extra day of service for going AWOL. So, when the day arrived, the entire group headed to the most popular nightclub in Lahti as civilians. They said their farewells to him with big grins on their faces, thinking that he who laughs last, laughs best.

Only their laugh was second to last.

"Some of the career officers came to me a few hours later and told me to get some civilian clothes on. We drove to the nightclub and the officers joined us. Guys were fuming when they saw me there. I slept over at an officer's apartment and picked up my stuff from the barracks the next day," Teemu said.

He had only one more thing to do.

"I had gotten out of the extra night by promising the two officers that I'd drive them through downtown Lahti in my Lincoln soft-top," Teemu said.

Teemu wouldn't be Teemu had he not put his entire first-season salary into his first car. Even though he had negotiated the use of a car from Jokerit, an Opel Ascona, as soon as he received his driver's license that September, he wanted to fulfill his biggest dream: to buy a big old American convertible.

He paid 80,000 Finnish markka ($13,500) for a red 1961 Lincoln Continental Convertible, known as a "Kennedy Lincoln" because John F. Kennedy was riding a similar—albeit a bit longer—car on November 22, 1963, when he was assassinated.

"Made for presidents and other tough guys. In other words, Linc's the car for me," Teemu wrote in a photo album.

The Lincoln he bought in March 1989 is still his most cherished car. He keeps it at his home in Finland. "Life is good when I'm behind that wheel," he said.

His military service ended on May 9, and to celebrate it, Selanne bought a motorboat with a 70-horsepower outboard motor.

He signed for one more year with Jokerit with an option for another year. He played tennis and water-skied every day—little did he know that in a few weeks, his life would change forever.

While Selanne and Sirpa Vuorinen officially met at Paavo's high school graduation party in 1989, their families' stories date back to when Teemu's mother Liisa—then expecting Panu—and Sirpa's mother Terttu—expecting Sirpa's sister Jaana—met at the hospital in 1966.

"We lived close to each other in Helsinki, and I even visited Terttu at the hospital when she was there for Sirpa, a year before Teemu was born," Liisa said.

The mothers bumped into each other weekly at the local playground, until the Selannes moved to another part of town. The fathers also became friends, and the families socialized for years and stayed in touch even after the Selannes moved to Espoo. Sirpa's sister, Tiina, used to babysit Teemu and Paavo.

Life at the Selanne household was slightly chaotic.

First there was the divorce, followed by Ilmari's move to Africa and Liisa's move back to Espoo to be with her children. Teemu had broken off his engagement to Anu, and Panu was in prison. Paavo was doing better—he had graduated from high school.

The day after the graduation reception, Liisa called Terttu and invited the Vuorinens to a party. The call brought Selanne and Sirpa together.

Sirpa said she hadn't paid any attention to the Selanne boys before then. "I just remember visiting their house once when I was 12, but not a thing about Teemu," she said.

When Terttu and Sirpa's father, Erkki, were about to go out, they asked Sirpa if she wanted to tag along, and she said yes.

Teemu came home from practice not knowing his parents had invited friends to a party. "I saw through the window how he drove his yellow Ford Escort across the lawn, and then he walked in wearing his worn-out track pants. We shook hands, and I developed a huge crush on him right away," Sirpa said.

They were both single.

"I wouldn't have recognized Sirpa as the girl we once knew. She had grown up to be a beautiful young woman," Teemu said.

Teemu's friends knew he often had crushes and that it was easy for him to get infatuated with women. This time it felt different, though. There was something special about this particular girl.

"She was open, happy, energetic, I knew right away she had all the qualities I liked," he said. "She was so open and gentle, and easy to talk to."

Sirpa didn't know anything about his hockey career. Liisa had just told them he was a pretty good player. "That's all," Sirpa said.

After the Vuorinens went home, Teemu asked her mother for their phone number. The first couple of calls went unanswered because Sirpa and her family were at their cottage. But soon enough, Teemu got a hold of Sirpa.

"I was so surprised that he called me that I teased him and asked him if he'd pick me up in his Lincoln," Sirpa said.

"I had two tickets to a Pink Floyd show in Lahti. I invited her to come with me and another couple, and I picked her up with the Lincoln," added Teemu.

Off they went. They saw the show on Friday and stayed at Teemu's drill sergeant's place. On Sunday, the couple headed over to a popular Helsinki club.

"We drove around the city all night and spoke about everything. It was really fun and romantic. Teemu dropped me off at home and started to drive toward Espoo. And then he ran out of gas," Sirpa said with a laugh.

"I guess I was so in love that I forgot to check the gas gauge. I walked the last [three miles] home and woke up Paavo so we could bring the car back," Teemu said.

What won Sirpa over right away was Teemu's kindness and boyish charm. They basically moved in together right away, splitting their time between Sirpa's parents' house and the Selanne home.

Sirpa had graduated from high school the year before and was working at a bank while studying psychology for the admission exam to the University of Jyvaskyla.

"I had made up my mind not to fall in love that summer, but it was such a fun summer with Teemu that I didn't even take the exam," she said.

That fall, Sirpa realized she wasn't dating just any hockey player.

"He was always nice with everybody, and I asked him several times why I had to share him with the whole world. It started to get on my nerves, but then I just had to deal with the fact that Teemu was a celebrity. But it wasn't easy," she said.

Sirpa had a habit of throwing temper tantrums and she was often jealous. Teemu's friends were sure the relationship wouldn't last.

"We're different in that I'm very detail-oriented, and Teemu is the exact opposite of that. It was infuriating in the beginning, until we learned to live with each other," Sirpa said.

The 1989–90 season was supposed to be Teemu's breakthrough season in the Finnish league. He was also expected to play at the World Juniors in Finland and then make his World Championship debut in Switzerland in the spring.

But it didn't happen.

Teemu (right) and Paavo, at the age of three, on the way to the park to play ice hockey.

Siblings Teemu (left), Paavo (center), and Panu, along with parents, Liisa and Ilmari.

Teemu, No. 13, breaks into the opponent's goal in youth soccer.

Teenaged Teemu on his prized
Honda MBX 125F.

Teemu on a boat trip
in 1987.

Prior to being drafted, Teemu decorated his room with the pennants of 15 NHL teams.

Teemu's first number on Jokerit was 11, the same as his idol, Jari Kurri. (Finnish Hockey Museum)

After his leg injury, Teemu had to wear a cast for 12 weeks. (Tapio Vanhatalo)

Two Hall of Famers: Teemu faced Sergei Zubov in a national team hockey match against the Soviet Union at the Helsinki Ice Hall on March 26, 1989. (Erkki Laitila)

Teemu and Sirpa pose with Teemu's Aarne Honkavaara Trophy as the best goal scorer in Finnish league in 1992. (Olavi Kaskisuo)

Teemu and Sirpa with their beloved puppy, Theodor von Flaschenburg, or "Teddy."

Eventually, Thunder von Domi (or simply "Domi"), named for Teemu's Jets teammate Tie, joined Teddy.

On July 19, 1996, Teemu and Sirpa were married at the Helsinki Old Church.

Teemu first asked to wear his beloved No. 8 with the Jets, but it was taken by veteran defenseman Randy Carlyle. He then asked for No. 13. (Getty Images)

Rally car driving was one of Teemu's favorite pastimes; "Teddy Flash" was his driving pseudonym.

Paul Kariya of the Mighty Ducks of Anaheim and Teemu had joked about playing together one day at the January 1996 All-Star Game in Boston. By February, they were teammates. They remain close friends. (Getty Images)

At the Salinas Airshow in October 2002, Teemu was able to fly the F/A-18D Hornet as part of the Blue Angels VIP flight.

Teemu played his first game as a Shark only 11 days after a minor knee surgery. (AP Images)

TO THE TOP

———

THE SELANNE BANDWAGON was packed and ready to go in the fall of 1989. Teemu was in love and playing fantastic hockey. In the preseason, the teenager on the verge of his first season in Finland's top league scored 13 goals and 16 points in six games.

"Teemu's gotten stronger over the summer and it's difficult for the opposing defensemen to knock him off the puck. He's a scoring machine, but even more importantly, he's oozing with joy. He loves what he's doing," wrote Ilkka Ala-Kivimaki, a veteran hockey writer at *Ilta-Sanomat*.

Matti Vaisanen had negotiated a raise for Selanne to 200,000 markka ($33,400) and the use of a car. Everything was going great.

"After last year, I'd really appreciate being able to sleep long nights and focus on hockey," Teemu said.

The team headed to the World Junior tournament began its preparations with two games against the French men's national team before participating in a four nations tournament in Czechoslovakia. Teemu played all five games.

"The World Juniors on home ice had been my goal for many years, and I wanted to be at my best in December. My goal was to win the gold and get myself a good negotiating position with the Jets," Selanne said.

He played his first Finnish league game on September 17, 1989, when Jokerit hosted Tampere Ilves at the Helsinki rink. Everybody wanted to see the kid play against men. *Ilta-Sanomat* ran a spread with the headline, TEEMU'S CANNON OR TAISTO'S GLOVE, with a reference to Ilves goalie Jukka Tammi, nicknamed Taisto.

"Teemu was hard to stop even though we all knew what he liked to do: drive to the net, with one hand on the stick, the other protecting the puck. He flew by everyone, and it wasn't just that he was fast. The way he skated, his powerful legs, and the attitude of a young man made him a confident player," said Raimo Summanen, who played for Ilves.

When the team skated out onto the ice prior to the start of the game, Teemu was the first Jokerit skater on the ice, right behind the goalie. He waved at the crowd and tapped the goal posts with his stick.

"Greeting the fans as the first player was a ritual that I continued in the NHL. The first Finnish league game was emotional, even more so than my first game with Team Finland, which I played in Switzerland. Now I was at home, and had lots of friends in the stands," he said.

According to league rules, Selanne was told to use a visor because he was still a teenager, a first in his career, and it bothered him a lot.

"The first period went in a fog, partly due to the visor, and partly because of all the ceremonies. I was just nervous and annoyed with the visor. It was like playing drunk," Teemu said.

In the second period, he pushed the visor up on his forehead. The referee didn't notice it, but the league forbade the trick after the game.

He scored his first league goal with a slap shot in the second period. "I fired with everything I had."

Teemu wasn't the only one making his Finnish league debut; both his linemates, Keijo Sailynoja and center Jan Langbacka, also played their first game in the top league. And all three scored in their first game. They posed for photos after the game, holding the pucks.

The score was 4–4 at the end of the third period and did not change after overtime. There were no shootouts.

The 19-year-old Selanne had now experienced three of the four big milestones in a Finnish player's career: his first game representing Finland, his first game with the men's national team, and his first game in the top Finnish league.

The fourth one, first NHL game, was a little further down the road than he was expecting.

A month later, Jokerit was playing its 11th regular season game and the opponent was league leader JyP from Jyvaskyla. The game was tied 2–2 after 60 minutes.

Then, less than 1:00 into overtime, time stood still for Teemu. "I remember the exact time, too—56 seconds into overtime," he recalls.

He had been on the ice for the entire overtime and had the puck in the offensive zone. He dished it toward the goal and collided with Jyvaskyla defenseman Vesa Kuha.

JyP recovered the puck and up ice it went.

Teemu stayed down.

He was grimacing and in pain. The referee whistled the play dead, and the arena went eerily quiet. When Teemu was carried off the ice on a stretcher, teenage girls in the stands cried.

"When I fell with Kuha, he squeezed his legs together and my leg got stuck between them. I just heard a snap and I knew that I must have broken my tibia," Teemu told the reporters.

Sirpa had come down to the dressing room. She wiped sweat off his brow.

"I tried to move my leg but the pain was too intense. It felt like my leg was in two pieces," he said.

Suddenly, there was a big roar in the arena, and Teemu understood that Jokerit had scored the game-winner.

The team rushed off the ice, and they all, led by captain Anssi Melametsa, wished Teemu good luck before he was taken by ambulance to the nearby hospital.

"If it is a case of a broken tibia, he'll be sidelined for months. If it's a broken fibula, he'll be back sooner," Jokerit doctor Esko Matikainen told team officials.

It was actually worse than that.

He had broken both the tibia and the fibula in his left leg. The doctors decided against surgery, instead opting to put the leg in a cast for 10 to 12 weeks. Teemu was going to miss the World Juniors, to begin the day after Christmas. The Finnish Ice Hockey Association had just lost its best player and the face of the tournament.

Selanne quickly made sure no one thought Kuha had done anything wrong.

"It was just an accident, a collision, and you can't blame him for anything," he said.

The media followed his recovery closely. He was flooded with presents, greeting cards, and visits. After about a week, he was in the mayor's box in a wheelchair to witness Jokerit's win over HPK Hameenlinna. Sirpa sat next to him.

"She tried to kiss me, and I told her to stop before the fans got upset. She was really mad," Teemu said with a chuckle.

When he spoke with reporters about his road to recovery, he sounded confident and optimistic, but inside, he was worried. "I was scared. I wasn't sure I was ever going to be able to play hockey again. I had way too much time to think about things when Sirpa and all my buddies were at work all day and I was home alone. I must have watched every single movie available on VHS back then," Teemu said.

The injury forced Teemu to reprioritize his life, and for once, he had time for his girlfriend.

"The injury was a good thing for our relationship because it brought us closer together since we had to spend so much time together," said Sirpa.

As soon as he was out of the hospital, Teemu also started his physical rehab. He was at an Espoo rehab center every day to work on the muscles in his other leg and upper body. The broken leg got electric therapy, designed to activate the muscles with short electric impulses.

The first cast went from his toes all the way to his groin, but six weeks into his recovery it was replaced by a shorter and lighter fiberglass cast, which allowed him to swim and do other aquatic exercises. At the end of January 1990, he was cast-free.

"When I got rid of the cast, I didn't know whether to laugh or to cry. The leg was just skin and bones. It took me five weeks of physical therapy to learn to walk again and seeing the poor shape of my body depressed me. Eight months after the injury, I was still limping," he said.

Teemu turned to his doctor friend Ismo Syvahuoko for help.

"I was involved in the discussions on when to take the cast off and how to best rehab the leg," said Syvahuoko, who worked at the Helsinki surgical hospital.

Teemu was optimistic that he could play a few games by the end of the season, but deep down, he knew the season would be long over before his rehab would.

"It was worst during the World Juniors because I really wanted to play there. During the tournament, I met Jets general manager Mike Smith, who said that I could play with the Jets' farm team in the spring, but obviously, that didn't happen," he said.

Finland finished fourth in the World Juniors, and Teemu's linemates Mika Valila and Keijo Sailynoja led the team in scoring. Canada defeated Czechoslovakia for the championship.

In February, the doctors gave Teemu the green light to get back on the ice. "I could only use my right leg; the left one just followed. It looked awful, and I'm sure the guys looked at me and though I was done. My skating was really brutal. But I loved to be back on the ice."

Jokerit finished 10th in the standings and missed the qualification round. But players, management, and fans were disappointed.

"We turned our attention to the next season. I decided to stay in the Finnish league for sure," Teemu said.

Jokerit fans organized support dinners after each season, which was something that Teemu truly appreciated.

The Winnipeg Jets kept an eye on Teemu's recovery, and when he finally had his cast removed, the team's vice president, Dennis McDonald, visited him in Helsinki.

In April 1990, Selanne traveled to Winnipeg to watch the NHL playoffs. The Jets' first-round matchup was a tough one against the Edmonton Oilers. The Oilers were a dynasty in the 1980s and, a month after facing Winnipeg, would win their fifth Stanley Cup in seven years—this time without Wayne Gretzky.

Teemu had met the Oilers' Jari Kurri the previous summer, but it was the first time he saw his idol on NHL ice.

"I saw three games, and it was an eye-opener. After that, I wasn't as confident that I'd be able to play in the NHL," Teemu said.

The postseason is a different beast than the regular season. The intensity is ratcheted up several notches and the toughness and the brutality of the game were more obvious watching the games in person than on television.

"It was crazy how much the teams hated each other and how dirty the game was," Teemu observed.

Seeing playoff hockey firsthand made him understand the hard work that was ahead of him to make it to the NHL. "It's a good wake-up call."

In July, Teemu was back at Jokerit's off-season workouts, even though he probably still wasn't ready. He even showed up for the team's 9.3-mile test run, to the surprise of each player. He wanted to do the same tests as everyone, even though his left leg wasn't close to being strong enough.

"I had never run that long on basically one leg, and yes, it was a crazy thing to do, but the risks of injuring the leg were really low. The bones in the leg had healed, but the muscles were gone. It was tough, and it must have looked silly. I had back spasms afterward," he said.

"I just wanted to prove to myself that I could do it."

Just like the year before, Teemu played tennis daily and water-skied. He was also an instructor at Jari Kurri's hockey school and cruised around in his Lincoln.

But he also worked harder than ever before. After such a long break, every workout—any workout—felt good. The most important thing was that he could actually do it again.

Finland had been awarded the 1991 World Championship, and a new arena was being built in Turku. Jari Kurri, now 30, sent shock waves through the hockey world when he signed a contract with HC Devils Milano in Italy after a contract dispute with the Oilers.

Teemu had been cut from Finland's World Championship team in 1989 and a year later was unavailable because of his leg injury. He was looking forward to finally making his international breakthrough, on home ice.

He was still officially a rookie in the Finnish league in 1990–91, having played just 11 games in his first season before the injury. Jokerit was coming off a 10th-place finish and set its sights on a playoff berth.

In the early 1990s, the top Finnish league was still considered semiprofessional. Teemu's salary was 200,000 markka ($33,400) and use of a company car was part of the deal. By most standards, he qualified as a professional hockey player—and when you consider Finland was about to enter the worst recession in its history and the average league salary was well below 150,000 markka, he was well paid, indeed.

Only two Jokerit players—Czech defensemen Mojmir Bozik and Frantisek Prochazka—had "hockey player" listed as their profession in the league's yearbook. The remainder of the roster included an MBA, an insurance salesman, a marketing planner, a salesman, a carpenter, a cook, an army conscript, and seven students.

And one kindergarten teacher.

"My mom had been the head of home day care in Espoo, and Paavo and I had worked at playgrounds in the summers since we were 15 or 16," Teemu said.

"I had tried to be a full-time hockey player after the army, but that wasn't for me then. I couldn't get out of the bed when Sirpa left for work, so I spent my days at home waiting for the practices to begin. I was so phlegmatic that I even yawned in practices."

He wanted to work, but he couldn't really take just any old job. The hours had to be flexible so he could leave whenever his hockey career required it. Liisa suggested Teemu try working at a kindergarten, and Marja Virkki, manager of an Espoo kindergarten, was more than happy to add Teemu to her payroll.

"We desperately needed male teachers, and the kids loved Teemu," Virkki said.

Selanne started as a part-time employee in October 1989, working from 9:00 AM to 1:00 PM. The injury cut his kindergarten career short as well, but he returned for two more years until it was time for him to go to the NHL.

"It was the best job. I played table hockey inside and road hockey outside with the kids. We had something going on all the time, just like when I was a kid. I really wanted to instill a sporty and positive attitude in the children.

"Plus, I didn't think about my hockey career at all when I was there. Another upside with only working mornings was that the kids were still upbeat and happy.

"They liked to play hockey with me but obviously, they didn't know that I was famous or anything, even though some reporters visited the kindergarten. To the kids, I was just Teemu."

He learned to truly appreciate the work, not just the play, and has often spoken for workers' rights for kindergarten staff. He would like to see more men in kindergartens and the teachers get more respect and especially higher salaries.

One day, he noticed each employee had an abbreviation next to her name on a board. A kindergarten teacher would have KGT and an early childhood teacher, PCT. Teemu added "KoK" next to his name.

"King of Kids," he said with a smile.

Up until this point in his career, Teemu had been a huge prospect, one who was drawing a lot of attention.

In the fall of 1990, he became a household name in Finland. Before long, everybody seemed to take an interest in this young, great hockey player, who had a fascinating and unusual softer side. All sorts of magazines, not just sports journals, published features on him.

Teemu was a role model who came up at the right time and with the right team. The country was in a recession after its trade business with the Soviet Union had collapsed. Teemu was there to show how difficulties could be overcome. But the demands for his time started to wear on him.

"I gave interviews every day and it was too much. A little less attention would have been enough, but I tried to turn it into something positive so that it would fuel me to try even harder on the ice," he said.

He had also received a 20 percent pay raise to 240,000 markka ($40,000) per season, along with the perk of the use of a car. His contract contained a clause stating that, should he move to the NHL, any transfer fees the Jets would pay would be split between Teemu and Jokerit 70–30. It was a big bonus, and a smart move for the future.

The Jokerit roster had also undergone some changes, and among the new faces on the team was his old linemate from Espoo, Antti Tormanen.

The Winnipeg Jets wanted Teemu to attend training camp, but Jokerit denied the request because the Finnish league was about to start. Teemu wanted to go to Winnipeg, but he also understood that Jokerit was his employer and that the trip would have been cut short in any case.

"I wouldn't have had time to play any games anyway," he said.

Kari Makinen remained as coach, but he was also the general manager of the team and the CEO of the franchise.

Makinen assembled a five-player unit that, with one change, would make Finnish hockey history a couple years later. Teemu and Keijo Sailynoja got Pekka Jarvela as their center, with Waltteri Immonen and Mika Stromberg as the defensive pairing behind them. A year later, Jarvela would be replaced by Czech national team center Otakar Janecky.

Jokerit lost the regular season opener to Kalpa Kuopio 3–2 but won Teemu's first game back in the Helsinki arena against Assat Pori 6–3. Selanne scored two goals and had an assist.

"The leg's as good as new, I don't even remember to worry about it," he said.

In keeping with his pregame superstition, he was still the first skater out after the goaltender. He still waved at the fans, but he rid himself of several other superstitions he had accumulated.

"I used to put on my gear in a specific order, but after the injury, my rituals changed," he said.

Despite the early optimism, Jokerit dropped in the standings after several one-goal losses. By the end of October, the team was dead last, and when it lost its eighth straight game in early November, the fans booed the team off the ice.

It was time for a coaching change.

Makinen stayed on as CEO, but the club found a new coach in the Soviet Union—52-year-old Boris Mayorov. He had coached the Helsinki team for two seasons in the 1970s when Jokerit finished fourth in 1974 and sixth in 1976.

"Boris always got changed in the players' dressing room and he was close to the players. He was a teacher and a father figure who made sure we all knew what was expected of us," Teemu said.

Mayorov won two Olympic gold medals as a player with the Soviet Union (1964 and 1968) and five World Championships (1963, 1965–67, and 1969).

Now his job was to take Jokerit to the playoffs.

As this was happening, Selanne made his national team comeback at the Deutschland Cup in Stuttgart in November and was on the top line. Finland lost its first game to Germany 3–2 but beat Czechoslovakia 2–0 in the second game. He scored the first goal—a one-timer—and picked up an assist on the second.

In the third game, Finland beat Sweden 4–2 and Teemu picked up another assist. His three points in three games made him the team's leading scorer in the tournament, and Finnish media declared his international breakthrough a fact.

"But for me, the highlight of the trip was a visit to the Mercedes-Benz factory," Teemu said with a laugh.

The Jets kept monitoring Teemu's development. Team psychologist Paul Henry visited him in October, and general manager Mike Smith and scout Wayne Hildahl came in November.

Alpo Suhonen had been the Jets' assistant coach the year in the 1988–89 season but returned to take a job as director of the Turku City

Theatre. He was working as a consultant to the Jets and was playing host to Smith and Hildahl when Jokerit beat SaiPa 10–4, with Teemu scoring three goals and ending the night with five points.

"I think Teemu will play in Canada next season," Suhonen said. Smith agreed.

"He's NHL-ready whenever he wants to come over. We've never been concerned about him, not even when he had his injury. Fortunately, the break was a clean one and the bones often heal to be even stronger than before," said Smith.

Mayorov started to use Teemu more and more. He double shifted him, and Teemu responded by climbing up in the scoring race. Regardless of how Jokerit fared, he was always worth the price of admission. When Jokerit lost to KalPa 5–4, for example, he scored all four Jokerit goals.

The media attention got even bigger when Teemu scored two goals and five points in four games for Finland at the annual Izvestia tournament in Moscow. He led the tournament in scoring, the second Finnish player to do so. Only Antero Lehtonen, in 1978, had previously done it.

"Reporters came to our house, my work, Sirpa's place, and the rink. I gave several interviews every day," he said.

Teemu never said no to an interview request. He had the media eating out of his hand, and the fans adored him. He was called Jokerit's "golden boy," "Super Teemu," "acrobatic entertainer" and the best hockey player playing in Finland. There weren't enough superlatives to describe Selanne.

In December, he had to skip a national team game due to a small injury, but he came to the rink in a tracksuit and signed autographs for a mob of kids.

He was everywhere.

He was one of the celebrity spokespeople in a campaign designed to motivate young people to vote in the parliamentary election.

By this time, it seemed certain the season was going to be Teemu's last in Finland, and when Jokerit played its last regular season home game—it missed the playoffs—in late February, he got emotional.

"I'm really bad at good-byes," he told *Helsingin Sanomat*.

Teemu was feted after the 9–6 victory. He got flowers and the crowd chanted his name, and an hour after the game he was still in the arena parking lot with hundreds of teenagers surrounding his Mitsubishi.

"You can't find a player to replace him, not even in the Soviet Union," said coach Mayorov, giving his star the highest praise in his vocabulary.

Jokerit finished ninth in the standings, which was still a step forward from the previous season. The team's attendance average was also better than Helsinki IFK's (with whom it shared the arena), but behind the scenes, not everything was running smoothly. Since joining the top league, Jokerit had lost 5.6 million markka ($940,000) and its future hung in the balance once again.

Teemu finished seventh in league scoring with 33 goals and 58 points in 42 games, 15 points behind the leader (and his old friend) Teppo Kivela, who played for HPK Hameenlinna. Teemu finished second in goals behind Arto Javanainen. He was voted to the First All-Star Team, and he was named the winner of the most gentlemanly player award.

He didn't, however, win the rookie of the year award.

The Finnish league board simply forgot Teemu was still eligible and gave the award to Janne Gronvall, the Toronto Maple Leafs' fifth-round draft pick in 1992.

Teemu did win a most prestigious award when the players voted him winner of the Golden Helmet as the league's most valuable player.

The Finnish sports paper *Urheilulehti* posed 50 questions to Teemu for its section aimed at younger readers.

Among the facts Teemu shared: he didn't like coffee, he did like NHL star Steve Yzerman, his favorite dish was a chateaubriand, and his favorite color red. He read Donald Duck comics—the biggest weekly magazine in Finland. He liked Tex Willer, a Western comic; he slept on a waterbed.

And he had three cars—the 1961 Lincoln Continental, a white Ford Escort, and the Jokerit car that was part of his contract.

Jari Kurri had been Selanne's idol for years. By the time their paths crossed for the first time in 1989, Kurri had won the Stanley Cup in 1984, 1985, 1987, and 1988. Kurri recalls the two had spoken on the phone before they first met.

"I was at Matti Vaisanen's office in 1989 when Jari called him," Teemu recalled.

"Vaisanen asked Kurri if he'd be playing in the World Championship. I told him not to do it because he'd take my spot on the team. Jari replied that he could play on the left wing instead," he said with a laugh.

Selanne had been the last player cut from the 1989 World team, and while Kurri did play for Finland, he didn't have to give up his spot on the right wing. After the tournament, Kurri asked him if he'd want to be an instructor at his hockey school. The invitation was accepted.

"We were roommates there and got to know each other better. I also played at the annual celebrity tennis tournament Bermuda Cup that summer for the first time, and Jari was there, too."

A year later, Teemu was back at Kurri's summer hockey school, and that's where they set a goal for themselves: to play for Finland in the 1991 World Championship in Turku.

"That was a stroke of luck. Jari had been my biggest idol and suddenly, I was his linemate at the national team camp. It was wild beyond my dreams," said Teemu, who spent the 1990–91 season on the Team Finland roster, including the Sweden Hockey Games tournament in Stockholm in February.

Kurri joined the camp in March, having played that season in Milan.

Teemu and Kurri were roommates at the World team's training camp. "I've jokingly said afterward that I used to look up to Jari—until I got to know him." The two became great friends; maybe it's a case of opposites attracting. Kurri is calm and contemplative, while Teemu is the exact opposite.

The 1991 World Championship was Kurri's third, and Teemu was about to make his debut. "I remember Jari telling me that I shouldn't sign with an NHL team until I was absolutely sure it made sense," he recalled.

The Finns traveled to North America, just like in 1989, and played six games in 10 days against teams from Canada and the Soviet Union. Again, the games were played in western Canada—Alberta and British Columbia.

It was during this trip Teemu and his agent, Don Baizley, met with the Jets, who offered him a four-year deal. He wanted to sign for a shorter time and he wasn't happy with the salary the Jets offered.

Most of all, though, Teemu didn't know what he wanted. He said he needed more time, and talked with reporters about his change of mind when he returned to Finland.

"Things have changed, and now it stands at 50-50 between staying in Finland and playing in the NHL next season. Should I stay in Finland, it doesn't necessarily mean I'll play for Jokerit," he said as he accepted the Golden Helmet award.

In 1990, Winnipeg Jets star player Dale Hawerchuk was earning $462,000, which made him the 20th-highest-paid player in the NHL. Teemu made almost $100,000 playing a lot fewer games for Jokerit, and you can imagine the Jets were not about to make a rookie their best-paid player ahead of a club icon.

And Teemu's comment about not necessarily playing for Jokerit was basically a thinly veiled way to open up an auction. Now every team in Finland was trying to figure out how to sign him.

One of the big clubs in Finland is TPS Turku. It had won consecutive Finnish titles in 1989, 1990, and 1991, and the city was about to host the World Championship in a brand-new arena that was going to double its capacity. It needed new stars, and it could afford them.

Teemu met with TPS chairman Hannu Ansas, CEO Jyrki Santala, and head coach Hannu Jortikka—who had coached Finland to its first World Juniors gold in 1987—at the Finnish League awards gala on the eve of the World Championship.

"Ansas asked me to join them in the TPS suite, and when I got there, they offered me a one-year contract of more than a million Finnish markka. I was stunned. It was an insane amount of money," he said.

It was.

The offer of a million markka was equal to about $170,000. Teemu told TPS he'd have to reconsider his move to the NHL.

"Had I only wanted money, I would have taken their offer. Except I didn't know I'd get an even better offer from Jokerit," he said.

TPS made another push in the middle of the World tournament.

"Matti Vaisanen met with Jari [Kurri] and me after one game to tell us that TPS would pay us a million markka each, if we'd sign right away. We didn't want to make any decisions that quickly, though," he said.

Teemu had informed both Jokerit and the Jets that he wouldn't negotiate a contract during the World Championship. He held most of the cards because the Jets had also had a change of mind and were ready to accept his demands.

The World tournament ramped up Finnish hockey fever to record temperatures, and everybody expected the team to finally win a medal at the World Championship. Finland had won Olympic silver in Calgary in 1988 but had never finished higher than fourth at the Worlds. Now, led by Teemu and Kurri, it finally had a Dream Team on the ice.

Head coach Pentti Matikainen wanted to take his team out of the media frenzy, and he opted to hold their last camp in Switzerland.

"That was a colorful trip. Quite a few guys had some late nights there, and some guys were still drunk during one morning skate. The first game at the World Championship was still a week away, so it didn't really matter, and maybe it helped bring the team together a little bit. At least we got some great stories out of it," Teemu said with a laugh.

The debut was memorable, thanks to the hype of a new arena, the play of Kurri, and Teemu himself, along with the performance of goalie Markus Ketterer. Last but by no means least were the matches against Sweden and the US.

The host team didn't play all its games in Turku, as Finland's national team was sent on a tour of the country.

The Lions played their first game in Turku, then three games in Helsinki and two in Tampere before returning to the main arena for the decisive game against Team USA.

The Finns beat Czechoslovakia in its opening game 2–0, but in its first game in Helsinki, Sweden brought back terrible memories from the 1986 World Championship by tying the game in the last 1:00 of play.

In 1986, Anders Carlsson had scored twice for Sweden in the last 40 seconds of the third period for a 4–4 tie. Instead of two points for the victory, Finland was given one for the tie. The lost point left Finland fourth in the standings.

In 1991, Finland again had a 4–2 lead, this time with 52 seconds remaining in the game. Mats Sundin made it a one-goal game with a wraparound that beat Ketterer. Sundin had already scored Sweden's second goal in the last 1:00 of play in the first period.

Finnish coach Pentti Matikainen took a timeout before the faceoff at center. When play resumed, Christian Ruuttu, then with the Buffalo Sabres, won the faceoff cleanly, and the puck was soon passed to defenseman Ville Siren.

"Ruuttu won the faceoff so cleanly that our players didn't even think to defend," Matikainen said.

Siren tried to fire the puck deep into the Swedish zone, but it hit Nicklas Lidstrom's shin pad and bounced to Sundin, who found himself on a breakaway. Sundin shot the puck into the back of the net with a classy backhander with 37 seconds remaining on the clock. Sundin had scored two goals in 15 seconds, another nightmare for the Finns.

"It was horrible," said Teemu, who watched the events unfold from the bench.

Finland only lost one point, and with losses to the Soviets, Canada, and the USA, it wouldn't have lifted the team into the medal round.

"This is the biggest disappointment of my career. Our team was way too good not to make the medal round," Selanne said.

"We failed and failed hard."

Despite allowing two late goals, Ketterer was named the tournament's top goaltender.

Selanne finished fourth in tournament scoring with six goals and 11 points in 10 games, behind Sundin, Kurri—both with 12 points—and Canada's Joe Sakic, who also had 11 points.

Head coach Matikainen said the team couldn't handle the pressure, that the desire to win the first World Championship medal was too much.

"Everything came down to one game, and that was too much for us to handle," he said.

Jokerit was bankrupt. Like the cartoon character Wile E. Coyote running off a cliff and not realizing it until it was too late, Jokerit had been running on air. The club couldn't find investors anywhere, and the company behind it was heavily in debt.

Kalervo Kummola, vice president of the Finnish Ice Hockey Association, encouraged businessman/adventurer Harry Harkimo—a lifelong IFK fan—to purchase a six percent share of Jokerit in August 1990. Harkimo had just captained a yacht in the Whitbread Round the World Race, his second in seven years. He had also sailed around the world solo in the BOC Challenge race.

Harkimo took interest in the team in 1990–91. He believed in Jokerit, and he went to work to save the franchise.

"I talked my old friend Henrik de la Chapelle into investing into Jokerit. We pooled all our resources, but still needed to borrow 3.5 million markka ($590,000). To raise that money, we started a company to oversee things and own players' transfer rights, because that was the only thing the banks would accept as collateral," Harkimo said.

By February 1991, Harkimo and de la Chapelle owned 74 percent of Jokerit. Kummola and other minority owners, including IFK CEO Frank Moberg, owned the remainder.

Harkimo understood that his business needed Selanne, and he was prepared to do almost anything to get Teemu to stay for another season.

Meanwhile, Teemu had narrowed his options down to Jokerit and the Jets.

He met with Jets general manager Mike Smith again, right after the World Championship, at a downtown Helsinki hotel. Teemu brought Baizley to the meeting, along with Kurri.

"I thought Smith was a little arrogant in the meeting, a bit like Moberg had been. He still offered me a four-year deal even though they knew I wanted a shorter deal, and I thought the money was still too low, too," he said.

Winnipeg offered him $175,000 for the first season, then $200,000, $225,000, and $250,000. Baizley wanted $25,000 more a year. "Smith said they had never paid that much to a rookie, but I didn't see myself as the 18-year-old kid they compared me to, either."

Back in Finland, Harkimo was making plans to try to sign Selanne for another season. Harkimo knew that Teemu would listen to his closest friends and he asked them to talk to him. "I knew Harkimo had asked the guys to call me, and it seemed to me he was obsessed with signing me. I don't know if he had told potential sponsors he had signed me or something, but he was on my case big time. One day, I drove around Helsinki with him and he said he wouldn't let me get out of the car until we had a deal."

Winnipeg had told Baizley it would be willing to do the one-year contract with an option for a second year, but the agent thought he could still squeeze more money out of the club.

Harkimo had made Selanne a great offer; all he had to do was make a decision.

"We went to a Helsinki nightclub, Kaarle XII, to talk—Harkimo, Syvahuoko, Sailynoja, Immonen, and I," said Teemu. "We were all a little drunk when Harkimo suddenly said that he'd throw in a motor-cycle for me for the summer and a car—any car—if I only stayed with Jokerit. Sailynoja and Immonen had told him toys like that could be the tiebreaker."

"I told him that I'd like a Mitsubishi Galant VR-4, the hottest rally car at the time. When he nodded his yes, I called Sirpa to see what she thought. She told me it was my decision, but that the offer sounded good."

He returned to their table and pretended to be mulling over things. Then he told the others he'd stay. "Everybody screamed in happiness. Harkimo gave me a hug and told me I had saved his life, that my staying was a bigger deal than the birth of his child," Selanne said.

Baizley informed the Jets about the decision and the next day— May 13—Jokerit held a press conference to announce Selanne's new contract.

"Many things played into my decision. Both Don and Jari told me to stay in Finland if I wasn't absolutely sure about what to do. I wasn't absolutely sure, but I felt that my place was still in Finland and that if I left now, I would miss out on something special. There's time for me to play in the NHL, but I've only played one full season in the Finnish league. I think I'm physically ready for the NHL, but maybe not mentally. So I signed with Jokerit," Teemu said.

The 1991–92 season would be special, with both the 1991 Canada Cup and the 1992 Albertville Olympics on the schedule, along with the World Championship.

Jokerit was expected to be in the playoff hunt, and Harkimo was raving about Teemu's importance for the team. "Teemu is the heart of this team, and nothing works without a heart," he would say.

The details of the contract were not disclosed, but Winnipeg was believed to have offered more money. Selanne was paid 1.3 million Finnish markka ($220,000) in 1991–92, an unheard-of amount. Jokerit's total salaries were just 12 million markka ($2 million). And he got the car, too.

Baizley wasn't worried. On the contrary, he predicted NHL salaries were about to skyrocket.

"Another year in Finland will only help Teemu's case. And the better he plays, the better it is for him in the future," he said.

In Winnipeg, Teemu's decision was met with shock. The Jets had finished last in their division and missed the playoffs. It had been three years since they had drafted him, and they were unable still to have him join the team while several players from his draft class were about to start their fourth NHL season. Trevor Linden, picked second overall in Selanne's draft year, had already scored 84 NHL goals and was the Vancouver Canucks' captain.

But Jokerit's future looked bright to Teemu, and he was excited about the upcoming season. Before training camp started, he took two trips. He joined Sailynoja, Immonen, Syvahuoko, and Eklund in Cyprus, and then he and Sirpa went on a vacation in Portugal.

Teemu and Harkimo also rode their motorcycles around Finland for a week. His summer schedule also included promotional and charity events, and he had to find time for the annual celebrity tennis tournament—known as the Bermuda Cup—along with the Jari Kurri hockey school.

He also played Finnish pesapallo—a baseball-like game—on a celebrity team, played soccer against Jokerit fans, handed out gifts after a Finnish soccer league game, and played in another charity soccer game.

Whenever and wherever Teemu showed up, hundreds of fans followed.

The Pietarinkatu Oilers, a celebrity hockey team that included Kurri, Esa Tikkanen, and Christian Ruuttu, played a charity game against a Helsinki Division 1 team and sold out the Helsinki arena.

"We raised around 170,000 Finnish markka [$30,000] for the Helsinki Children's Hospital and their intensive care unit," Selanne said.

Selanne had been the spokesman for Nintendo's Game Boy since 1988. Now he took that role for Finnish dairy giant Valio. He also represented Sokos Hotels, one of the country's biggest hotel chains. Valio made him its official milk drinker and shot TV commercials with him—a first for Teemu.

Selanne also spent two weeks at the Vierumaki Sports Center. Mayorov gathered the Jokerit players for a weeklong camp.

Teemu and Jokerit goaltender Markus Ketterer then attended Finland's preparation camp for the best-on-best Canada Cup tournament. NHL pros were not competing at the Olympic Winter Games at this time, and participation in the World Championship was limited because it conflicted with the Stanley Cup playoffs.

"I was so excited to play against the biggest NHL stars, such as Wayne Gretzky," Teemu said.

Finland had played in the 1976, 1981, and 1987 Canada Cup tournaments, but was excluded from the 1984 tournament because of its poor showing at the 1983 World Championship. West Germany received that invite.

The Finns did not help themselves with their poor showing in the Canada Cup. Heading into the 1991 event, Finland had finished last every time and had won just one of its 15 games, an 8–6 victory over Sweden in 1976.

When Finland traveled to Canada in late August, there were six NHL players on the roster: Jari Kurri and Esa Tikkanen of the Edmonton Oilers, Christian Ruuttu of the Buffalo Sabres, Petri Skriko of the Boston Bruins, Teppo Numminen of the Winnipeg Jets, and Jyrki Lumme of the Vancouver Canucks. Eight other players had NHL experience.

Teemu was one of eight players who had only played in Europe.

During training camp, Finland played four exhibition games, meeting the Soviets and the Swedes twice each. One game has stuck in Teemu's mind for a special reason.

"I had my first hockey fight in one of the games against the Soviet Union. I checked Vladimir Malakhov and he cross-checked me back and then attacked me, so I had to defend myself. He was really strong," he said.

Teemu didn't get knocked out, but Malakov was the clear winner of the skirmish.

When the tournament started, Finland delivered the biggest shocker—a 2–2 tie with tournament favorite Canada at the storied Maple Leaf Gardens in Toronto. Janne Ojanen scored both goals, and Ketterer was solid in net. Teemu had an assist on Ojanen's first goal and missed scoring on a great opportunity.

"The puck hit my blade so suddenly that it caught me by surprise, and I shot the puck over the crossbar. The poor quality of the ice surprised us, but the final score was great," he said.

Finland beat Czechoslovakia 1–0 in its second game for its best start at the Canada Cup. Teemu received the credit for the goal with 17 seconds remaining in the third period, when the puck deflected off the skate of Czech player Martin Rucinsky when Ruuttu tried to pass it to Petri Skriko at the far post.

In the third game against the Soviets, Teemu had a scary moment.

Frustrated at not being able to contain Teemu, defenseman Mikhail Tatarinov hit him on the head with his stick.

"Suddenly everything went dark. I was concussed and I took 10 stitches. I really didn't expect it, suddenly everything just went dark," he said.

Soviet assistant coach Vladimir Yurzinov, who had been a player-coach in Finland in the early 1970s, spoke Finnish, and he apologized for Tatarinov's act. "Sorry about the crazy guy. Nobody knows what he's thinking," he said.

Teemu was medically cleared to play Sweden the next day. He just had to keep an ice pack on his eye to keep the swelling down. "If nothing else helps, we can lift the swollen parts and sew them on my forehead," Teemu joked.

Finland beat Sweden 3–1 and advanced to the semifinal against the USA. The Finns lost 7–3, but Teemu claims he missed about 10 scoring chances. "And I usually bury them. I've never missed as many chances in one game," he said.

Both Teemu's and Kurri's play was considered a disappointment. Expectations had been high and for Teemu to get just two points—a goal and an assist—and Kurri to score two goals wasn't good enough.

Unfortunately for Teemu, Finland took a lot of penalties, which cut into his ice time. "It was hard for me to get going, and I didn't until the semifinal. I wouldn't trade this experience for anything, though," he said afterward.

Teemu's first contact with the best players in the NHL convinced many he had what it took to play in the world's top league. But there were doubters, too, who thought he was too soft for the NHL.

He was happy with his tournament.

"It was such a trip to play against Wayne Gretzky, Mark Messier, Paul Coffey, Brett Hull, Dominik Hasek, and many other superstars. I learned at least two things. First, how to play in the smaller North American rink and second, that the ice isn't always great there," he said.

For Finland, making it to the semifinal and finishing third in the tournament was one of the country's greatest hockey achievements. The Albertville Olympic Winter Games were eight months away, and Selanne was one of 16 players on the Canada Cup roster available for the tournament.

In the Finnish league, TPS Turku had won three consecutive league titles and was favored to make it four.

Jokerit started the season strong, even if Teemu's play wasn't up to par. The Canada Cup had been an ordeal for him, both mentally and physically, and he even had trouble getting over jet lag. He scored two goals in his first seven games, and Finnish papers commented on his struggles.

"I'm not as loose as I usually am. I'm used to practicing with the team in the fall, but this year, I had to be in great shape in August," Teemu said.

He started to pick up his effort in Jokerit's eighth game of the season with a goal and an assist in a 4–1 triumph over TPS. In his next game, Teemu scored twice and added an assist in a 5–2 win over Lukko. Two straight victories put Jokerit atop the standings.

"Everyone in the room had great confidence. Things looked really good," Teemu said.

When the league stopped for the Christmas break, he was the leading goal scorer and was in the top five in the scoring race.

It was a happy Jokerit team that gathered at its annual Christmas party, even if Teemu couldn't enjoy it as much as he'd wanted to. The next day, he had to report to national team training camp to start preparations for the Olympics.

Finland played four games before the New Year, but a fatigued Teemu was nursing a slight groin injury and he appeared in only two games. He had also given up his work at the kindergarten, but he still paid regular visits to play games with the kids. He became more involved with the children's hospital and visited the children there three times a week. He also bought a semidetached home in Espoo for himself and Sirpa. "It was our first home together. Sirpa was 22, I was 21."

When Teemu made his decision to stay in Finland for another season, there was no suggestion the NHL would allow its best players to participate in the Olympic Games. He knew he was bound for the NHL, and Albertville could be the only chance he would get to represent his country at the Winter Games.

"I really wanted to experience the Olympics. Reporters thought it was funny when I joked that I hoped they'd be my last Olympics, too."

Finland had won silver in Calgary in 1988, and after the Canada Cup bronze, a medal was a reasonable goal for Finland in the Albertville Games.

The Soviet Union had been dissolved, but its successor, the Commonwealth of Independent States (CIS), was allowed to use players from across the former Soviet states. With the collapse of the Berlin Wall, many top Soviet players had moved to the NHL, and their absence from the 1992 Winter Games boosted Finland's medal hopes.

As the Finns gathered for their training camp, Selanne let it be known that he was still bothered by the lack of ice time in the Canada Cup.

"I'm in great shape, and the Worlds and the Canada Cup have made me even hungrier to win something big. I think the coach could have used me better. Even a young player can carry a team," he told a Finnish newspaper.

In the Olympics, Selanne didn't have to share ice time with Jari Kurri, who was back in the NHL, reunited with Gretzky on the Los Angeles Kings.

Matikainen built his first line around Teemu, with Hannu Jarvenpaa as left wing and Mika Nieminen as the center.

"We must play responsible two-way hockey. Jarvenpaa is a grinder, and we need one on the line with Nieminen and Selanne focusing on the offense," Matikainen said.

For Teemu, it was important that Sailynoja was on the team, even if they didn't play on the same line. The longtime friends hung out together outside the rink. Teemu was able to experience the true Olympic spirit, too, by spending time with Finnish ski jumpers, whose mental toughness was similar to a hockey player's.

Finland finished third in its group and faced the CIS in the quarterfinal, which had been introduced to the tournament for the first time. CIS won the game 6–1, and Finland finished seventh in the tournament, its worst finish since 1960.

Teemu scored seven goals and had 11 points in eight games, finishing fourth in tournament scoring. "The Olympics was a great experience, and having played in the Olympics, the Canada Cup, and the World Championship, I felt I was ready for the NHL," he said.

Three days after the team returned home, Selanne was back in a Jokerit jersey for the final seven games before the playoffs. Jokerit was chasing the regular season title, home ice advantage, and the big cash prize the winner would receive.

"I wouldn't have minded a short rest, but we really wanted to finish first in the regular season," he said.

Jokerit needed a point in its last game against last-place Joensuu to clinch the title, and the team flew to eastern Finland on two chartered planes. They were planning to get back to Helsinki that night to celebrate their regular season championship.

But Joensuu scored the game-winner with 39 seconds remaining in the third period, and afterward Teemu smashed his stick against the locker room door, putting a dent on it. It was reported that Teemu punched a hole in the door, but reporters didn't know he had also broken a sink in the shower room.

Meanwhile, JyP beat TPS and, with that, clinched the top spot in the standings.

Teemu led the league in goals, with 39 in 44 games—10 more than the runner-up, Juha Riihijarvi. Teemu finished fourth in the scoring race with 62 points.

The Jokerit first unit topped the plus/minus statistics, with all five in the top six, and Immonen leading the league with plus-38. The team's average attendance, 7,363, was second in the league, behind TPS and its new arena. The Helsinki arena's capacity was 8,308.

Six teams qualified for the playoffs, and the regular season winner JyP and runner-up Jokerit each received a bye to the semifinal. The teams that finished from third to sixth place in the standings met in the quarterfinal. In its semifinal, Jokerit took on Assat Pori (Aces) in a best-of-five series and had to go the full five games after both teams won their home games.

Game 5 was played in Helsinki, and Jokerit won 5–0. Teemu and Jokerit were in the Finnish league final, which would have sounded unbelievable just nine months earlier, not to mention two years earlier.

The final was a best-of-seven series between regular season winner JyP and Jokerit. Teemu's Jokerit beat JyP in the first game in Jyvas-kyla, and in the second game at home, taking a 2–0 series lead. JyP clawed its way back into the series by winning Game 3 in overtime.

In Game 4, Teemu scored twice, and Janecky also scored in a 3–3 lock after regulation time. Then, in the sixth minute of over-time, Teemu got a partial breakaway and his shot sent Jokerit to a 3–1 series lead.

"I thought the arena was going to explode," Selanne said.

Jokerit could clinch the championship in the next game, but it would mean doing so on the road.

"If that was my last goal in this arena, it was a dream come true. I can't leave a better memory to the fans," said Teemu, who got a fine top hat from the fans to commemorate his hat trick in the game.

"Maybe I've had better games, but I can't remember any of them right now. The hockey gods were on my side today."

Team owner Harkimo chartered two planes again, and Jokerit was off to a flying start on the ice in Game 5 as well.

Teemu scored in the second period to give his team the lead. Sami Wahlsten made it 2–0 a little later. In the third period, Teemu scored his second of the game on a breakaway, and Heikki Riihijarvi sealed victory with a goal into an empty net.

Jokerit was the Finnish league champion, a Cinderella story ending, winning its second Finnish title 19 years after the first one.

The fans stormed the ice and everybody wanted a piece of Teemu, who scored five goals and had six points in the last two games. He also led the playoff scoring with 10 goals and 17 points in 10 games.

Teemu pointed to three reasons for success.

"Leo Aikas has taught us everything we know, Harry Harkimo built the organizational foundation, and [Jokerit head coach] Boris Mayorov knew how to put together a team," he explained.

And then he added a fourth: "We have players on the team who have been to the rock bottom, and they don't give up at the first setback."

Two days after Game 5, Jokerit was honored with Finland's first championship parade that started from the House of Parliament and continued along Helsinki's main street to the arena.

The championship trophy traveled in style, on the backseat of Teemu's red Lincoln convertible.

Teemu was named Best Forward in the league and was voted to the First All-Star Team.

Teemu was planning to head to Winnipeg, sign a contract with the Jets, and play a few late-season NHL games. But an NHL player strike put a damper on the plans. As part of the collective bargaining agreement that ended the strike, there were changes in the transfer payments for Europeans to sign with NHL teams.

Four days after Game 5, Selanne called Finland coach Pentti Matikainen to tell him that he'd decline the invitation to play at the World Championship because of fatigue.

"He pushed me and I told him that if I have to make up my mind right now, I'll say no," said Teemu, who, instead, went on a skiing trip with Sirpa and the Harkimos.

Matikainen told the press Selanne had declined the invitation, but Kalervo Kummola, the strongman of Finnish hockey, refused to take no for an answer. Together with Harkimo, he talked Teemu into playing in the Worlds. He informed Matikainen about Teemu's decision to play.

"I told Kummola that Teemu was not going to play in the tournament, because I had named my team. It wouldn't have been fair to the guys who had been on the roster throughout the camp. He hung up on me," said Matikainen, who is convinced that the phone call was the beginning of the end for him as Finland's coach.

Kummola denies that, but added he thought it was a strange decision since Matikainen was prepared to add players from the NHL. Selanne thinks he was just pushed too early.

"I had no energy then but I don't think anyone would have minded had I joined the team a little later," he said.

Finland won the nation's first World Championship medal, a silver, with Teemu's best friends on the team.

That summer was his first as a true pro in that he trained on his own—and he loved it. "It was so much more fun to work out according to my own schedule," he said.

He also worked out with Kurri, following a 10-week program that Juhani Salakka, a Finnish Olympian weightlifter, had drafted for them.

In June, he was back on the ice at Kurri's hockey school. Then it was time for the Bermuda Cup tennis tournament—he won it—before Teemu and Harkimo hopped on their motorcycles and roamed around Finland for a week.

While the expectation was that he'd play in the NHL the following season, there were still some unanswered questions regarding Teemu and the Jets.

The Jets had drafted him in 1988, but, according to the new rules, the team had to sign a player within four years from the draft or he'd become a restricted free agent. Winnipeg could still match any other offer if another club signed him.

"The Jets made several offers that summer, but we wanted to see what the marketplace would be like for me. Winnipeg knew it could match a better offer, so they were happy to just monitor the situation," Teemu said.

His agent, Don Baizley, suggested a North American tour, and in August, Sirpa and Teemu went on an eight-day trip through Canada and the US. They started in Winnipeg and then flew to San Jose because the Sharks had shown interest in Teemu.

"They said they'd pay me so much that the Jets could never match it, but they never made a concrete offer," said Teemu.

Calgary Flames general manager Doug Risebrough called Baizley and invited the Finnish star to Alberta. Teemu was still in San Jose, and San Francisco was the closest airport with a connecting flight to Calgary. The airport was less than an hour's drive from San Jose, but Baizley booked them on a flight to San Francisco instead.

"It was a seven-minute flight. So funny," Teemu remembered.

The Flames really wanted to sign him. Head coach Dave King had coached the Canadian Olympic team and had seen Teemu in several tournaments. He pleaded with Risebrough to sign him.

"I thought it was a done deal. They offered me a three-year deal worth $1.2 million and a $1.5 million signing bonus. We accepted it."

However, Selanne was a Flame for only a day. The Jets matched the offer. After four years of waiting and negotiating, the Jets finally had their man.

"The difference between that contract and the offers I had gotten the year before was significant. Obviously, staying in Finland for another year had been a good investment. The Jets paid me about three times as much as they had originally offered," Teemu said.

It was also about three times his Jokerit salary. In fact, the Jets contract was so big that many predicted the team would eventually be forced to trade Teemu elsewhere for financial reasons. Teemu wanted to play in Canada and not the US.

"I wanted to play in Winnipeg or Calgary, because I knew they loved hockey in Canada.

"Don said don't come over before you are 100 percent mentally ready to do it. That is what I did. I said I wanted to play the Olympic Games and the World Championship, and then we won the Finnish national title, and after that I said the only thing I want to do was go to the NHL.

"I was the highest-paid player when I came over. I didn't realize it until later, but there was a lot of pressure. But all my career I never felt pressure. It was just a challenge. I always said in a hockey team, if you do not know the players and you come to a practice and you watch these guys, you would say this guy and this guy and this guy are the best players. And then when you go to the game, you don't even notice them. When they don't feel pressure, they can be great. And then when it is time to do something, they can't deliver.

"I was not a normal rookie when I came. I played in the 1991 Canada Cup, the 1992 Olympics, and the World Championship, and that helped me so much. When I came over of course I was excited and nervous about how things would go. But the thing is, I felt ready for the NHL."

In his first season, Teemu made $1.48 million and was one of 33 NHL players making a million dollars. Three years earlier, only Wayne Gretzky and Mario Lemieux had million-dollar deals. The highest-paid players when he signed were Eric Lindros ($3.5 million), Gretzky ($3.0 million), Lemieux ($2.41 million), and Mark Messier ($2.38 million).

Before leaving for the NHL, Selanne played a farewell game with Jokerit, an exhibition game against Malmo from Sweden. Jokerit lost the game 3–2, but 7,000 spectators stayed in the arena to give Teemu a standing ovation at the end of the game. Hundreds of them stormed the ice, and an hour after the game he was still at the rink, surrounded by fans.

"Unbelievable. I'll never forget it," he said.

Afterward, Teemu and Harkimo bought the team dinner.

Teemu was happy. The story was perfect. He'd played for Jokerit for eight years and had won the major juniors title, got promoted to the Finnish league, and then won the league title.

"We came from the brink of bankruptcy and won the Finnish championship. We were like a family."

The feeling of being a part of a family was something he never really felt in the NHL. Pro hockey in North America is simply business. "They don't have any loyalty to a player, and I learned that the hard way when I was traded from Winnipeg to Anaheim," Teemu said.

But more about that later.

The Jets' camp opened on September 10, and Selanne got into town a week earlier. Sirpa had begun her physiotherapist's studies, but she could divide them into six-month periods, and so followed him to Winnipeg in October.

"We can't replace Teemu as a person or as a phenomenon," said Harkimo, who would benefit from Teemu's North American contacts at a later time.

"But we'll have to replace him as a player. If nothing else, then we need to find three or four players to do it."

Everything was set. Teemu was a member of the Winnipeg Jets and he wasn't alone in a new city. His agent lived in the same city and Teemu says he was like a second dad. Finn Alpo Suhonen was an assistant coach. Longtime friend Teppo Numminen was a teammate, and his mom moved over to make sure there was support on the home front.

"I think support is so important, especially for young players," Teemu said. "There are so many moving parts, there are so many things you have to worry about. I felt I never had to worry about a thing. There were people to look after things, and that helped me. I can only imagine how things would have gone without the support and the opportunities they gave to me.

"You are young, and if things do not go right right away and you have to fight through things and face the issues by yourself. . .the biggest difference between the normal life inside the team in Finland, which I was used to, and when I came to the NHL is that you feel you do not have true friends on the team. You feel how hard the competition is and how much somebody wants to take your job.

"In Finland it is more like a family. Here, right away you feel that the guy next to you might be hoping you don't play well that night."

The pressure was on.

PART TWO

THE FINNISH
FLASH IS BORN

———

WHEN TEEMU SELANNE, a 22 year-old Olympian and Finnish champion, signed with the Winnipeg Jets, he knew he had done everything in his power to be ready. He accomplished everything he could at home and learned from the pressure that comes with achieving your goals.

He wasn't a raw 18-year-old moving away from home to chase a dream. He wasn't a wet-behind-the-ears rookie who had a Plan B if he didn't make the team.

He was ready for prime time.

There is no shortage of NHL rookies from Europe bombing when they join their NHL teams. NHL teams learned from their mistakes, and measures were put in place to make the transition as seamless as possible.

In Teemu's case, the Jets were well placed to have the welcome mat out. Winnipeg's good relationship with Finnish hockey players dated back to the 1970s, when the first Finnish pro players, Veli-Pekka Ketola and Heikki Riihiranta, signed with the Jets, then in the NHL-rival World Hockey Association.

"Hockey was like religion in Winnipeg, almost everybody in the city was a huge hockey fan, and they were really knowledgeable about the game," Teemu said.

The move, and everything that comes with it, was eased thanks to the presence of two Finns already in Winnipeg—Jets assistant coach Alpo Suhonen and defenseman Teppo Numminen, who was getting ready for his fourth NHL season. Selanne lived in Numminen's new house for a few weeks while waiting to move into his own abode.

The Jets also assigned team official Lori Summers to help Selanne with things like fan mail and even laundry until Sirpa arrived from Finland.

For his part, Selanne had prepared for the next step in his hockey career by taking English classes from Jarmo Kekalainen, now general manager of the Columbus Blue Jackets, who had been his teammate in the 1991 Canada Cup and had spent four years in North America as a college and pro player. Kekalainen put together a folder that included the most important answers to media questions and the hockey glossary. "I had even taken some French classes just in case I was going to end up in Quebec. I had also worked on my English by subscribing to The Hockey News for years," Selanne said.

He even took some boxing lessons from Erkki Meronen, a former top boxer from Finland, to get ready for the rougher style of game played in the NHL.

Teemu hit the ground running, and he credits his teammates for his easy transition. He didn't have problems with adjusting to the smaller ice surface in the NHL. "The smaller rink suited me better than the Olympic-size rink. It's a different game in the NHL," he said.

The difference in area is about 2,690 square feet.

"In Europe, you can always take a shortcut. There's more space behind the net and the game is slower. When you win a one-on-one in a small rink, you have a scoring chance, and if you make it out of the corner with the puck, you have a scoring chance."

Teemu had one focus: to show everybody he was going to be a star. While Teemumania had raged in Finland, there had been some scathing criticism, as well. "'He's too soft,' 'He'll never make it,' 'He'll be back in no time.' Those are the comments I remember. I wanted to prove to myself—and everybody else—that I belonged in the best league in the world," he said.

Just like when he played for Jokerit and the Finnish national team, he had to wait to get his beloved No. 8 jersey, which at the time was taken by veteran defenseman Randy Carlyle—the same person who would be behind the Ducks' bench when Selanne won the Stanley Cup.

Then, to everybody's surprise, Teemu asked for No. 13, albeit because of a brain cramp. He thought that Finn Veli-Pekka Ketola had worn No. 13 when he played for the Jets in the days of the WHA, but Ketola had famously worn No. 13 in Finland. Ketola had asked for No. 13 when he joined the Jets, but he was denied because it was at the time considered an unlucky number in hockey circles. As a Jet, he wore No. 12.

One big change from when Teemu had attended training camp in 1988 was that players no longer reported to camp out of shape. The Jets also put the players through rigorous conditioning testing performed by another Finn, Juhani Hirvonen, Alpo Suhonen's contact from Vierumaki.

Of the 24 teams in the NHL at the time, the Jets had the most players from outside North America thanks to their five Russian players, two Swedes, and two Finns, as well as Suhonen, the assistant coach. Their biggest star was an American, Phil Housley, who had been nominated for the Norris Trophy as the league's top defenseman a year earlier.

While the Jets had waited patiently for Teemu for a long time, he wasn't the only young star with high expectations. Russian Alexei Zhamnov and US-born Keith Tkachuk were other top prospects facing high expectations.

Teemu didn't notch as many goals as fans and team executives expected in his first handful of exhibition games, but Suhonen told the media to calm down. "It'll take at least a year until we can expect Teemu to truly blossom," he said.

Teemu didn't score but picked up two assists in his NHL debut at the Winnipeg Arena on October 6, 1992, a 4–1 victory over the Detroit Red Wings.

"I'll remember that day forever. I was not as nervous as I was in my first NHL training camp game in 1988. But I was really, really excited; at last my dream came true, I was playing my first game in the toughest league in the world," Teemu said.

He scored his first NHL goal in his second game against the San Jose Sharks at the Cow Palace in San Francisco. The Jets lost 4–3 in overtime, but Selanne put the Jets up 2–1 in the first period, with Housley and Tkachuk drawing assists. "I was in my sweet spot at the top of the circle on the left side, and I one-timed it in under Jeff Hackett's blocker. What a feeling it was."

The first NHL goal was the first of many to come in his rookie year.

The next time Teemu played in front of his new home crowd, he had them on their feet all night, scoring a hat trick in a 7–3 victory over the Edmonton Oilers, who dominated the Jets in the 1980s. The ice was full of hats, and he received his first standing ovation. The Jets fans were thrilled, but the Oilers wanted to teach the Finnish kid a lesson. In the third period, they sent Tyler Wright over the boards to do that. Wright dropped his gloves and started to hammer Teemu with a series of punches, but Selanne pulled Wright's jersey over his head. That didn't sit well with the Oilers' brass, and Wright was sent back to his junior team for the rest of the season. As is often the case in NHL circles, Wright's and Teemu's paths crossed again almost 15 years later when Wright was traded to Anaheim, and he ended his career as Teemu's teammate.

In his first five games, Teemu had scored five goals and nine points, and the media couldn't get enough of the affable Finn.

"You can't tell he's a rookie, it's unbelievable. And he gets along with everybody. People love him," said *Winnipeg Sun* writer Ed Willes.

Teemumania was in full swing.

Jets head coach John Paddock described it this way in Randy Turner's 2011 book on the return of the Winnipeg Jets, *Back in the Bigs*: "There's great players and there's great players with a flair. His personality and exuberance and excitement to play the game it certainly caught on with everybody in the city and province. Dale Hawerchuk was a great player, Keith Tkachuk was a great player, but neither of them had that personality that people just swarmed to. We were big news wherever we went. Big News."

By the end of October, Selanne had 11 goals and nine assists in just 12 games. He had five more points than the NHL's most-hyped rookie heading into the season, Eric Lindros, who began his career with the Philadelphia Flyers after refusing to sign with the Quebec Nordiques, who had drafted him No. 1 overall in 1991. Neither Wayne Gretzky nor Mario Lemieux had produced as many points in his first dozen games. Nine of Teemu's 11 goals came on the power play.

He scored just six goals and added five assists in November, but he made amends in December when he had his second hat trick of the season en route to an 11-goal, eight-assist output in 14 games.

Winnipeg has a well-earned reputation as one of the coldest cities in Canada in the winter, but the Jets were hot in January, going on a 9–1–2 run, thanks in part to Teemu. He put together a stretch that saw him record multiple points eight times in a 10-game span and finished January with 12 goals and 15 assists in 12 games.

Selanne quickly became the talk of Canada. Hockey fans marveled at his acceleration, and seeing Teemu on a breakaway several times in a game was nothing unusual. He was dubbed the "Finnish Flash."

"Scoring that many goals early on boosted my confidence, and once the snowball got rolling, there was no stopping it," he said.

By this time, Sirpa had arrived in Canada and got to work decorating the house Teemu had bought. Selanne may have been the Finnish Flash, but there was nothing flashy about his home, located in the River Heights area of Winnipeg on Campbell Street. That only made neighbors and Winnipeggers more appreciative of Teemu. Every year, residents of Campbell Street would hold a street party and one time they knocked on Teemu's door to invite him to attend a barbecue. To their amazement and delight, Teemu did.

"He sat down with us and had a drink and a hot dog," said Frank Rizutto, who lived just a few homes away. "He stayed with us for a while chatting, and then afterward played ball hockey with the kids on the street."

Teemu was a happy camper. "It didn't look like much, but it was 120 square meters [1,290 square feet] and I had a sauna built there. We had four bedrooms upstairs and a nice basement with a pool table, TV, and a bar. It was really cozy."

The Selannes had company over from Finland practically all the time. Sirpa left for Finland in February. Paavo and Liisa moved in, and there was always a friend visiting. The first ones were the Harkimos and Sirpa's sister Jaana with her daughter, who came over for Christmas. Right after that, Ilmari paid his first visit. For Harkimo, the visit was a chance to make some new contacts at the Jets organization, which also gave him the idea to build a new arena in Helsinki. "On Christmas Eve, Teppo Numminen was our Santa," Teemu said.

By the end of January, Selanne had already scored 40 goals. Mike Bossy's record in his rookie season of 1977–78 with the New York Islanders was 53. It was considered to be unbeatable. Yet with 30 games to play in the regular season, Teemu was only 13 goals away from surpassing Bossy.

Teemu was logging big minutes and was naturally the front-runner to win the Calder Trophy as the rookie of the year. Wayne Gretzky took notice of the remarkable rookie. "Teemu has to win the Calder, and he should also get votes for the Hart Trophy [as the league MVP]," he said.

Teemu was living his dream.

The only thing that had surprised him was the league's tough travel schedule. Winnipeg had one of the longest travel distances in the NHL, and in 1993, the Jets traveled mostly on commercial flights.

After a road game, the players stayed at a hotel before leaving for the next city in the morning. Their postgame relaxation often took place in a local club. Alcohol and partying were a big part of an NHL player's life. "It was taxing. Now it's completely different, since all teams have chartered planes and they fly to the next city right after the game. That's why there's less partying. . .and longer careers," Teemu said.

The Jets were no different. The players were a part of the Winnipeg nightlife, and some of them developed drinking problems.

"One time, I was driving behind one of my teammates when he crashed his car into a streetlight. The police officers saw who was driving and let him go. They drove him home and told him to stop driving while drunk because the team needed him on the ice. Any other person would have been in jail," Teemu said. "Other teams' players liked Winnipeg, too, there was always a good party going on. Canadians are like Finns, they like to have fun."

Teemu wasn't your prototypical Canadian winger, and his style wouldn't have gone over well on many NHL teams. Fortunately for him, Suhonen was there to assist him by making sure he could use his strengths on the ice. "Head coach John Paddock and I made a deal that I would talk to Teemu about his defensive play so that he wouldn't think he could do whatever he wanted. I'd tell him, 'I guess you forgot your D skates at home today,' or 'The Zamboni driver sure is pleased when he won't have to go to the right winger's D zone at all,'" Suhonen said with a chuckle. "In some other teams, he would have had to defend more or he would have stayed on the bench."

But the Jets knew what they had and they knew how to get the best out of Teemu.

"If Teemu was evaluated by his defensive play, we wouldn't even have a Teemu. He's like Lionel Messi or Usain Bolt. He radiates positive energy and that's what you have to use," said Suhonen, who summarizes Selanne's rookie campaign in two sentences: "He had the world's fastest first 3-4 strides on skates. He was also physically ready."

And when Selanne gives credit to his teammates, he's not just paying lip service. The Jets team did have high-end talent, as well. "You can't overestimate Phil Housley's value to Teemu; he must have scored 40 goals off Housley's passes," said Suhonen.

"It was incredible how everything started," Teemu said. "I was so quick and the Housley factor was perfect. I knew if I could get open, he would find me. He was the best passer. It was unbelievable how he could find me."

Teppo Numminen witnessed Selanne's dream season from up close and was as impressed with it as everybody else. "He did things that nobody had ever seen. He caught defensemen by surprise, leaving them flat-footed behind him. I'll never forget some of his moves. His acceleration was so fast that he basically changed the game. It took other teams until Christmas to scout him, and even then he could do whatever he wanted."

After home games, Teppo and Teemu, who roomed together on the road for three years, headed over to the Wise Guys nightclub. Even at 22, Teemu didn't put too much thought into what he was wearing, according to Teppo. "Teemu used the same suit all year, and it was one he had got from Team Finland years earlier. The pants were ripped between the legs, and his style, or lack thereof, became the team joke," Numminen said. "The more guys gave him flak for it, the more determined he got to not buy a new suit. He had one tie. I made the knot early in the season, and he used that the rest of the year."

In Winnipeg, Teppo was to Teemu what Paavo had been to him as a kid. He made sure Teemu knew where to be and when. Selanne had two other close friends on the team. One was Darrin Shannon, and the other Tie Domi, whom the Jets acquired, along with Kris King, from the New York Rangers for Ed Olczyk in December 1992. The trade brought much needed heavyweight presence to the Jets' lineup and protection for their young stars.

Selanne needed friends, because although he was a fan favorite, he was also being criticized for his lack of defensive play and for being selfish. "There were days when I was the last one to arrive at the arena and the first one to leave, which wasn't appreciated in the NHL, where the optics are important. You should stay on the ice or get on the bike. To me, that's sucking up to the coach," Teemu said. Numminen added, "He was always late for everything, which annoyed the rest of the guys."

According to Suhonen, several players were jealous of each other, and the atmosphere was very competitive. Some veteran players simply didn't like Selanne's attitude. It rubbed them the wrong way. "If I hadn't scored in the game," said Teemu, "I sometimes didn't celebrate afterward, even if we had won or tied it. Some of the guys on the team were wondering why I wasn't happy."

"He walked into the locker room like he was walking into a bar. Randy Carlyle, for example, couldn't stand it," Suhonen added. "He'd tell Selanne that 'the f-----g Laplander' should be the first one on the ice and the last one off it. Somehow, Carlyle couldn't let Teemu be Teemu.

"Teemu couldn't stand it, and he didn't understand it or didn't want to understand the old NHL culture in which veteran players made the team's rules," said Suhonen.

"Looking back, Carlyle was right. I didn't understand the standards and habits expected for young players. Carlyle, in turn, didn't understand that Zhamnov and I weren't just any rookies," said Teemu about the former Norris Trophy winner. Carlyle was playing in the last of his 17 NHL seasons. "He was trying to make us skate at the end of practices without understanding that we played big minutes each game and needed rest. Then he got furious when we didn't do as he said."

Carlyle retired at the end of Teemu's rookie season, having played only 22 games. And, naturally, their paths would cross again when Carlyle was named the Ducks' head coach in 2005, a position he held when they won the Stanley Cup.

Carlyle wasn't the only one not loving the new kid. Some younger players were bad-mouthing Teemu behind his back and trash-talking him on the ice. Both problems disappeared when Tie Domi was traded to the Jets. He may stand only 5-foot-10, but Domi was strong as an ox and impossible to get off his skates. With Domi on the ice, Teemu didn't have to worry about being slashed or hit, and in the dressing room, Domi made others accountable for their words. "I couldn't stand some guys talking about Teemu like that. They were jealous of everything Teemu had," Domi said.

"If somebody was bad-mouthing another teammate, Tie would just go and fight them," said Teemu with a laugh.

Domi's temper flared up often—teammate or opponent, he didn't really discriminate. Once during a practice he managed to dangle his way past defenseman Igor Ulanov only to see the Russian throw his stick and knock the puck off Domi's stick. Domi dropped his gloves and fought Ulanov. When the Jets visited Helsinki in the 1994 preseason, he fought Neil Wilkinson in the scrimmage, breaking his teammate's cheekbone. Teemu may have been a rookie, but he wasn't afraid of the fierce Domi. One morning, the rest of the team was already on the ice and coach Suhonen was wondering where Teemu was when he suddenly emerged from the dressing room.

"He was wearing a bucket—a real bucket—on his head. He had written DOMI on it," Suhonen said.

"Tie does have a big head and no neck. He got really mad and chased me around the rink," Teemu recalled. Suhonen let them run around the rink, Domi chasing Teemu in vain, until everybody started to laugh. "That said everything about Teemu's confidence," Suhonen said.

As soon as Teemu and Tie became friends, Domi wanted to learn Finnish cuss words. Teemu taught him one—the Finnish equivalent of the F-word—but then got tired of the Canadian yelling it to everybody. "I told him there was one more word that was even worse, 'hirvi.' I told him the Finnish word for moose. Since then he's been yelling 'moose' to everybody," Teemu said with a laugh.

Tough guy Tie Domi is one of those players who can say Selanne is a close friend. "I forgot to mention him in my Hockey Hall of Fame speech. I wrote it down in advance, and Tie was in there, but because I didn't use my notes in the speech, I just forgot. I'm really sorry about that," Teemu said. "It has also been really interesting to follow Tie's son, Max's, NHL career. What an awesome story it is."

Teemu had brought the mania along with him from Helsinki to Winnipeg. The Jets' average attendance went up by 2,000 fans a game, which was almost a miracle, considering that Canada was in the middle of a recession. Selanne was to Winnipeg what the Beatles had been to America—an import everyone wanted a piece of.

He became the fourth Finn to play in the All-Star Game, following in the footsteps of Pekka Rautakallio, Kurri (six times), Reijo Ruotsalainen, and Christian Ruuttu.

"It was a fantastic experience to play in the All-Star Game in the legendary Montreal Forum and to meet people like Gordie Howe and Bobby Hull. It felt really good to hear them talk about me," Teemu said.

CBC made a documentary about Teemu. "The handsome rookie scores goals at will, wants to become a kindergarten teacher after hockey, and is the spokesman for milk in Finland. He's almost too good to be true," reporter Peter Jordan said.

The happy-go-lucky Selanne had Bossy's record for most goals by a rookie in his crosshairs, and the pressure was mounting.

"I did not realize there was pressure until I had 47 goals and then I didn't score for a couple of games. I wasn't playing bad, but I wasn't scoring. Then Mike Smith called me in the office and he said, 'Sit down. What are you doing?' I said, 'What do you mean? Not playing well. I just can't score right now. It is only two games,'" recalls Selanne. "Then he said, 'Okay, I will give you two more games.' There were two games before we had four or five on the road. He said, 'I will give you two games to show something or I might send you to Moncton,' the minor leagues."

Teemu was speechless, although he knew deep down it was an empty threat.

"I didn't say anything, but I was thinking, *what a fucking asshole.* And then the same day he saw my wife in the mall. She came home and said, 'I saw Mike in the mall and he came to ask me whether I knew where Moncton was. Do you know where Moncton is?' Fucker! Are you fucking serious?"

"I needed six goals to tie and seven to break the record, and everyone was thinking it was going to happen on the road. But then we played Minnesota and I scored four goals. The following day, we had a fan fest and I signed autographs from nine in the morning to five in the afternoon. I was so tired, but the line never ended."

Teemu was now the third player in NHL history to score 50 in his rookie season, joining Mike Bossy in 1977–78 and Joe Nieuwendyk in 1987–88. Wayne Gretzky had 51 in his first NHL season, but he wasn't considered a rookie by the NHL because he had played one season in the WHA. Selanne had now scored 91 points in 63 games. He was only 19 points away from Peter Stastny's record for most points in a single season by a rookie, 109, with 21 games remaining. So he had another record to surpass.

Two nights later, the Jets were back on home ice against the Quebec Nordiques. This was Teemu's first opportunity to make NHL history, as Bossy's record was just two goals away. The fans made sure not to be late getting to their seats for the start of this game, and it was a good thing they did—Teemu scored 15 seconds after referee Ron Hoggarth dropped the puck at center ice.

The play started in the Jets' end with a faceoff in the left circle won by Thomas Steen. The puck went back to Phil Housley, and from the corner goal line Housley fired a pass right onto the stick of the speedy Teemu. He would go to his backhand to score on Stephane Fiset for goal No. 52.

The record-tying score came in the second period as Teemu came out from behind the net and tucked the puck into the wide-open goal, catching Fiset out of position.

Teemu's next goal, midway through the third, would make NHL history. The game was tied 3–3 and the puck was again in the Jets' zone along the boards to the right of goaltender Bob Essensa. Tie Domi got to it first and spotted Teemu racing up the middle of the ice. Domi lofted the puck into the neutral zone with Selanne a step ahead of Nordiques defenseman Adam Foote, who was desperately trying to catch him. Sensing Teemu would not be caught by Foote, Fiset came charging out of his net to beat Teemu to the puck now entering the Quebec end of the ice. With only his left hand on his stick, Teemu deftly lifted the puck a few inches over Fiset's stick and into the vacated net, igniting the loudest roar of delight heard at the Winnipeg Arena since Dave Ellett's double-overtime goal against the Oilers in the 1990 Stanley Cup playoffs.

As Teemu started his celebration, a banner at the south end of the rink where he had just scored summed up the moment best. The banner read: 52...53...54...BOSSY'S RECORD IS NO MORE!

Teemu threw his glove in the air and "shot" it down with his stick. It was an iconic image that defined Selanne's reputation as a marksman.

"It was like a snowball going downhill how everything started. The whole city and media got excited, and my personality made it bigger. I was so pumped. Even that celebration after I broke Bossy's record, I wasn't planning to do it but now when I look back at it I am a little embarrassed. But it has become me.

"A lot of guys don't celebrate when they score, but I am always so happy and excited, whether it was my 10th goal or my 600th goal. It was my passion. I think the way I lived in the first year created a little jealousy, because I was just myself and some people thought this should not happen for a rookie. I think I realized this later, but I was just myself," Teemu said.

The game was paused for 10 minutes for celebrations. Teemu received several standing ovations and Jets owner Barry Shenkarow handed him a gold-plated stick.

"Never in my wildest dreams could I imagine scoring seven goals in two games and setting the record at home. Maybe Mike Smith's mind game [about demoting Selanne to Moncton] really worked; maybe he was smarter than we all thought. He definitively deserves some credit. But maybe he thought the goal outburst was all because of him," Teemu said with a laugh.

"I had no idea before the season started what the record was, and I could never imagine scoring so many goals. Jari Kurri was my idol and he scored 30 goals as a rookie, and I thought I'd like to score 30, too. I scored 20 goals just in the month of March. Every time I went to the rink, I was confident I was going to score. I was fast on my skates and I was getting two, sometimes three breakaways a game. I knew I was going to get the chance to score.

"I didn't really realize what happened [at the time]," Teemu said on a conference call to celebrate his induction into the Hockey Hall of Fame. "Now, the [goal] number is so big... I really don't know how that happened."

After the ceremony, the Nordiques went to work and, with a strong lineup including Joe Sakic and Mats Sundin, were not bothered by all the hoopla, but instead inspired by it. They scored the next four goals to win 7–4. Despite the loss, the night belonged to Teemu, who also surpassed former Jets captain Dale Hawerchuk's club high for goals in a season with his record-setter.

Jets head coach John Paddock was ill that day, and so assistant Alpo Suhonen guided the team in Selanne's record-breaking game. "[Paddock] came to the arena the next day as if nothing had happened. He just wanted me to get to coach in that historic game," said Suhonen.

That same day, the Jets had new T-shirts for sale featuring an image of Selanne and the text THE NEW BOSS. The Jets merchandise was flying off the shelves, and the owner was excited about the possibilities for the next season. Mike O'Hearn, the Jets' vice president of communications, said that "Teemu Fever" happened organically, just like in Finland.

"We didn't have much to do with his popularity. On the contrary, we had trouble keeping up with it," he said. "Teemu was a great player, of course, but he was also good-looking, smart, friendly, spoke good English, and was a great guy. He was the first Jet to be popular nationwide."

Amid all the frenzy, Selanne would offer these comments to the media that would sadly all too soon foreshadow what was to come for the Jets team in Winnipeg: "Every time you set a league record, there is something of significance that goes along with it. I think it's great. It brings attention to the team and it brings attention to the city. Now I just hope the city and the team take advantage of it."

The Jets gave Teemu another present a few weeks later when Paavo drove a Jeep Grand Cherokee onto the ice before their game against Vancouver on March 12. And on March 23, Teemu broke Peter Stastny's rookie record for points in a game. Teemu scored two goals and picked up an assist on a Zhamnov's goal but Toronto won 5–4.

The Jets planned a Finland Day in late March when Jari Kurri came to town with his Los Angeles Kings. Fans were handed a Finnish flag when they walked in, and the Finnish national anthem was played before the game. The game was broadcast to Finland with a 73-minute delay, even though it was marketed as the first live NHL broadcast outside North America.

The Finnish Flash had no delay, as he scored twice and had three points in the 3–3 game. Now Teemu was not only breaking rookie records, he was in the race to lead the league in goal scoring. Before the last regular season game, Teemu had 75 goals, one more than the Buffalo Sabres' Alexander Mogilny. That evening, the Jets were at home facing the Oilers and Teemu scored his 76th goal off a breakaway in the second period.

"The Sabres played their game on the East Coast, so I heard during our second intermission that Mogilny had scored two goals and that we were tied. I tried to get one more like crazy, and the guys were trying to set me up with chances. I had 11 shots that night, the most in any game that season, but could only score that one time. We had a two-man advantage and I stayed on the ice for the entire power play, but I couldn't beat Bill Ranford for that 77th goal. I hit the post twice," Teemu said.

Winnipeg won 3–0 and Selanne added another assist for a two-point game, but he was angry at himself for not scoring a second goal. "That just goes to show how hard it is to play hockey if you try to force it," he said.

Selanne put together the most incredible rookie season in NHL history, racking up 76 goals and 132 points to establish a pair of records that haven't been challenged since. In fact, no first-year player has even come within 20 goals of Selanne's mark—making it one of the most incontestable records in league annals.

Selanne finished fifth in the scoring race with 132 points in 84 games, 28 points behind leading scorer Mario Lemieux. Teemu accounted for 24 percent of the Jets' goals, and was involved in 41 percent of the team's 322 goals during the regular season. Housley had 97 points, a personal best, with so many coming from assists that led to Teemu goals. "I just knew where he was at all times. Chemistry like that is hard to find," Housley said.

Only Gretzky, Brett Hull, and Lemieux had scored more goals in a single season than Teemu. Phil Esposito also had one 76-goal season in his Hall of Fame career. Since 1993, only one rookie has scored 50 goals—Alexander Ovechkin, when he scored 52 in the 2005–06 season.

Teemu's game was analyzed and talked about everywhere. "He moves like Mike Bossy or Brett Hull in the offensive zone, he can be out of the picture a while and then suddenly he gets the puck and— bang!—the puck's in the net," Jets head coach John Paddock said.

"He's always where the puck will come next, like Gretzky. If you try to stay on him, he moves to the other side, which leaves the lane wide open for Phil Housley."

Teemu's physical play was even praised by the legendary Don Cherry, infamous for his distaste for European players and who once referred to Alpo Suhonen as "dog food" during his Coaches Corner segment on *Hockey Night in Canada*. About Teemu, Cherry said, "He was a positive surprise."

Maybe Teemu wasn't that soft after all. Canadian hockey fans appreciated Teemu's resilience and that he never complained about being hit or getting challenged to fights.

"He must be the toughest superstar in the league. He delivers checks as much as he receives them. Look at Gretzky or Lemieux, they never hit anybody," said Paddock.

Selanne did give as much as he received. In one game versus Chicago, Teemu went right after Blackhawks defenseman Chris Chelios and knocked him off his skates and down twice with textbook open-ice hits in a span of seconds.

Because of Teemu's incredible season, the Jets made the playoffs, but would lose their first-round series to the Vancouver Canucks in six games. Teemu scored four goals and six points during the series, highlighted by a hat trick in Game 3, his sixth in the NHL (five regular season and one playoffs), and the overtime winner in Game 5 with the Jets facing playoff elimination. "We gave our all but it wasn't enough. The game was completely different in the playoffs, and all means were allowed to stop the other team's players," Teemu said.

No surprise that Selanne was the unanimous winner of the Calder Memorial Trophy as the NHL's top rookie, being named first on all 50 ballots. He was also selected to the First All-Star Team with Luc Robitaille of the Kings, Mario Lemieux of the Penguins, Chelios, Ray Bourque of the Bruins, and Ed Belfour of the Blackhawks.

Teemu said he'd never been as nervous as he was when he delivered his acceptance speech in Toronto. "I had seen the Oscar gala on TV so I knew what the deal was. It went okay, I guess."

He gave nods to the other candidates—Joe Juneau, Felix Potvin, and Eric Lindros, and then thanked his Jets, teammates, coaches, trainers, and equipment managers, and of course Jets fans. He also praised his agent Don Baizley "and all the people in Finland who made this possible."

Teemu returned home after the Jets were eliminated and told a Finnish newspaper that he was simply going to rest.

But he didn't. He had a full slate of events.

Everywhere he went, a crowd surrounded him. At the Tampere theme park, 8,000 fans stood in line to get his autograph. He said he gave more than 20,000 autographs that summer.

How crazy was it? So crazy that he even had to leave the Bermuda Cup tennis tournament afterparty and take a helicopter to Savonlinna to make an appearance at a youth event. "I couldn't say no. I was too nice and went to any event that wanted to have me," Selanne said.

He was racing from one event to another on August 1 when he made the news after he was pulled over for speeding, passing a car in a no-passing zone, and having a radar detector. He received a hefty fine—20,000 markka, about $6,000—and lost his license for a week.

That made news in Canada, and a year later, he was still appealing the fine. The negative publicity got to Teemu, who for the first time was annoyed with the media. He had tried to work out, but it wasn't easy. He had spent a week on the ice with Jokerit, and lifted weights with Kurri, but in August his schedule simply blew up.

"I had to skip almost all my regular workout sessions. I used to call Sirpa and ask her to meet me with my running shoes at an intersection on the way to our house. Then I'd run home with Sirpa driving a car behind me so I could see the road," he said.

"That summer I was looking forward to getting back to the NHL— for some rest."

———————

When Teemu left home for Winnipeg at the end of summer he was a little unsettled, and maybe it was a sign of changes and troubles ahead.

He was on his own, as Sirpa stayed in Helsinki for her studies, and expectations were high for a second record-setting season.

His second training camp was average, at best, but all the talk about a sophomore slump went out the window when he scored a hat trick in his first regular season game. "The reporters asked me if I thought I could score 200 goals that season," Selanne said with a laugh. "It was such a crazy notion, but they meant it."

Then, for some inexplicable reason, he went five games without a goal. Everybody could see something in his game was off, something was missing. Head coach John Paddock knew about Teemu's busy summer and suggested he take some time off, which in NHL terms might be one of the strangest offers ever.

"About a month into the season, he told me I could take two weeks off. He told me to go to the Bahamas with Sirpa and then come back and start afresh," Teemu recalled. He turned down the unusual offer. "I told him that I appreciated the offer, but that it was my own fault. I had never heard of such a thing."

The NHL had realigned the makeup of its divisions, and the Jets were now part of the Central Division along with Chicago, Dallas, Detroit, St. Louis, and Toronto. Those teams played what is known as "heavy hockey," and their grinding physical style was difficult for the slick Winnipeg Jets to handle. Smith was facing criticism for building a team that was "too European," that had too few role players and too many Russians. Smith was fired and Paddock became both general manager and head coach.

Selanne offered up another opinion. "Our problem was defense. Teppo was all alone back there."

In November, the unthinkable happened when Teemu sputtered through a four-game goalless streak, although he still had scored 20 points in the Jets' first 16 games. Teemu was never one to hide from the media, who were desperate to know his thoughts about how his scoring touch had gone cold.

"I'm a little desperate. I'd like to help the team, but I just can't score right now. It's hard to say why," he said.

Paddock then threw fuel on the fire when he criticized his star publicly. "He's spreading himself too thin by doing interviews, charity work, and business deals. He didn't have time to work out properly in the summer."

The local media jumped on that.

Tim Campbell of the *Winnipeg Free Press* wrote, "Selanne has been on time in front of the media, but he's been late on the ice. There's no twinkle in his eye anymore, and apparently pressure gets to him as well. He should learn to politely say no."

Adding to Teemu's woes was that Phil Housley—the skilled defenseman who could feather a pass to Selanne like no other player on the Jets—was dealt to the St. Louis Blues in the off-season.

Like many Jets, Housley didn't get along with general manager Mike Smith. His main gripe was a contract dispute. Housley was looking for ways to structure his contract to avoid the higher taxes in Canada. The matter came to a head the previous season at an end-of-year party the Jets held for their staff and the players and their wives as a thank you for the season that had just concluded. At this party, with alcohol most likely a contributing factor, the goodwill turned to blows as Housley and Smith had a fight and had to be separated. The bad blood played a role in the trade, which saw Housley sent to the Blues with Nelson Emerson and Stephane Quintal coming back in return. In a totally bizarre move, the Jets, looking to quiet growing fan discontent and to justify the trade, issued a press release suggesting Housley played a less significant part in Teemu's record-setting rookie season than he actually did.

Teemu's goalless streak didn't last, and he was on pace to score a respectable 40 goals when he suffered an 80 percent tear in his Achilles tendon in a freak accident during a game against Anaheim in late January. The blade of Ducks defenseman Don McSween's skate cut Selanne just above the right boot. The injury, which required surgery, ended Teemu's season.

It was tough to take. Selanne still believed he could still return and play the last regular season games and possibly join Finland's national team for the World Championship in Italy. But he couldn't do either. He missed the last 33 games of the regular season and ended up with 54 points in 51 games. Looking back at his second year in the NHL, Teemu said, "The highlight of that season was playing with Wayne Gretzky in the All-Star Game in Madison Square Garden."

Truth be known, Selanne was cutting himself short. He became the second-fastest player in league history to score 100 goals when he hit the milestone in his 130th game. The record is Mike Bossy's 100 goals in 129 games. Teemu's 100th was against Sabres goaltender Dominik Hasek, who was on his way to the first of his six Vezina Trophy awards as the NHL's top netminder in 1994.

Without Selanne, the Jets spiraled out of control and went 19 consecutive games late in the season without a win. When they finally snapped the streak, beating Dallas on March 2, Teemu said the fans celebrated like it was the Stanley Cup Final.

Only 10 days after his surgery, Teemu started his rehabilitation. "I was at the rink every day between 11:00 AM and 1:00 PM working on my upper-body strength and rehabbing the ankle. I swam a lot, too," he said.

Suffice it to say it was an unhappy season for the Jets. They finished last in the Western Conference, and there was no shortage of rumors about the financially challenged franchise being moved to the United States. Paddock didn't help the firestorm surrounding the team when he used the media to put some pressure on Selanne to live up to the promise of his rookie season.

"He'll be one of the truly great players only when he leads his team to a Stanley Cup championship," Paddock said.

Teemu went home to promote a couple exhibition games at the end of the summer in Finland by the Jets. He also watched some of the Finnish league playoffs and had discussions with executives about working the World Championship as a TV analyst. When he didn't get cleared to play, he went to Italy as a representative of the media instead. The Finnish company PTV compensated him by paying for his rally racing costs that summer.

Finland went to the championship final but lost to Canada in a sudden-death penalty shootout after the two teams were tied at 1 after regulation and tied again after the first 10 shots, with each team scoring twice. It was Canada's first hockey World Championship in 33 years.

Hockey isn't Teemu's only sports love, and car racing is one of his passions. He had visited the San Marino Formula 1 Grand Prix in Imola as Team McLaren's guest and had met their ace driver, Ayrton Senna. The next day, the Brazilian driver was killed in a crash on the track. "It was a truly sad day. I had just shook hands with him before the race," he said.

Selanne cut back on his off-season appearances to focus on rehabbing his injury so he would be ready to go when training camp opened in September. Selanne was pumped about getting back on the ice, but there was a cloud hanging over the resumption of hockey—labor unrest between the NHL and the NHLPA over a collective bargaining agreement.

Selanne and the Jets were scheduled to start their preseason games in Helsinki at his old home arena in a tournament with his old team, Jokerit, along with IFK and Teppo Numminen's alma mater, Tampere Tappara. The Jets would be the third NHL team to visit Finland. The New York Rangers and the Washington Capitals had played exhibition games against IFK and Karpat in 1981.

Selanne played the host role to perfection. He took the entire team and their players' girlfriends and wives on a cruise from Helsinki to Porvoo, where they enjoyed their time at the Hotel Haikko Manor and Spa. "It was the first such cruise for many of the players. The guys were excited to visit a traditional Finnish smoke sauna," he said.

The tournament was a great experience for the team and a wonderful homecoming for Teemu, who scored four goals in the Jets' game against Tappara and another goal in the game against IFK. The Jets won both games 8–2 and 5–3, respectively.

After two seasons with No. 13 on his back, Teemu finally got the number he had been waiting for when Randy Carlyle, who had worn No. 8 for many years, retired. "There's usually a moratorium on a veteran player's number after he retires. I asked Randy if it was okay to take his number, and he said yes. I also made sure the team was not going to retire his number. Finally, I got the number I'd been waiting for, and I was happy," Teemu said.

The Jets wanted to put their disastrous previous season behind them as quickly as possible, and coach John Paddock tried to make amends with Selanne by praising his star for his training camp performance. "He's been more alert here than in any practice last season. I think he's matured, but he still likes to have fun," he said.

Whatever momentum the Jets wanted to take from their successful trip to Finland and an upbeat training camp was stalled when the NHL postponed the start of the regular season by two weeks in the midst of contentious contract talks with the players' union. Then, the league locked the players out.

NHL players looked elsewhere for employment, and Selanne and Kurri signed with their former Finnish team, Jokerit. Teemu stayed at a downtown hotel with Kurri, since now it was Sirpa who had to stay in Winnipeg for an internship as part of her studies.

The lockout dragged on, and on December 6, Teemu and Kurri played a game in Kuopio, then flew back to Helsinki for the annual Independence Day gala at the Presidential Palace. "I had played golf in the same charity golf group with President Martti Ahtisaari every year for a few years. I once drove over his foot with my golf cart," said a grinning Selanne.

The NHL lockout lasted 103 days. Team owners failed to push a salary cap through, and player salaries continued to skyrocket.

An abbreviated season opened in January, and Teemu got off to a great start before he suffered a concussion on a blindside check by Vancouver's Mike Peca, who broke his jaw on the play and had to leave the game.

"He was deliberately trying to hurt me. I was hit in the head. I flew through the air and hit my head on the ice. I lost my memory for a while, and didn't know what day or year it was. It was scary," Teemu recalled.

It would be another 20 years before the NHL would act to remove those types of hits on unsuspecting players from the game.

Five years after the first incident, Peca, then with the Buffalo Sabres, took another run at Selanne, who then was a member of the Anaheim Mighty Ducks. Peca knocked Teemu off his skates with a low check that infuriated Teemu so much he chased the Sabres' captain to the Buffalo bench, yelling at him.

"He went right at my knees," Teemu told reporters after the game. "It could have been a really serious injury. It's a joke. It's the same thing with hits from behind. If you don't call them, the guys are going to keep doing them."

Teemu's strengths are his speed and his amazing scoring touch. It was his bread and butter. But toward the end of his third season, the points started to come further apart, and his acceleration just wasn't there.

Teemu was puzzled, but his body told him what was wrong.

"That's when my problems with the left knee began. I had to take anti-inflammatory medication half the season," he said. "The schedule in the Finnish league was easier, so my knees were fine there, but it got worse when I got back to the NHL. I played 12 games with injections."

An ailing left knee didn't stop Teemu from playing his part in the Jets' production. Selanne was on a line with Alexei Zhamnov and Keith Thachuk, and they had combined for 74 goals. Their output was second only to Philadelphia's "Legion of Doom" line of Eric Lindros, John LeClair, and Mikael Renberg, who combined for 80.

"We were linemates also as rookies in 1992–93, and it was unique how we were able to dominate the game. It was always a great pleasure playing with Alexei and Keith," said Teemu.

The Jets sputtered and were on track to miss the playoffs for a second straight season. That predicament saw Paddock step away as head coach to focus on his duties as general manager. Terry Simpson took over as interim head coach, and in late June, the interim tag was removed.

The Jets' future was uncertain, and the rumor mill was working nonstop about the team leaving Winnipeg. Prior to their last game of the regular season against Wayne Gretzky and the Los Angeles Kings on Tuesday, May 2, there were reports that the Jets were likely headed to Minneapolis to replace the Minnesota North Stars franchise, which had moved to Dallas following Selanne's rookie season.

Winnipeg lost the game 2–1, with Winnipeg native Randy Gilhen scoring the Jets' lone goal. As the horn sounded to end the game, Gilhen attempted to get the game puck, but he wasn't quick enough. Referee Kerry Fraser quickly scooped it up and handed it to Gretzky in what was surely a planned event by the two. Gretzky then quickly left the ice with the memento and was caught on camera mouthing the words "last puck" as he entered the Kings' dressing room. Jets team officials were so upset that they refused to let the Kings' team bus leave the Winnipeg Arena until Gretzky promised to return the puck.

The next few days and weeks were chaotic for players and especially the fans. A final farewell celebration was held at the arena. Veteran Thomas Steen had his No. 25 jersey retired and Ed Olzcyk promised to bring the Stanley Cup back to Winnipeg if the team went on to win the Cup in their new home.

Steen, who had played all of his 14 NHL seasons with the Jets, had been imploring local politicians and fans to step up to save the Jets. Little did anyone know at the time that there were steps already being taken to do just that. That night, the players had one last loud and very long blowout party at Wise Guys. DJ Kyle Irving was spinning records and at one point, Jennifer Hanson, the anthem singer for most Jets home games, took the stage to sing the Canadian anthem. Later in the evening, the players gathered on the stage and sang "Sweet Home Manitoba" to the tune of 'Sweet Home Alabama' by Lynyrd Skynyrd. Quietly, and quite illegally, the bar stayed open until 4 AM.

As news of efforts to save the Jets became public, there were fan rallies held at the Forks and then at Portage and Main, where the Jets had signed their two biggest stars of the franchise, Bobby Hull and Dale Hawerchuk. Then came the word that a deal was in place—the Jets weren't going anywhere. The team had been saved—sadly, that wasn't the case for the Nordiques, whose fans watched as their team left Quebec City for Denver, Colorado.

But the Jets fans' joy was short-lived. The deal fell apart, but by this time it was too late to move the franchise to Minnesota. The NHL announced there would be one last season for the Jets in Winnipeg.

Teemu and Sirpa were happy to spend another year in Winnipeg. They had made their home in the city and had several close friends, even outside the Jets family. Sirpa had become close with Kathleen Leipsic, an Olympic gymnast, and life in the NHL came full circle years later when the Nashville Predators drafted the Leipsics' son Brendan in 2012. Four years later, Brendan, who at this point was with the Toronto Maple Leafs, scored his first NHL goal in his first NHL game. Teemu's photo of a young Brendan at the Selannes' breakfast table dominated social media.

When Teemu returned to Finland, he rehabbed his knee every day and played tennis with Ismo Syvahuoko, his tennis partner and physician. Teemu also started his own hockey school, and his foundation organized a sports marketing seminar. Having learned the lessons of spreading himself too thin in the off-season, Teemu again scaled back on his activities.

By NHL standards, Teemu was underpaid. The $1.5 million signing bonus he had received when he signed with the Jets camouflaged the fact. His salary in his second season was only $400,000, way under the league average, which was $600,000. "Even I made more money than he," said enforcer Tie Domi, whose salary was $450,000.

In the Canadian media, Selanne's stoic attitude was praised. Star players' salaries were taking off, and several players without his star status had wanted to renegotiate their contracts. Teemu received high praise for honoring his deal and not making his salary a nagging issue with the team.

"I was praised for reporting to camp, but I had simply made up my mind to honor my contract even though my rookie season had gone beyond expectations," Teemu said.

To say Teemu was a bargain is an understatement. Peter Forsberg, for example, had signed a four-year contract with the Quebec Nordiques, worth CAN$6.5 million, even though he spent the first season of the contract in Sweden. Teemu made $2.7 million for the same period.

On the other hand, Selanne also knew he'd have his big payday eventually. Each new contract other stars signed would raise his value. Selanne and agent Don Baizley had planned to renegotiate the contract in the summer of 1994, but the lockout postponed their plan by a year. Teemu did get a $1.6 million raise for his option year, but he lost half of it due to the lockout.

Teemu wanted a longer-term deal. The Achilles tendon injury had reminded him, once again, of the fragility of a career. Everything can be over in a heartbeat. "I figured that if I could make $15 million in five years, my family and I, and my extended family, could live on that. Probably I would've made more money on shorter-term contracts, but that wasn't what I wanted," he said.

Baizley thought his client was worth more and reminded him often that a $3 million annual salary would actually make him an underpaid star. "I told him that I had a pretty good life if that was true," Teemu said.

Even with the injuries, Teemu had averaged a point a game, which by NHL standards was more than acceptable, but he wanted to get back to the 100-point level.

Teemu and Sirpa were expecting their first child and, with the help of Kathleen's husband Greg Leipsic, Teemu proposed to Sirpa by hiding an engagement ring in a salad they had ordered in from a restaurant. She said yes.

Teemu was still loyal to the Jets and to the fans—so much so that he started the 1995 training camp without a contract, and finally signed a five-year contract worth $15 million on the eve of the regular season opener.

He did have a good life and no complaints.

The only dark cloud was the future of the Jets. During the "Save the Jets" fundraising campaign, the players pitched in as much as anybody else. Even Teemu gave some money.

Canadian teams were in financial trouble due to the weakened Canadian dollar. Virtually all the teams' revenues were in Canadian funds, but their big expense, the player salaries, was almost always in American dollars. The NHL had expanded into the so-called US Sun Belt. Teams were now in California—the Anaheim Mighty Ducks and the San Jose Sharks—and Florida, with the Panthers and the Tampa Bay Lightning.

The Jets played in the NHL's smallest market, and the financial numbers spelled doom.

Jets owner Barry Shenkarow and his partners sold the team to Richard Burke and Steven Gluckstern, two American businessmen, who had planned to move it to Minnesota. However, they would change their minds and instead relocate the franchise to Phoenix at the end of the 1995–96 season and rebrand the Jets as the Coyotes.

The new owners loved having Selanne on the team. Who wouldn't be happy to have a superstar going to another All-Star Game? They went out of their way to let Teemu know he was a big part of their plans.

"We are in Washington having a pregame meal, and our PR guy gives me the phone. It was Richard Burke, our new owner, and he said, 'Teemu, I know there have been a lot of rumors that we can't afford to have three guys who make so much money, with Keith [Tkachuk] and Alex [Zhamnov]. But I just want to tell you that you are not for sale and you will be a huge part of our success in Phoenix. Just keep playing.' I said I appreciate the call, and he said, 'The team will go to Phoenix at the All-Star break, but we will fly you and your wife to Phoenix after the season and we will show you around.'"

"I was sure he'd tell me he had traded me, but he told me that the rumors weren't true and that I should just enjoy playing because I was going to be a big part of the new team in Phoenix. After that, I didn't take the rumors seriously," Teemu said.

Selanne went to the All-Star Game in Boston, where coincidentally he and Paul Kariya of the Anaheim Mighty Ducks met, became friends, and joked about playing together one day. Their styles of play complemented each other, and they shared the same agent in Don Baizley.

While there was talk in hockey circles about the Jets wanting to trade Teemu, few expected the team to actually do it, although it was almost certain that they'd have to move one of their high-paid forwards. Keith Tkachuk had signed a $17 million offer sheet with Chicago prior to the start of the season, which the Jets matched, while Zhamnov was playing out the option on his contract, meaning he would be a free agent when the season ended and thus harder to deal.

After the All-Star Game, Teemu returned to the Jets, confident that he would move with the team to Phoenix based on his conversation with the new owners.

Three weeks later, that confidence was shattered.

Teemu had scored 24 goals and 72 points in 51 games. The Jets had played five games after the All-Star break and were getting ready to play against the Ottawa Senators at home. They had a morning practice on an off day when head coach Terry Simpson asked Teemu to step inside the coach's office. There was a phone call for him. It was Paddock.

"I still had my gear, so I took off my helmet and gloves and took the phone. [Paddock] was very quiet and he did not know how to start the conversation. I thought *fuck, what is this?* He said, 'This is the toughest day of my life. I just traded you.'"

What followed was deafening silence.

"We went a minute without talking. Total silence. I said, 'Where?' and he said Anaheim. 'All right, thanks.' As I hung up I heard him say, 'Teemu, Teemu, Teemu.'"

Teemu was in shock. "It was probably the saddest day of my career."

He headed back to the Jets' dressing room, took his gear off, and showered. He saw Nummimen, took him aside, and whispered what had just happened to him. He also saw some other teammates and let them in on the news.

"I'll never forget the looks on their faces. It was tough for all of us."

Selanne left the arena, and headed home to tell Sirpa, who was having a baby shower and was looking at baby clothes with Ottawa Senators forward Antti Tormanen's girlfriend Minna Rautanen. Teemu decided to wait for a better moment.

"Our captain, Kris King, called and asked to speak with me. I told Sirpa to tell him I wasn't at home. She realized what had happened and burst into tears," Teemu said.

More and more friends gathered at the Selanne house. "It broke my heart," Kathleen Leipsic said. "Our Brendan was a year old, and Sirpa was pregnant. We had looked forward to taking care of the kids together."

Teemu now smiles when he talks about breaking the news of the unthinkable.

"It was so funny," Selanne recalls. "A week before, my wife asked me about some TV thing about a holiday trip to Disneyland, and she kept asking me if I was ever going to take her to Disneyland. I said of course. I said now you can go to Disneyland every day."

But there is no doubt that the trade shook Selanne to his core.

"That night I could not sleep the whole night. I was shaking. Is this for real? I felt I had failed. I heard the first trade is tough, and they are right. It is not something you can describe. It is such a disappointing season."

Sirpa was nine months pregnant. She and Teemu had talked with the doctor about the due date, looked at the NHL schedule, and saw he had a two-day break between games. They decided the baby would be delivered then. He would be home for the birth and then rejoin the team in Calgary.

"There were so many things going on, and I thought, *This is so unfair. I am so happy here.* I wanted to finish the season and have the chance to say goodbye to the fans. It was very sad, anyway, and I turned over and I tried to get close to my wife. I was shaking."

Selanne had accumulated 306 points in 231 regular season games and six points in six playoff games as a Jet. None of that mattered anymore.

"The normal people who work in companies, they have no idea how it feels and how brutal the situation is when somebody comes and tells you, 'Here's your ticket, thank you. Now go.'"

Two decades later, Selanne is no longer bitter.

"They traded Gretzky. I remember Esa Tikkanen telling me he was with the Oilers on the bus to the rink to play the New York Rangers when he found out he had been traded to the Blueshirts. He got off the bus and went to the other dressing room. Guys have been traded during games."

Paddock faced the local media and explained the reason he had traded Selanne instead of Tkachuk or Zhamnov was that "Tkachuk can't be moved due to his contract and Zhamnov is our only world-class center."

As hard as it is to believe, the knives were soon out for Selanne.

Montreal-based French columnist Yvon Pedneault wrote in a Finnish paper that the Jets' players didn't like Teemu and that there were those who even hated him. He was considered a selfish player who cared more about his stats than the team's wins. According to his sources, the teammates had demanded the team make the trade. "Nobody's going to go on the record, but they don't think Teemu cares about the team. He only cares about Teemu," Pedneault wrote.

Teemu didn't lack confidence and many people misinterpreted that. He could be brutally honest when talking with the media about, for example, the team's defense.

Reporters wrote about other so-called issues. It was said some players didn't like how Paavo used the Jets' gym and sauna as if they were his own. Among some players, Paavo's nickname was "Billy," a reference he didn't understand until he innocently asked Winnipeg's CKND-TV sports director Joe Pascucci what it meant. Paavo was told it was likely a reference to former US President Jimmy Carter's brother Billy, who promoted himself on the coattails of his brother's fame.

Teemu has heard all the stories, but he doesn't think they're true. Having said that, he does say he's met coaches and players who have been jealous of him. "I still don't think that was the case with the trade," he said, almost 25 years later.

The trade was emotional, but it wasn't completely unexpected. The Jets couldn't afford three players making more than $3 million. "I was the easiest one to trade. I had just signed a five-year extension."

"It would have been easier had Burke not called me and lied about the rumors. They betrayed me, and that hurt," he said.

The Jets received Oleg Tverdovsky, a 19-year-old defenseman; Chad Kilger, also 19; and Anaheim's third-round pick in the 1996 draft, which they used to draft Per-Anton Lundstrom, but the Swede never played in the NHL. The Mighty Ducks got Teemu and Marc Chouinard, 18, and the Jets' fourth-round pick in the 1996 draft.

Jets fans were furious. In their first game after the trade, against the Senators, the attendance was only 8,673 and the fans demanded that the trade be reversed and that Paddock be fired.

Teemu put on a brave face, but inside, he was upset and had difficulties getting over the trade. "I was so naïve, and I thought that Winnipeg was always going to be my home. I did everything I could to make them happy and to put the city on the map. That trade changed everything. I woke up and realized that the NHL was all business. It completely changed the way I see the world."

Lori Summers, the Selannes' friend and the director of the team's charitable work, thinks the trade changed Teemu as a person. "He was as open a person one can be, and I consider myself lucky to have known him before the trade. It was the end of his innocence. Teemu made us Winnipeggers better people."

Like the Leipsic family, Summers and her husband Lance, who passed away in 2017, were close friends, and they didn't allow one of the most famous and lopsided trades in NHL history to drive a wedge between the families. "I´m really grateful Lori was asked to take care of me when I was in Winnipeg. She became like a big sister to me and helped me so much. She took care of everything I needed off the ice and that allowed me to focus on hockey. Lori and Lance were both an enormous help and they played an important role. We became lifelong friends. We miss Lance, and we still see Lori regularly," Teemu said.

Anaheim general manager Jack Ferreira tells this story about the deal. He told ESPN.com in January 2015 that he and Ducks coach Ron Wilson were shooting the breeze when the conversation turned to rumors that the Jets were thinking of shopping Selanne.

"So, we were talking about our team, and then talking about Teemu, and I just said, 'The hell with it.'"

He called Paddock at his house and asked him flat out. The rest is history.

The Ducks' GM had sent details of Selanne's contract back to Anaheim, where it was being reviewed by the rest of the front office. "His contract, as I kept hearing from our people back in Anaheim, was quite inflationary," he said. "It was, but he was also going to change the franchise, too. We needed something to restart the franchise."

Rob Scichili, the Ducks' public relations official, told the Finnish newspaper *Helsingin Sanomat* that Wayne Gretzky would one day leave the Kings and then Teemu would be "the king of California."

In Anaheim, people couldn't believe how the team could have pulled off such a trade, and Ferreira was treated like a hero. He had been on a "fishing expedition" and was caught by surprise when Paddock took the bait.

Going from Canada's coldest major city to California sun wasn't all bad for Teemu.

Little did he know at the time, but the trade would end up having a profound impact on Teemu's life.

QUACK, QUACK, QUACK

PAUL KARIYA WAS LINGERING in the Mighty Ducks' dressing room after a morning practice when head coach Ron Wilson came out of his office with a smile on his face that could have lit up a dark hockey arena.

"He called in Oleg Tverdovsky and Chad Kilger and we were all like, what is going on?" Kariya recalled.

He didn't have to wait long for an answer. "I don't remember if it was [general manager] Jack [Ferreira] who came in, but somebody told us that we just got Teemu Selanne."

Jaws dropped.

"We were all like, 'No way, we got Teemu,'" Kariya said. "We could not believe it, and our minds were blown. Then these guys came out and we knew what happened and it was kind of awkward. What do you say? Do you say we just got Teemu Selanne, one of the best scorers in the NHL?

"I still remember Ron's face."

The trade came less than three weeks after Teemu and Kariya sat next to each other on the Western Conference bench at the All-Star

Game in Boston. They were like two kids in a candy store as the player introductions were made.

"We just sat there and when every player came into the ice, we were just, 'Look, there's Brett Hull, can you believe how great a shot he has.' Then there was Wayne Gretzky, the greatest player in the game. We just talked about how great these guys were, and I remember saying here is a guy who scored 76 goals and he is such a fan of the game, and that just stuck with me," Kariya recalled.

The Ducks were headed out on an East Coast road trip, and Selanne caught up to his new team when they were in Uniondale, New York, to play the New York Islanders.

It was 24 hours since his life had changed, albeit for the better in the end, but Teemu still had a few lingering, raw emotions. He still felt betrayed.

"When I got there, I started feeling better. It was pretty good. But that 24 hours, my body and my mind had never felt like this," Teemu said. "I stopped and thought about it later and realized I played great in Winnipeg. But still, I felt they lied to me. I get there was no feeling. There are no feelings. They do not care how I feel. They do not care how the fans feel. It is brutal. They don't care about how you feel and your family issues.

"But a lot of people said, 'Hey, they want you.' I was going to a team that wanted me."

It was, in hindsight, one of hockey's worst trades.

Kariya is a fastidious, dedicated athlete, while Teemu was just the opposite.

But opposites attract, and Selanne and Kariya clicked immediately.

"I did not know it was going to happen so soon. We were roommates, and right away in the first practice you could see that this would be awesome. We were so fast," said Selanne. "Playing with him was so easy. We both felt the game the same way. We did everything at high speed and it was the easiest hockey I ever played. It was unique."

"Our playing styles matched perfectly. Speed was biggest, but we were thinking exactly the same way, how we want to play this game. We made each other better with passing and we were very unselfish together. We knew we were going to help each other."

Kariya finally had someone to play with.

"It was instant chemistry, and we both saw the game the same way. We both played an up-tempo game," added Kariya. "I knew how great a goal scorer he was, but he was underrated as a pass-maker and that was one of the first things I noticed, how well he saw the game.

"He helped me in every facet of my game possible, but he made me a better scorer for sure, seeing how he did things in practice. Teemu would be going on a breakaway, and Ron would say, 'Paul. Watch how he opens his stick like this and the goalie doesn't know if he is going to go on his backhand or shoot.' Little adjustments like that, I would make to my game just by watching him."

"I taught him about life," Teemu said. "He was used to avoiding fans. Every time we checked into a hotel he wanted to know where the emergency exits were, and he ordered food from room service so that he could be alone. He even had a cook at home. But I made him come out, and I think it opened up his eyes."

Selanne may have taken his career seriously, but compared with Kariya, he was a mess. Kariya was a perfectionist.

"Every morning at 8:15, he meditated, no matter where we were. And he went to bed at 10:00 PM, wearing wrist supports so that his arms wouldn't get sore," said Teemu, who couldn't resist the temptation to poke fun at his buddy's habits.

"One night, I put on my shin pads when I was going to bed. Paul was wondering what I was doing, so I told him that I once hurt my knee in my sleep."

When Teemu joined the team, the atmosphere in the dressing room immediately changed. "Before that, guys didn't really laugh in there, but he knows how to loosen things up," said Kariya.

Television color analyst Brian Hayward saw a difference in Kariya.

"He was like a kid in a candy store. Suddenly he had a duo that would always create havoc for the opponent. With one trade, Anaheim's offense became credible," Hayward said.

"Until then, it had been simply dump-and-chase. With Teemu's arrival, they had a line that could keep the puck with their team and create chances in every shift."

For center Steve Rucchin, being put on a line with Kariya and Selanne was like winning the lottery.

"He told me he didn't want to touch the puck at all. He just said he'd drive to the net and create some room for us. Don't pass the puck to me, he said," Teemu said with a laugh.

Rucchin might seem an odd fit for Selanne and Kariya, but his strengths blended well with the pair of skilled speedsters.

"A lot of people said, 'Think about what it would have been like if you had a great center,' but me and Paul thought we had the best center. We did not need Adam Oates or Wayne Gretzky," said Teemu. "Steve Rucchin was the guy who did so much. He made room for us, and we always thought this was perfect for us."

Rucchin did get the puck and he knew exactly when to pass it to them. It was a little easier to get it to Kariya, because he always wanted it; Teemu only wanted it when he had a scoring chance, although he was a much better playmaker than people give him credit for.

Teemu joined his new teammates on Long Island, where the Mighty Ducks were set to play against the New York Islanders. The Finnish Flash scored a goal in Anaheim's 4–3 loss, but not all was lost. Teemu looked at the schedule and liked what he saw.

"The team was on a two-week road trip, which gave me a good chance to get to know the guys. I roomed with Kariya, who had been my linemate in the first game but not in the next few games, and that was fine because it gave us an opportunity to observe each other's play."

Playing for a new team and getting to know his new teammates wasn't the only thing on Teemu's mind. Sirpa was about to give birth to their first child, and Teemu wound his way back to Winnipeg shortly after the Ducks' five-game road trip.

After he played his first home game in Anaheim against Boston, he took an overnight flight to Winnipeg to be at Sirpa's side for the delivery. She had been in Victoria General Hospital for a day, with her friend Kathleen Leipsic at her side, and Teemu desperately wanted to be with his partner for the birth.

He made it.

"I landed in a snowy, cold Winnipeg and Greg Leipsic picked me up and we drove to the hospital. It was strange to drive through Winnipeg, knowing that just a few weeks earlier, this was my hometown. I loved the city, it was full of friendly people. We really had a good time there. Suddenly, I'm there again for the birth of first child. Everybody can surely understand what confusing feelings I had."

Teemu and Sirpa had worked things out with her doctor so that the baby would be induced after he arrived at the hospital to allow him to be part of the delivery.

"The hospital was busy, and the moment before the birth the doctor went to another room. Sirpa was doing her part, she was pushing, and doctor came back in about five minutes before the baby was born," Teemu recalled.

Eemil Selanne was born at 3:30 AM on February 23, 1996.

"Childbirth was completely inconceivable, how it all happened, and I will never forget the feeling I had when I held our baby in my hands for the first time. Tears were falling, and hockey was the furthest thing on my mind. It was the most wonderful experience of my life," Teemu said.

A few hours later, Greg Leipsic picked Teemu up at the hospital. Teemu decided he needed a massage, so he called his old EJK Espoo teammate, Jukka Nieminen, who was the Jets' massage therapist. He asked them to come to the rink, even though the Jets had a game against the Chicago Blackhawks. The game was underway when Teemu and Greg took the arena's back door to get to the room where Nieminen had his massage table. Teemu was getting massaged when Chicago center Jeremy Roenick came into the room for medical attention.

"He asked Teemu what the f--k he was doing there," said Leipsic.

Selanne told him he was getting a massage after his firstborn's birth.

"The look on Roenick's face was priceless. I don't think anyone ever knew I had been there, except for Jukka and Teppo [Numminen]," Teemu said.

Teemu took Numminen, Nieminen, and Leipsic out on the town to celebrate, and after another hospital visit to Sirpa and Eemil, he caught a flight back to Anaheim. He only missed one game, on the road against Calgary.

He was in a Ducks uniform for their next home game against San Jose.

"I was really tired after a few nights of no sleep at all, and Coach Wilson told me I didn't have to dress," Teemu said. "I thought after the warm-up that I can't play, but I decided to try. I don't know where I got that feeling and energy."

Teemu scored a hat trick and had an assist in a 4–3 win. He dedicated his three-goal performance to Eemil. He had the pucks framed, and they hang in the Selannes' living room in California.

A week later, Sirpa, Eemil, and Teemu's mother, Liisa, along with Teddy and Domi—Sirpa's and Teemu's dogs—flew to Anaheim and checked into an apartment in a hotel next to Disneyland.

"Everything was great. I couldn't have been happier," said Selanne. "That made me realize how bad the relationship between the management and the players had been in Winnipeg. Anaheim had a great organization, and Southern California was a great place to live. Plus, the team traveled on chartered planes."

When Selanne joined the team in February, the Mighty Ducks faced a 20-point gap to a playoff berth, but they clawed their way back into the hunt and had a two-point lead on Winnipeg heading into the last game of the season.

An Anaheim win would leave them tied in points, but the Jets went into the last game of the season with 36 victories, two more than the Mighty Ducks.

The tiebreaker when two teams ended the season with the same number of points was wins, so a Mighty Ducks win would not allow them to advance.

"We beat them 5–2. That was a good end to the season, and Paul and I traveled to Vienna for the World Championship," Teemu said.

When Selanne joined the Mighty Ducks, Anaheim had only had one true star—Kariya. Now the team had two.

Playing a full 82 games in his second season, Kariya scored 50 goals and finished with 108 points, which was twice as many points as his next teammate. Rucchin was second in scoring with 19 goals and 44 points. Teemu was fourth with 16 goals and 36 points in 28 games as a Mighty Duck.

"Kariya was all alone, and while he doesn't like to show his emotions, it was easy to tell that he was excited about Teemu's arrival. Finally, he'd have someone to play with," Hayward said.

Hayward followed Teemu's career from beginning to end, first on the ice as a goaltender with the San Jose Sharks, then as Anaheim's goalie coach, and finally as a member of the Ducks' broadcast team, a job he took in 1995.

"My first memory of Teemu is from the fall of 1992, when the Sharks played an exhibition game against the Jets in Winnipeg. [Sharks] coach George Kingston warned the team of this young Finn who would beat any defenseman if he was given space," said Hayward.

"He was the fastest player I had seen, and by then I had played 10 years in the NHL," added Hayward.

Teemu and Sirpa had bought a new house in Yorba Linda, California, about a half hour's drive from the arena, before they headed back to Finland for the summer.

That summer, Teemu had knee surgery to deal with an issue he had with the meniscus in one knee and a torn joint capsule in the other. It was the first time Ismo Syvahuoko operated on his friend's knees, but not the last.

"During the seasons 1994–95 and 1995–96 I took more anti-inflammatory medication than in any other time in my career," he said.

But it was a memorable summer in other ways.

Selanne had his bachelor party and wedding, and the same priest who had baptized Teemu and Paavo baptized Eemil Jalo Ilmari Selanne at home.

And there were friends' weddings, as well.

"I was mostly nervous about the bachelor party because I knew Waltteri Immonen was looking forward to payback, given what happened at his bachelor party earlier in the summer. In Finland, bachelor parties are a little bit too crazy," Teemu said with a laugh.

On July 13, Selanne was at Keijo Sailynoja's bachelor party when his friends grabbed him, put a towel over his head, and headed out on the town. They drove him to sauna and to party in the Helsinki clubs. The next day, they took Teemu to the Helsinki Olympic Stadium and he played the first 5:00 of a Finnish soccer league match. After that, they dressed him up as Elvis and he sang at a Helsinki nightclub. Last but not least, to cap a great night, he was taken to a tattoo parlor.

"When the tattoo artist recognized me, he got so confused that he tattooed the Swedish flag onto my right ankle instead of a lightning bolt going through the Finnish flag," Selanne said.

Years later, the tattoo became a talking point between teammates.

"Peter Forsberg thought it was particularly hilarious, when we were together in Colorado. He said that I have secretly always wanted to be Swedish," Teemu said with a laugh. "I'll get it fixed one day."

On July 19, 1996, Teemu and Sirpa got married at the Helsinki Old Church, with his brother Paavo and friends Ismo Syvahuoko, Waltteri Immonen, and Kai Eklund sharing the duties as best man. Antti Tormanen's partner Minna Rautanen sang "Can You Feel the Love Tonight" from the movie *The Lion King*.

Selanne saved one surprise for Sirpa. The newlyweds took a helicopter to their wedding reception on the small island of Klippan, a stone's throw from the Helsinki cruise terminal.

A friend sold photos of the wedding to a Finnish tabloid, ending that friendship.

The coming 1996–97 season would begin with the World Cup of Hockey, a new tournament modeled on the Canada Cup. Finland finished fifth, having lost the quarterfinal to Russia 5–0. Teemu had three goals and four points in four games.

When the players returned to their NHL teams, Teemu had a new teammate in Anaheim—Jari Kurri.

"Anaheim was one of my three options. I listened to my family before making the decision, and Teemu's part of my family," Kurri said.

Ron Wilson, who had coached Team USA to the World Cup win, had promised Kurri a spot between Teemu and Kariya.

"If you can keep up with us," Teemu teased Kurri.

"I don't have to. I'll just dish out the puck, and you guys can go after it," Kurri said.

The Finnish media went crazy; the magazines were filled with stories of Teemu and Kurri hanging out in Disneyland. Sirpa hosted a one-hour NHL TV special that was broadcast in Finland.

"I didn't realize last year how lucky I was to get traded here. The only downside is the traffic," Selanne said.

"Jari and I could walk around Disneyland without anybody recognizing us. It was fantastic," he added.

Kariya was out of the lineup for the first 11 games with a sports hernia, but Kurri and Selanne found chemistry right away. Besides playing on the top line, they were part of the Mighty Ducks' first power play unit.

Everything seemed to be going fine until Kariya resumed playing.

"When Paul returned to action, Jari's ice time went down and we didn't play on the same line. It was a curious decision by Wilson, as if we only had two players on the team," said Teemu.

Kurri finished the season playing all 82 games and left Anaheim after the playoffs for a final NHL season in Colorado.

"It was a great season, though. It was nice to be on the same team with Jari and be his roommate on the road," Teemu said.

Wilson was on solid ground in having faith in keeping Selanne and Kariya together. Kariya had 44 goals and 99 points in 69 games while Selanne contributed 51 goals and 109 points in 78.

Both were voted to the First All-Star Team, and Kariya was up for the Hart Trophy as the league's MVP, finishing second to Dominik Hasek.

Selanne and Kariya were one of the most dangerous duos in the NHL. They had speed to burn, and their skill level was scary. They were not easy to contain offensively.

Teams used clutching and grabbing to counter offensive flair, and this boring-but-effective style of play was being used more and more, especially since the New Jersey Devils had used the style to win the team's first Stanley Cup in 1995. Head coach Jacques Lemaire employed a defensive system that won games.

The next season, Florida coach Doug MacLean used a similar style of smothering defense to guide his team to the Stanley Cup Final.

"Before that, the stars had had more time and space, but now there were teams that didn't even try to create anything, and simply focused on defending," Selanne said.

The Ducks made the 1996–97 playoffs, and, as fate would have it, they met the Phoenix Coyotes, who were playing their first season in Arizona after moving from Winnipeg, in the first round. The series went the distance, but the Ducks won Game 7. Teemu tallied eight points in the seven games.

In the second round, Detroit swept the Ducks, and Teemu and Sirpa took off on their honeymoon in Hawaii.

———

By the annual Bermuda Cup celebrity tennis tournament in Finland, Teemu was already looking forward to the new season, the birth of their second child, building on the team's success the previous season, and the 1998 Olympics in Nagano, when NHL players would compete at the Olympic Winter Games for the first time.

"For the first time in my career, nothing about the previous season bothered me," he said.

THE MIGHTY DUCK

I N THE FALL OF 1997, Kariya and the Mighty Ducks couldn't agree on a new contract, and Teemu started the season as team captain.

Wilson, the only coach the team ever had, was fired in May due to "philosophical differences" with management over bolstering the Ducks' roster through free agency. Pierre Page was behind the bench when Anaheim flew to Japan to open the regular season with two games against the Vancouver Canucks.

The games in Japan were a prelude to NHL players participating in the 1998 Nagano Winter Olympics. The NHL had hoped Kariya's presence would generate interest in Japan. Kariya was a fourth-generation Japanese-Canadian. Teemu's international stardom was a bonus. The Vancouver Canucks were hyped as the "Pacific Rim" team, and they featured Russian star Pavel Bure and Mark Messier, who was a member of the Oilers and Rangers Stanley Cup teams before he signed with Vancouver.

Kariya wasn't the only star player not reporting to training camp. Some players under contract even sat out to get more money or to force a trade.

Others took advantage of a system of restricted free agency to get massive salary increases.

Joe Sakic of the Colorado Avalanche didn't crack the top 20 in league scoring in 1996–97, but that wasn't an issue when the New York Rangers signed him to an offer sheet worth $21 million over three years as a restricted free agent. The Avalanche were not about to allow their star center to leave, and they matched the offer.

But Sakic's new contract cast a shadow over contract talks overall.

Teemu was making $3.4 million a year and had finished second in goals to former Jets teammate Keith Tkachuk and second in the scoring race to Mario Lemieux the previous season.

"I respect my contract," he said publicly.

And he did.

Even without Kariya, Selanne picked up where he left off the previous season. The Finnish Flash was flying high and led the league in goal scoring after 18 games.

"I had scored a goal in 11 consecutive games. The NHL record was 13. On the night before the 12th game, Sirpa went into labor, we drove to the hospital, and I didn't sleep at all that night," Teemu recalled.

Eetu was born at 1:00 PM on November 12, 1997.

"I went home, showered and got changed, and played that night against Montreal. We lost the game 4–3, and my streak was over. I left all my energy in the hospital," said Teemu, who scored 17 goals and had 19 points in 11 games between October 21 and November 10.

"There are bigger things in life than hockey, and that day, my wife was the first star. The birth of my second son was of course much more important than the NHL record," he said.

The Hockey News editor-in-chief Steve Dryden wrote in an editorial that nobody had ever done more with less.

"Selanne's goal streak is in a class of its own because he doesn't get any help in Anaheim. He's basically scored his goals on his own, playing against the toughest defensemen in the league. In addition, his goals have been highlight-reel material. He's at least as good as in his rookie season," he wrote.

Kariya finally signed a new deal—two years, $14 million—and returned to the lineup in December. Teemu called it a great Christmas present, having played 32 games without his friend.

Anaheim beat Washington 6–4 in Kariya's first game back. Teemu scored two goals and had three points; Kariya had two goals and four points.

This was a marriage of teammates made in hockey heaven.

"I'm sure a lot of players could do what we did, but nobody else did [it] as fast and unexpectedly as we did," Kariya said.

As is often the case, great players push each other to even greater heights.

Both Selanne and Kariya had a competitive edge.

"It is scary. It is not very often that two players find that chemistry. You know what he thinks. He knows where I am going to be and sometimes he knew where I was going to be before I did," Teemu said. "And when you realize that chemistry it is the greatest feeling. We were working so hard together. We did every drill as hard as we could possibly do. If we did 2-on-1s, we were always the first to go. Since we knew we would be playing together, we wanted to do everything together at practice. We were like a team. We watched tape together. After every shift we talked and sometimes we were yelling at each other. We were like brothers.

"And we were competing. Everything was a competition: who scores the most goals in a drill, who puts the most pucks through the five-hole, everything. After the practice, the loser would have to take the other's skates off and get him something to drink.

"The thing that really made us successful was that we were unselfish players. We talked about the game and gave each other honest feedback. We knew that if he played well, it'd help me, and vice versa. Sometimes I thought we shared a brain out there."

Selanne played in the All-Star Game, scored a hat trick, and was named MVP of the showcase event, the first European player to be so honored. He played on a line with fellow Finns Saku Koivu of the Montreal Canadiens and Jere Lehtinen of the Dallas Stars. The trio was reunited a couple weeks later in the Nagano Olympics.

As the NHL shut down for the Winter Games, Teemu was loving playing with Kariya and was playing the best hockey of his life. He had nine points in the three games before the break and led the league in both goals and points.

A couple weeks before the Nagano Games were to open, Kariya took a brutal cross-check to the head from Gary Suter of the Chicago Blackhawks. He suffered a concussion—not his first—and he missed the Olympics and the rest of the NHL season. Suter was suspended for four games.

"We only played 22 games together," Teemu said sadly.

The Nagano Olympics were expected to focus worldwide attention on hockey and also to be a North American showdown for the gold medal between the US and Canada.

They fell short on both counts.

All three medals went to European countries, with the Czech Republic, behind Dominik Hasek's brilliant goaltending, beating Russia in the final.

"That the NHLers were able to play in the Olympics was like winning the jackpot for hockey. The World Cup or the Canada Cup is played in the fall, when the players still haven't found their stride," said Selanne.

Teemu loved putting on Finland's jersey and representing his country and played what he calls his best game of his career in the quarterfinal against Sweden, which featured Peter Forsberg, Mats Sundin, and Nicklas Lidstrom, while Finland countered with Selanne, Teppo Numminen, and Saku Koivu.

The game was scoreless after 40:00 of play, but 4:00 into the third period, Teemu scored his first goal, assisted by his former Jets team-mate Teppo Numminen. Eight minutes later, the Finnish power play unit of Selanne, Koivu, and Jere Lehtinen gave Finland a two-goal lead when Koivu and Lehtinen set Selanne up with a chance he didn't miss, beating goaltender Tommy Salo cleanly.

Peter Forsberg scored for Sweden with 12 seconds remaining in the third period, and they kept coming. Mats Sundin won two offensive faceoffs in the remaining time, but the Finnish defense smothered the Swedes and Finland went through to the semifinal.

"I thought nothing was going to stop us," Teemu said.

The Finns were scheduled to have the day off before the semifinal against Russia, and the veteran players had told team captain Koivu—then 23 years old—he should make sure they were given the whole day off. Coach Hannu Aravirta and team manager Heikki Riihiranta thought it was a bad idea.

"In hindsight, that was a mistake," said Aravirta.

After a postgame team dinner, the players were taken back to the Olympic Village for rest and relaxation, but that did not sit well with some of the players. They described going back to the village as akin to wearing handcuffs.

Some of the players bolted and headed downtown to enjoy Nagano's nightlife. They didn't think going out on the town would hurt the team since they had the next day off.

"We had agreed that we couldn't afford to get drunk. We were after the biggest dream a player can win with the national team," Teemu said. "It was the first time all the best players participated in the Olympics and we had made it to the semifinal.

"And yet, some guys couldn't wait a few more days."

At the morning skate the next day, part of the team clearly suffered from hangovers, a fact the coaching staff somehow missed. The lineup in the semifinal was the same as in the quarterfinal game against Sweden.

Finland controlled the game but Pavel Bure—"The Russian Rocket"—also had a night to remember, scoring five goals in the game: three on breakaways, one on the power play, and an empty-netter that sealed Russia's 7–4 win.

Russia had held a 3–0 lead, but Finland rallied back and tied it, and even tied it again after Alexei Zhamnov's goal had put Russia back in the lead. But Bure and Andrei Kovalenko scored to the seal the win.

Finland outshot Russia 32–21, but defensive lapses allowed the Russians to capitalize.

After the game, Aravirta heard about the players' night on the town.

"Had I known about it, of course I would have done something about it," he said.

The memory of what could have been leaves Teemu filled with remorse.

"We were so much better than Russia in the semifinal, it was a huge disappointment. I've never got drunk during a tournament; it's a matter of professional pride. It takes at least three to four days to recover from a night out. It's crazy to do in the middle of a tournament."

Teemu led the tournament in scoring, with four goals and 10 points in five games, but he couldn't play in the bronze medal game against Canada due to a groin injury.

Teemu had had problems with his back, and the Anaheim physiotherapist had suggested he start to work on his core muscles, which in turn made a new muscle group sore.

"I shouldn't have taken up such a vigorous gym program. I had the same injury many times after that, including in 2007, until we found a new method to cure it.

"In 1998, I would have given anything to play in the bronze medal game, and I even asked the team doctor to give me an injection, but he thought I shouldn't risk the rest of the season. Had it been the Olympic final, I would have played. That would have been so special," he said.

Finland beat Canada 3–2 in what was Jari Kurri's last game with the national team. Teemu finished second in the MVP voting behind Dominik Hasek, who led his Czech team to gold.

Teemu missed five games after the Olympics, and then the last four games of the regular season, when he pulled a muscle in his thigh. Playing without Kariya and with a less-than-healthy Selanne, the Ducks missed the playoffs.

In mid-March, Dallas Stars defenseman Craig Ludwig, whose task it was to keep Teemu from scoring, hit him with his elbow and knocked Selanne unconscious. "It was a brutal act and it was no accident. I was out cold on the ice."

However, the Mighty Ducks weren't going to take it lying down. They had already lost Kariya to a concussion, and the team had lost eight of its 10 games since. A line brawl broke out on the ice as Teemu lay there unconscious.

"We had to respond in a very aggressive way," said Brent Severyn, the Mighty Ducks enforcer.

Teemu was one of the best players in the NHL in 1997–98 and he was one of the three finalists for the Hart Trophy—the only time in his career he was a finalist for the prestigious award. Buffalo Sabres goaltender Dominik Hasek was named the MVP. Teemu was third in voting, with Art Ross Trophy winner Jaromir Jagr finishing second. Teemu won the goal scoring title and was named to the Second All-Star Team.

The Hockey News named Selanne its Player of the Year. The *Toronto Sun* called Peter Forsberg the best in the league, followed by Teemu and Jaromir Jagr.

Brian Hayward thinks Teemu should have won the Hart Trophy.

"He carried the whole team on his back. He wasn't just fast, he was also strong. I remember seeing him score goals with more than one defenseman trying to stop him," he said.

Even with Kariya out of the lineup, and one less thing for the opponents to worry about, Teemu scored 52 goals and had 86 points in

73 games and finished eighth in the scoring race. He played 51 games without Kariya, and of his 52 goals, only seven came on the power play.

He was the fourth player in NHL history to score more than 25 percent of his team's goals in a season, after Maurice Richard of the Canadiens, Brett Hull of the St. Louis Blues, and Peter Bondra of the Washington Capitals.

Selanne's 52 goals represented 25.4 percent of the team's 205 goals, and only Hull's percentage had been better than that. He had scored 27.7 percent of the St. Louis Blues' goals in 1990–91 when he netted 86.

Selanne's offensive output and his stellar leadership caught the attention of Anaheim's home newspaper, the *Orange County Register*. "Teemu won't win the Hart Trophy because the Ducks missed the playoffs, but if the award was called the Heart Trophy, he'd be a shoo-in to win it," read an editorial. "His positive attitude has made an impression on thousands of fans. He always has time for everyone, from homeless people to sick children."

Hockey players are unselfish when it comes to making time for fans and sick children especially. Teemu felt that having time for the fans was the easiest part of the job. "Anyone can give autographs, and it feels good to make people smile."

Selanne signed an extension with the Mighty Ducks after the season. His new two-year contract was worth $17.5 million, but it would not kick in until 2000. "I was happy to continue my career in California, but I also told the management that I wished they'd build a stronger team."

Management, in turn, had its concerns about Teemu, specifically his hobby of rally driving. They had invested millions in their top player and pointed out to him that his contract actually forbade it.

"The contract only said I can't do anything dangerous," was Teemu's reply. "They knew they couldn't stop me, but Ferreira also said that I shouldn't get any speeding tickets now that I was making so much money. I told them I'd skip one race for each newly signed good player."

That summer, Teemu did participate in his third Rally Finland race, but his life had changed now that he was a father to two boys. He talked about his life with Finnish *MG* magazine. "I relax by driving go-carts and jet skis. I read car magazines and watch rally videos and watch other sports in general. One day, I watched seven hours of the US Open tennis tournament," he said.

In July 1998, Teemu turned 28. He had been up for the Hart Trophy and had led the league in goal scoring twice. He had more than proved that he belonged in the best hockey league in the world. Injuries had bothered him, but he had returned to the top stronger than ever.

But there was one nagging issue.

"Our roster didn't get better, even though the management had promised us new players at the end of the season. I started to feel that I was wasting my best years on a team that couldn't win the Stanley Cup," he said.

But there were some good times too.

After the 1998–99 season, he traveled to the annual NHL awards gala for the first time in six years and received a new honor, the Maurice Richard Trophy for the leading goal scorer. A highlight was receiving the honor from Richard himself. "The Rocket" died a year later, leaving Selanne the only player to have the award presented to him from the man for whom it is named.

"It was a great honor to meet him. We agreed that it was time to have a trophy that celebrated goal scoring, instead of just those who try to stop scorers," Teemu said.

He was fast racking up individual awards but was still looking for team success. A headline in a Finnish paper described Teemu's feelings best: Is it never Teemu's turn to win?

He played in the 1999 World Championship in Norway, when Finland lost to the Czech Republic in a two-game final. Teemu was named tournament MVP and to the All-Star team.

He led the NHL in goals for the third time (1993, 1998, and 1999) and had played in the All-Star Game every year since he joined the league. He made the First All-Star Team twice (1993 and 1997) and the Second All-Star Team twice (1998 and 1999). In 1993, he finished fifth in league scoring, and then eighth in 1996, second in 1997, eighth in 1998, second in 1999, and fifth in 2000.

But the individual accolades didn't mean much without team success.

The Mighty Ducks had made it to the second round of the 1997 playoffs before being swept by the Red Wings. The year after, they missed the playoffs entirely. In 1999, the Red Wings swept them in the first round, and in 2000, the Ducks didn't make the playoffs.

"It was annoying. We made the playoffs but couldn't get past the Detroit Red Wings. And then the year after that, we were on the outside looking in again," he said.

According to Teemu, the management's focus was in the wrong place.

After the 1998 season, the front office fired another coach and this time, the general manager as well. Craig Hartsburg took over from Pierre Page and Pierre Gauthier from Jack Ferreira.

The new coach and general manager didn't have to worry about Teemu's dangerous rally racing hobby after their first season in charge in 1998–99.

Unfortunately for them, and for Teemu, the rally racing came to an abrupt end after the thing management had feared most came to pass.

Teemu was in a crash.

He was getting ready for a Channel Four race and was driving a Toyota Corolla WRC car on a private road rally car drivers used to sharpen their skills, just as he had done the year before.

"We had agreed to test the car after all the Toyota team Europe's other drivers on a Friday night, on the eve of the race. We had all the mechanics and big trucks that Toyota had arranged for us there," Teemu said.

Finnish Ice Hockey Association president Kalervo Kummola had always wanted to see rally testing up close and he drove to the test area with his son-in-law, his brother-in-law, the son of Teemu's co-pilot, and former NHL player Raimo Helminen.

"We had been testing for about an hour, driving back and forth on the road that had been closed to the public, and they all had had their chance to sit next to me in the car, and we had changed tires many times when "Kale" [Kummola] told me they had to go home.

"But since we had about 10 minutes left on our agreement to keep the road closed, we agreed I'd drive first and wait for them at the other end of the road before I'd drive back to the Toyota service area," he said.

Teemu took off in his Toyota. Kummola followed. Selanne was so excited about the car and the testing and so anxious about running out of time that he forgot their agreement. When a friend asked him questions about his car, he wanted to show him how it worked.

He turned around and headed back toward the pit stop area.

"I was testing the brakes and got closer to the only jump on the road. And I didn't remember what I had told Kummola," he said.

It was the only spot on the road where the drivers couldn't see the other car.

"I accelerated a little and luckily was going only about 90 miles per hour when the car became airborne. You could make a 300-to-420-foot jump there, but I didn't want to break anything, so we were in the air for about 32 feet.

"The second our wheels left the road, I saw Kummola's car at the bottom of the hill. When we landed, I had 20 feet to do something."

Kummola turned his wheel so his car headed toward the ditch. Selanne's vehicle hit the front corner of Kummola's car and landed on the other side of the road.

"Had I been driving faster and Kummola not turned the wheel, we all would have died. My car would have gone right through their windshield. It was a hard collision as it was. I saw stars and I remember checking that my arms and legs worked before I ran to see how the others were," said Teemu.

"Kummola said his elbow and both heels hurt, but I was relieved that they all were alive. Fortunately, his Toyota Camry was one of the safest cars in the world.

"After that, I went into shock and almost passed out. I just sat in the middle of the gravel road thinking about what could have happened."

Somebody called an ambulance and the paramedics helped Kummola out of the car.

"We agreed that we wouldn't talk about the crash. Our service team took care of the cars and we all went to the hospital for a checkup. While I was there, reporters from both big Finnish evening papers called me. Somebody had tipped them off. I just said that we had a minor accident, nothing serious."

"I got back from hospital to the hotel at six in the morning, and was shocked to see the papers," Selanne said.

One of the papers speculated about the size of the fine and wrote that it could be a million markka ($250,000).

"The guy who had tipped off the papers worked for Toyota and got fired for it," he said.

It turned out that Kummola had broken his elbows and heels and had to use a wheelchair for a long time. Raimo Helminen's season was painful, and for months there was blood in his urine.

"It was completely my fault, and a human error. I forgot. Fortunately, somebody was watching over us. It wasn't our time yet," said Selanne.

He was going to continue his rally career later that summer in the Rally Finland race. Toyota wanted him to race, as did his copilot Pekka Huolman, whose son Mikko had been in Kummola's car.

"I told him to do it, too," said Kummola.

However, the media attention and the public opinion were too much for Jarmo Mahonen, the general secretary of the Finnish motorsport governing body. He didn't want to give Teemu the needed license.

"I gave up. And I haven't been in a rally race since," Teemu said.

In the end, he was fined 257,229 Finnish markka (around $75,000), a record fine in Finland, for not reporting to the police that the road had been closed. The fine system in Finland is progressive and based on your income. The two other drivers were fined 300 markka.

Selanne's copilot did not think much of the punishment.

"It was a complete miscarriage of justice. We were driving on a private road that the team had rented from the owner. We had taken all safety measures, and I heard from a Finnish rally legend that they never used to report closing of roads to the police, and he had done it dozens of times," said copilot Huolman.

The accident made Teemu realize how precious life is. He decided to do things he had always dreamt about but hadn't done.

"I bought myself a Ferrari. Well, it wasn't the first thing that came to my mind, far from it, but I started to live in the now more than before. You just never know when it is your turn to go.

"I've always said a prayer at night, and I thanked my guardian angel for nobody getting more seriously hurt."

The accident bothered him, but he tucked it away into the back of his mind. It took him almost five years to talk about it.

"Kummola and I finally went through everything on Team Finland's World Cup flight from Toronto in 2004. Sometimes I still wake up from a nightmare in which my Toyota is airborne and I see Kummola's car in front of me," Teemu admits.

By the time Selanne was making preparations for training camp, Disney had put the team up for sale. Any chance of ownership re-investing in the club was slim to none.

Life as a Mighty Duck was sometimes challenging.

The team lacked depth. It had Selanne and Kariya, but it didn't have a second line that could support them in goal production. The players tried hard, but they just weren't skilled enough.

"Winning the Stanley Cup was a distant dream. It was my biggest dream, but I felt Disney was more interested in having a sold-out arena where they sell as much merchandise as possible rather than winning."

By the time the new millennium came knocking, Selanne also began talks about the end of his career.

His line of thinking was, "I don't care about scoring a certain amount of goals. All I want is to win the Stanley Cup. But I'll retire by the time I'm 35. It's just too hard out there."

While Teemu was getting frustrated with the Mighty Ducks, it was also true that he had been in the league longer than his team, and it takes time to build a Stanley Cup contender.

The salary cap stopped teams from adding top-tier players and their million-dollar salaries that teams not headed to the playoffs would peddle by the league's trade deadline.

One philosophy was to build through the draft, develop prospects into star players and key role players, and then add key players via free agency.

The Mighty Ducks drafted in the top five positions four times in the first six years, but they had also traded away one of their top picks—Oleg Tverdovsky—in the deal that brought Teemu from Winnipeg.

Players were getting bigger and faster than ever before, and there was constant debate about the players' lack of respect for each other, a topic that had been visited and revisited many times.

"There's not enough respect out there. Maybe it's natural when everybody's competing for a place in the league," Teemu said.

In January 2000, he spoke with Finnish sports paper *Veikkaaja*, and the tone was not his usual one.

"It's been a different season. It's hard to find that hunger all the time. Basically, I have nothing to complain about, but at the same time, something's missing," he said.

Trade rumors swirled around Selanne, who picked up his game toward the end of the 1999–2000 season and finished fifth in league scoring, a point behind Kariya and 11 points behind the Art Ross Trophy winner, Jaromir Jagr.

As the world got over the Y2K computer scare and prepared for life in the 21st century, Teemu and Sirpa welcomed their third child.

Leevi was born on April 22, 2000.

"He came three weeks ahead of schedule. The season was over, and we were celebrating at Newport Beach with my friends and just sitting in a limousine when Sirpa called and told me that she wouldn't want to spoil my party, but she just got a baby water. I asked her if she was sure and she answered yes," Teemu said.

Teemu ordered the limousine driver to drive to their home in Yorba Linda immediately to get Sirpa.

"We took Sirpa on board and went to the hospital. The limousine was full of my friends, and they were quite nervous Sirpa would give birth to a child in the car," Teemu said with a laugh.

Leevi's birth is related to another funny story that shows how difficult it is for Teemu to say no.

"Leevi was already born and the whole family was at home when Hannu Aravirta, the head coach of the Finnish national team, called me and asked me to play in the World Championship in Russia. In my distress, I lied and said I probably can't come there because we will have a family addition in the next few days," Teemu remembered, laughing.

Right after the call, when Teemu, Sirpa, and the baby were in the kitchen, their doorbell rang.

"There was a Finnish magazine reporter and photographer who asked when our baby's due date was. I said that it will probably be in the next few days, at the same time hoping that Leevi will not cry in the kitchen," Teemu said with a laugh.

Aravirta did not give up, trying to call again and again.

"Eventually I had to send him a fax. I politely refused to call. I wrote that I know he would have talked to me in to the World Championship if I had answered his call."

The Selannes started to look for a bigger house for their bigger family, and they found it in Coto de Caza, where they still live.

"We had bought a semifinished house in Anaheim Hills in the spring of 2000 and had picked the floors, the wallpapers, and the other details when a friend showed us an ad in the *Orange County Dream House*, about this beautiful place in Coto de Caza," Teemu said.

He wanted to have a look at the place, if for nothing else then at least to get inspiration for the decoration of their new house. Once there and having walked around the house for a couple of hours, he was sold.

"I told Sirpa that we couldn't take the Anaheim Hills house. We only live once," he said.

He pulled out of the other house deal and had to pay a penalty fee, but it was worth it to have found the house of their dreams. Sirpa, too, was more than pleased.

"I thought he was quite the family man to invest so much in our home," she said.

The house went for $4.3 million and it's in a gated community about 90 minutes south of Los Angeles and an hour north of San Diego. The Honda Center and Disneyland are about a half an hour from the Selanne estate.

The estate includes a big main house, a guesthouse, a pool area, a tennis court, a three-hole golf course, and horse stables. And, of course, a Finnish sauna, which was the first thing Teemu had built there.

"California is a wonderful place to live. You can go surfing in the morning, play golf during the day, and go skiing the same evening," Teemu said.

While their new California home was being renovated, Teemu enjoyed life in Finland. The highlights included Leevi's christening, the Bermuda Cup tournament's 20th anniversary celebration at a Helsinki Kalastajatorppa Hotel, and Teemu's 30th birthday party.

"And I was given green light to run again for the first time in seven years, just not on hard surface," he said.

The 2000–01 season was Teemu's ninth in the NHL, and it was a roller-coaster ride. He scored seven goals in the first 13 games—and was on pace to hit 45—but in November he scored four times in 14 games and had no goals in the 10 games in December.

"I'd never experienced anything like that. I played 14 consecutive games without a goal. I had chances, but I just couldn't get the puck into the net."

In mid-December, Kariya broke his foot blocking a shot and missed 16 games.

Selanne was on his own, again, and he missed participating in the All-Star Game for the first time in his career.

Fan attendance started dwindling, and there was a coaching change. Guy Charron replaced Craig Hartsburg after 33 games.

And Selanne was hampered by a knee injury.

"My left knee had been giving me trouble all season long and right after Christmas was when the hell of pain began," Teemu said. "I had to skip two games in February and March, and after that, I only played one more game as a Mighty Duck."

On March 5, five years and 28 days after the trade that brought him to California, Selanne was on the move again. The Mighty Ducks sent him an hour's flight north to the San Jose Sharks. In return, the Ducks received left wing Jeff Friesen, goaltender Steve Shields, and future considerations.

Teemu wasn't as bitter about the deal as he was when he felt betrayed by Winnipeg.

"Probably the hockey was the most fun I've had since joining the NHL, but with Disney me and Kariya never felt that they wanted to build a winning team. It was funny because we would have lunch with management at the end of every season and they would say they would be aggressive and would go after free agents, and they never did.

"Pierre Gauthier was the second guy to lie to me. At least he did tell me he was shopping me around, but he told me there was nothing he liked and nothing will happen between now and the end of the season. Same thing happened; I was traded 10 days later. Both times I was told I was not going to be traded and both times I was traded."

The Sharks were thrilled. "Selanne is an elite player who is one of the top offensive threats in the game and a major weapon on the power play," Sharks general manager Dean Lombardi said. "He should address several major needs for our club. This is a big step for our organization."

Selanne was added to provide instant offense for a team that had been limited to just 18 goals over its last eight games at the time of the deal.

When he was dealt to the Sharks, he was leading the Mighty Ducks in goals, assists, and points with his 26 goals and 59 points in 61 games. In his last game, against the Los Angeles Kings, Teemu scored a goal and picked up two assists—Kariya scored twice and assisted one—in front of the home crowd.

For the Sharks, it looked to be a great trade. They acquired a proven superstar for a second-line forward and a backup goalie, thanks to the emergence of Evgeni Nabokov in the Sharks' net.

Anaheim also picked up $3 million of Teemu's $8.5 million salary the following year.

There had been rumors about Anaheim trading Teemu, to be sure, but it was still hard to believe the deal was done.

"I received a lot of calls [from general managers] about Teemu. It was at the point where I felt it was my duty to listen," said Gauthier.

The GM then gave the obligatory line about trading a top player and getting less than value in return.

"The objective of the trade was to improve the club immediately and for the future. We believe it will make our team better. The team needed a change. We have to look at what the team needed as it goes forward, not what it had in the past," Gauthier said.

Fans didn't think trading away Teemu was the way to build a winning team. They were furious.

At the time of the trade, Selanne had scored more goals than any other player in the league since his rookie season, 372. Many of his goals had come against the Sharks—36 goals in 41 games—including his first NHL goal.

Nobody at that time could imagine that in six years Anaheim would win the Stanley Cup—with Selanne again one of the team's most important players.

"I was surprised he was available," said Lombardi. "Usually, they don't move too much within [the same division]. Given that there's a bit of a rivalry here in California between San Jose, Anaheim, and Los Angeles, that's one of the things that crosses your mind.

"He fills a box in terms of our blueprint here. I don't know if you're going to see 70 goals from him, but we do consider him to be an elite scorer."

Brian Hayward gets nostalgic thinking about Kariya and Selanne's time in Anaheim.

"When they played together, they were the best duo in hockey. They were so fast. If you compare them to, say, Wayne Gretzky and Jari Kurri, their game was completely different. Kurri was a great goal scorer and Gretzky the greatest playmaker there ever was. Paul and

Teemu did the same, only faster. They had breakaways all the time, and the other team couldn't tell which one of them was Kurri, and which one Gretzky," he said.

In his four and a half seasons with the Mighty Ducks, Teemu scored 225 goals and had 482 points in 393 regular season games and added another nine goals and 14 points in 15 playoff games.

"A trade is always a surprise, even if there are rumors," Teemu said. "But that time I was relieved. San Jose was a great option for my career. I don't think I would have had many other teams in mind," he said. "Kariya was more shocked than I was."

Moving to San Jose did not mean Teemu and his family had to abandon their new dream home. Their estate's three-hole golf course and tennis court had just been finished when Teemu was traded.

"We knew, though, that Coto de Caza would be our home. The boys were so small that moving wasn't difficult. Eemil was five, Eetu three, and Leevi a little under a year old," Teemu said.

The trade was completed on a Monday, and the day after, Teemu had a minor knee operation in San Jose. After spending a couple of days back home, he drove his Ferrari the 400 miles from Anaheim in four hours, thanks to the 485-horsepower engine under the hood.

Ismo Syvahuoko, Teemu's friend and doctor in Finland, spoke with Sharks doctor Arthur Ting about the knee. "I suggested that maybe it was time to have a major surgery and consider the long-term effects of Teemu's well-being, but they decided to just do another arthroscopy instead. Maybe they figured that even a less than 100 percent Teemu helped the team," he said.

"San Jose wanted to fix the knee immediately so that I'd be ready for the playoffs. I played my first game as a Shark 11 days after the operation," added Teemu.

He didn't complain, but he admits the knee was in a bad shape when he was traded.

"Basically, I played with one leg. I had to take anti-inflammatory medicine before every practice and game for years," he said.

The Sharks lost Teemu's first game to the Kings 1–0 in overtime. Teemu had only three assists to show for his first six games. He scored his first goal as a Shark in his seventh game, at home against Anaheim.

"We won the game 7–4, and I scored a hat trick, but so did Paul. We were laughing after the game. We talked about how I was going to come back to Anaheim and we would play together again, but Paul got so pissed off about the management of the Ducks, and he wanted out."

The Sharks made the playoffs but lost their first-round series to the St. Louis Blues in six games. Teemu ended up scoring seven goals and had 13 points in 12 games in the regular season as a member of the Sharks, but picked up just two assists in the playoffs.

"I broke my thumb in the first game. I could play, but they had to freeze my thumb before every game. I couldn't really shoot," he said.

———————

Like in California, Teemu had always wanted to have a home base in Finland, a place where he could do all the things he loved to do without leaving home, and they eventually found something. The Selannes lived in a semidetached house in Espoo before they found the place they wanted in the village of Hila in Kirkkonummi, Finland, near the sea 35 minutes southwest of Helsinki.

The Selannes paid $570,000 (in 2019 dollars) for the house, which included a sauna, a boat shed, a smaller cottage, a garage, a beach, and two piers.

But Teemu did not like being so far from downtown Helsinki, so he bought another house by the sea, in Lauttasaari in downtown Helsinki, for $3 million (in 2019 dollars).

"The plan was to move there and have the Hila place as a summer cottage. Then we decided to build our dream house in Hila instead, so I sold the Lauttasaari house."

Selanne had been in the NHL for nine seasons, and his hunger for success had never been bigger. The trade to San Jose had just made him hungrier. "Everything I saw in the first few months told me I had gone from a business to a true sports team," he said.

His off-season training had gone well, and he was looking forward to the 2001–02 season, which would also include the 2002 Winter Olympics in Salt Lake City.

"I felt great. For the first time in a long time I had high expectations for the season. It was like I was a rookie again," he said.

But things around him quickly turned into a nightmare.

First, his good friend Saku Koivu, the Montreal Canadiens' captain, was diagnosed with non-Hodgkin's lymphoma in his abdomen.

Then came the terrorist attacks on 9/11.

"Fortunately for Saku, he got better fairly soon and he could make a comeback in the last game of the season, but the 9/11 attack really affected our family. We told each other that we'd never live in the US after my career was over. Also, having the Olympics in the US—and playing there—seemed crazy," Teemu said.

"We visited the World Trade Center area when we played the New York teams. It looked like an atomic bomb had been dropped there."

That was the backdrop as Teemu headed into the 2001–02 season.

CUP HUNT IN
THE WILDERNESS

SELANNE ENTERED THE LAST SEASON of his contract as the league's sixth-highest-paid player, with a $9.5 million salary, $1.1 million less than what Jaromir Jagr was paid with the Washington Capitals, which topped the NHL list.

Most importantly, he believed he had a real shot at winning the Stanley Cup as a Shark. "We had two great offensive lines, a great defense, and good goalies."

Teemu played on a line with Patrick Marleau, then a 22-year-old prospect who had scored more than 20 goals twice in his four previous seasons in the league, and Adam Graves, who had won the Stanley Cup with the New York Rangers in 1994.

The other offensive line had Marco Sturm, a German forward; Vincent Damphousse, a Stanley Cup champion with the Montreal Canadiens in 1993; and team captain Owen Nolan.

On defense, the Sharks had veteran defenseman Gary Suter (who had abruptly ended one of Paul Kariya's seasons with the Ducks and would retire after the season); Bryan Marchment, who had amassed 204 penalty minutes the season before; and a 22-year-old Brad Stuart, who had made the All-Rookie team just two years prior. And in goal, Yevgeni Nabokov was backed up by two Finns, Vesa Toskala and Miikka Kiprusoff.

But what looked good on paper wasn't as good on the ice.

When the NHL shut down for the Olympic break, Selanne had scored just 18 goals and had 36 points in 57 games. He also averaged just 15:00 of ice time per game, well below his career average.

The Sharks' coach, 43-year-old Darryl Sutter, one of the legendary six Sutter brothers who had played in the NHL, liked to rotate his lines, which created a situation that wasn't ideal for the Finnish veteran. Also, Sutter wasn't a fan of a creative style in which offense was the best defense.

"I couldn't find my legs at all because in Winnipeg and Anaheim, I had played so much," Selanne said. "I was really disappointed because I had been so pumped before the season. The worst part was that I didn't think I was helping the team."

Sutter knew Nolan and Damphousse and trusted them just like the Ducks' coaches had put their faith in him and Kariya.

In San Jose, Selanne was suddenly the fifth wheel.

The Sharks' decision to go after Selanne was questioned since everybody knew he was not a third-line player.

According to a *New York Post* story, Sutter had words with Selanne in front of the team.

"I don't care if you get into your Porsche and drive back down to Anaheim right now," Sutter had said, according to the *Post*.

Both Selanne and Sutter deny the story. Sutter blasted the author, veteran hockey writer Larry Brooks, and claimed that Brooks just wanted to see him traded to New York.

"We simply had a discussion about my ice time and production," Selanne said, but added he had told Sutter that if he wanted more goals, then he needed more ice time.

Whatever words were said, Teemu was in the doghouse. His career seemed on a downward slope, but there was light at the end of the tunnel.

"I'm looking forward to the Olympics," he said at the time.

Suddenly, the tournament didn't seem so crazy anymore.

With Saku Koivu sidelined by his cancer, coach Hannu Aravirta made Selanne captain of the Finnish team. Antti Aalto took Koivu's place between Teemu and Jere Lehtinen on the team's first line.

Finland finished a disappointing sixth in the tournament, losing 1–2 in its quarterfinal game against Canada, which went on to win Olympic gold under Wayne Gretzky's leadership. Kariya added an Olympic gold to his resume, which already included a World Juniors gold (1993) and a World Championship (1994).

Selanne scored three goals in four games for Finland, but the highlight—or the lowlight—of his Salt Lake City tournament was his hit on Chris Pronger in the quarterfinal. Pronger chased a puck into the corner; Teemu followed and shoved the bigger player from behind. Pronger hit his head on the glass and staggered back to the bench. Teemu was not penalized.

"Finally I was able to pay the debts to Pronger, but he was still leading 71–1 when it came to dirty, nasty plays," Selanne said.

When the regular season ended, Teemu was averaging 16:58 of ice time with the Sharks, fifth most of the team's forwards. Since he did not kill penalties, his ice time was 2:30 less than captain Owen Nolan's and Damphousse's.

He finished third in team scoring—behind Nolan and Damphousse—with 29 goals and 54 points in 82 games.

The Sharks beat the Coyotes, now captained by Teppo Numminen, in five games in the first round of the playoffs, but lost Game 7 of their second-round series to the Colorado Avalanche 1–0. Peter Forsberg scored the Avs' lone goal, while Patrick Roy recorded the shutout. Teemu scored five goals and had eight points in 12 playoff games.

On July 1, Selanne became a free agent for the first time in his career, and while there would have been other options, he re-signed with the Sharks. He even took a $3 million pay cut because he truly believed in the team. Also, his relationship with coach Sutter had gotten warmer.

"I had a good feeling about the season in the end, because I got to be a part of a winning team. I thought the series against Colorado showed that we had potential. Also, my family liked San Jose," Teemu said.

"I really wanted to win the Stanley Cup."

The Sharks were one of the Cup favorites in the 2002–03 season, and Selanne was full of energy. "This is the year. Now or never. I'm in the best shape of my career," he said.

Expectations were high again, but the gap between the expectations and reality couldn't have been bigger. The Sharks didn't win the Stanley Cup. They didn't even make the playoffs.

The team got off to a poor start, and when Sutter was fired after 24 games, the team had won just eight. The new coach was Teemu's old coach from Anaheim, Ron Wilson.

"Wilson was a great Christmas present. He didn't rotate all four lines equally and my ice time was closer to 20 minutes a game again," Teemu told Finnish media.

And the team did play better for a while, losing just two of its first 10 games with Wilson behind the bench in regulation time. One of the hottest pairs in the league was Selanne and Marleau. "Patrick is so fast, strong, and talented that he can be the best in the world," Teemu said.

But by March, the Sharks were out of the playoff race. Teemu went 15 consecutive games without scoring a goal, and picked up only eight assists in that span.

"There's nothing to say. We have a great team that's playing lousy hockey," he said.

He led the Sharks in scoring with 28 goals and 64 points in 82 games.

He felt he still had some hockey in him and told management of Finland's World Championship team he wanted to join the team at the Worlds in three Finnish cities, with the final in Helsinki.

Finland put together an outstanding team with 14 NHL players on the roster, its most ever, including Selanne and Saku Koivu.

No team had won the World Championship gold on home ice since the Soviet Union did it in Moscow in 1986. That Finland would do it was Teemu's dream.

"I even told [then–general manager] Jari Kurri that if we win the World Championship, I'll call it a career. And I meant it," he said.

If the Sharks' season had been a disappointment, Finland's tournament was a disaster.

Finland took on Sweden in the quarterfinal in Helsinki. Halfway through the game, Teemu had scored a hat trick and led the team to a 5–1 lead over the rival they loved to hate.

Sweden, led by Forsberg and Mats Sundin, rallied back and won the game 6–5.

"It was the biggest nightmare of my life. I still can't quite wrap my head around it," Teemu said.

If anything, the game once again proved that hockey is a fast sport in which the biggest high can quickly turn into the lowest of lows. Thirty minutes into the game, Teemu was a national hero, thanks to his three goals. Thirty minutes later, a nation of hockey-mad fans was in shock.

"I remember thinking that hockey couldn't get any better than that. We completely steamrolled Sweden and played fantastic hockey. We were in the zone, it was almost supernatural. The whole arena seemed to be shaking," Teemu said.

"You can only feel that in your home arena. Also, I knew that another two million Finns were watching the game on TV [in a country of 5.2 million people], and my family and all my friends were in the stands."

With the stands shaking and with all of Finland ready to celebrate, Sweden's coach, Hardy Nilsson, made a goalie change when his team trailed 5–1. Out was former NHL player Tommy Salo and in was Mikael Tellqvist, who played for the Toronto Maple Leafs.

Then Sweden scored its second goal.

"We had everything under control by that point, but when they scored their third goal, we panicked. The coach should have called a timeout, for sure," Selanne said.

Selanne had a breakaway in the middle of the middle period, but Tellqvist turned away his backhander. A few minutes later, Sweden made it a one-goal game, and then tied the game halfway through the third via Forsberg's solo effort, in which he carried the puck from one end of the ice to the other, skated around the Finnish defense, and scored with a wraparound.

With 4:54 remaining in the game, P.J. Axelsson scored the game-winner on a deflection.

"We made terrible mistakes and the silence inside the arena after each Swedish goal was deafening. No words can describe the pain. It was horrible," Teemu said.

Selanne was shocked. The crowd was shocked. The nation was shocked.

"I felt like a traitor."

He shook hands with the victors and walked straight to the locker room without talking to the media, which was very unlike him. He took off his gear and then broke a dressing room table with his stick. Bottles, rolls of tape, everything that had been on the table went flying around as Teemu took his frustration out on the furniture. Nobody had ever seen him like that before.

He got dressed without showering, called Ari Lehto, who handled his affairs in Finland, and told him to pick him up at the arena back door. Then, 10 minutes later, he was gone without speaking to anyone.

"I was in a state of shock. I couldn't believe anything like that could happen at the highest level of hockey," he said.

"He barked at me to get driving. I asked him where to, and he said, 'Anywhere,'" Lehto said.

While team captain Saku Koivu was addressing the media, Selanne was chowing down on bar food.

"I just wanted to be alone. I probably would have gone home but fortunately, I called Sirpa, who was out with her friends. She told me to go back to the team so that the teammates wouldn't misinterpret my behavior," he said.

He arrived back at the team hotel at 3:00 AM, but the tournament was over.

Finland didn't win gold, and he didn't have to consider retirement. It was time to make new plans. The Selannes had enjoyed living in San Jose and had made a lot of new friends.

"It was a fun time, we were just the right age, and most of Teemu's teammates were in the same phase in their lives so we spent time with our families during days and went out in the evenings," said Sirpa.

"It was a party team. Once a month, when we had a day off, we went out in San Francisco," added Teemu.

The Selanne boys were two, five, and seven years old, and liked to hang out with their father at the rink.

"Sutter was a tough coach, but he was very patriotic and he loved children. My teammates often told me after a loss that I should bring the boys to the rink the next day because that way, the coach wouldn't have the heart to be angry at us," Selanne said.

The fans also loved Selanne so life was good, except for one thing: that ongoing pursuit of the Stanley Cup.

His old team, the Mighty Ducks, had gone to the Stanley Cup Final in 2003, led by rookie coach Mike Babcock and goaltender Jean-Sebastien Giguere, who, according to TV analyst and retired goalie Brian Hayward, "put on possibly the best goaltending performance in NHL history."

The New Jersey Devils won the Cup in seven games. Giguere was voted the Conn Smythe Trophy winner as the playoff MVP.

The end of the season also marked the end of Paul Kariya's contract with the Mighty Ducks. He was unhappy with the way his extension negotiations were going and was ready to test the market as a free agent.

Kariya called Selanne, who had an option for another year with the Sharks but was free to sign elsewhere, as the option was only his to exercise.

"I had been thinking of maybe returning to Anaheim. We had our home there, the Ducks had made it to the Final, and I really wanted to play with Paul again," said Teemu.

"Paul called me and said he wouldn't re-sign with the Ducks because their offer wasn't good enough. They couldn't come to terms. We realized we were both free agents and could sign with any Stanley Cup contender."

That started a wild game of what-ifs.

"We put money issues aside and focused on finding the best team for us. Our dream team. We both said Colorado. We had dreamt about playing with Peter Forsberg or Joe Sakic and had joked that even if you played poorly with Forsberg, you'd only get 'demoted' to Sakic's line," Teemu said.

Once linemates on the Mighty Ducks, Kariya and Selanne became business partners on the open market. They called Don Baizley, who represented them both, and asked him to design an offer that the Avalanche couldn't refuse. The plan was to sell them to the Avs as a package.

"Either they sign both of us, or neither of us. Money won't be the obstacle," they told Baizley.

Baizley went to work with one of the most special contract negotiations in NHL history. Colorado's GM Pierre Lacroix told him right off the bat that they couldn't afford to sign them both.

"They only had about $7 million left in their budget. Teemu and Paul had made $16.5 million the season before," said Baizley, who passed away in 2013.

Some creative accounting was needed. Kariya was 29 years old, and if he played one season for less than the average salary, he'd become an unrestricted free agent, which would give him a chance to really cash in.

They joined the Avalanche as a package deal and they took major pay cuts in agreeing to sign there. They joined an Avalanche team that had finished first in its division each of the eight years since moving from Quebec City. The two stars wanted a Stanley Cup, and they felt that joining Joe Sakic, Peter Forsberg, and the rest of the talent there would be the best way to do it.

"When we both became free agents, we made a hockey decision," Kariya said at a news conference at the time. "We both said, 'Forget about the money, where's the place we want to play?' And Colorado jumped out at both of us immediately. So we made things work monetarily."

Kariya agreed to a $1.2 million contract. He had earned $10 million in his final season with Anaheim. Selanne, who declined his option at $6.5 million with the San Jose Sharks, agreed to a $5.8 million contract.

Lacroix couldn't believe his luck. Suddenly, his roster included forwards Forsberg; Sakic; Milan Hejduk, who was the NHL's leading goal-scorer in 2003; Alex Tanguay; defenseman Rob Blake; and now Selanne and Kariya.

"Detroit's general manager Ken Holland called me and said that if I had any more superstars for sale, I should let him know," Baizley said.

Not everybody was happy. The Ducks, for example, were furious.

"Paul stunned them. He could have gotten $10 million from the Ducks but he chose to sign with the Avs for a million," said Bryan Hayward.

But once again, Selanne thought he was on a team that was a true Cup contender.

The Avalanche had been a strong factor in the playoffs each season for almost 10 years, winning two Cups in that time, and many of the key players from those teams were still in Denver.

But once again, it wasn't meant to be. In fact, the season turned into the worst nightmare of Selanne's storied career.

"If I could, I would erase that season from my mind," he said.

The season started well, as Selanne and Kariya finally got a world-class center in Joe Sakic. "It was the best line I've ever played in, but it didn't last long," said Selanne.

Kariya broke his wrist in the fifth game of the season, and Selanne slid down the lineup.

"What made matters worse was that I could be the first star in a game and still be in the fourth line in the next. It drove me crazy," he said.

He was back in the doghouse, only much deeper than in San Jose.

"When me and Paul went there, the first time we met the coach, Tony Granato, he told me, 'Guys, remember you have not won anything in this league yet.' He said this before he said hi. We both said how about start by saying welcome. I almost said, 'You have not won anything, either.'"

"Almost right away I felt he did not want us there," Teemu continued. "That year I learned how lucky I was before, how much fun hockey was, and now here is somebody taking the fun and passion out of it."

After Kariya broke his wrist, Selanne found himself sliding down the Avalanche depth chart. "I went to the third line and then the fourth line. And then I was a healthy scratch. To see that, it was terrible. I wanted to quit. This is not right. Even though I was not 100 percent, I knew I could still be a factor. I felt like I did not want to play anymore."

Granato was cutting into what made Selanne a star player.

"I lost my passion for hockey. And a lot of times when I drove to the rink, I looked at myself in the mirror and I saw a sad person. This was not me."

As part of his summer conditioning program, Selanne played a lot of tennis and squash in Finland prior to joining the Avalanche. His knee wasn't 100 percent healthy when the season started. Teemu suffered a lateral meniscal tear playing squash just as he was about to report to camp in Colorado.

"We had to make sure his knee was in good enough shape for him to report to camp so that the club wouldn't terminate his contract. We made another arthroscopy, but that was just patchwork. He needed a surgery that would have taken months to recover from," said Ismo Syvahuoko, the Helsinki physician who knew Selanne better than anyone else on the planet.

Irked by how Granato was treating him, the phone lines between Selanne and Ismo Syvahuoko were busy. Syvahuoko has always been the person he calls first when things aren't going right.

"His knee was in a bad shape and he was in pain. That he had almost gotten used to, though, because he had used painkillers for years. What was worse was the mental pain," Syvahuoko said.

Teemu's knee had been patched up for years, but there was never time to do it right. He helped his friend find medication that was powerful enough to dull the pain so he could at least get some sleep.

Syvahuoko estimates Selanne only had about 50 percent power left in his left leg.

Kariya recalls meeting Granato in the dressing room. "I remember Tony came in and said Teemu's knee is toast."

Behind the scenes, the Colorado management was furious. They had committed to paying $5.8 million to a player and had received damaged goods. They took their anger out on Baizley.

"Nobody will ever believe that Teemu can play in the NHL," Baizley told Syvahuoko.

There's one phone call that Syvahuoko remembers better than the others.

"Teemu told me that had he been a racehorse, he would have been shot already."

Sakic was close to Selanne, and when he saw how his friend was bothered by what was being said, he asked Coach Granato to have a chat with the Finnish veteran.

"He told me I should be happy to play 10 minutes a game. I decided never to speak to him again," Teemu said.

"Teemu was a pro about it. Not many players of his stature could have taken it so well," Sakic said.

Teemu scored 16 goals and 32 points in 78 games, ninth on the team. Kariya finished seventh in team scoring, with 11 goals and 36 points in 51 games. The longer the season went, the less Teemu played. The humiliation reached its peak in the playoffs.

The Avalanche advanced to the second round after beating the Dallas Stars in five games. Teemu's ice time in the five games was 11:17, 11:14, 9:59, 16:56, and 10:39.

Riku Hahl, a fellow Finn in his third season on the team, explained the situation like this: "Teemu had played on the third line with Matthew Barnaby and Chris Gratton. I played in the fourth line with Andrei Nikolishin and Dan Hinote. In the playoffs, Granato promoted Hinote to the third line and put Teemu on the fourth line.

"So, one of the legends of the game stayed on the bench and played only on 5-on-5, whereas Nikolishin and I played on 5-on-5 and short-handed. Sometimes Teemu had to stay on the bench for seven to eight minutes between shifts."

The Avalanche faced the Sharks in the Western Conference semifinal and lost the series in six games. Teemu played 10:49 in the first game. And then in the second game came the shocker.

"I was a healthy scratch," Selanne said.

He had been a big star for the Sharks in the three previous seasons but now had to watch a playoff game from the press box. He called Syvahuoko, who was Finland's doctor in the upcoming World Championship, and told him he'd be interested in playing if the Avalanche were eliminated from the playoffs.

Teemu was back in the lineup for Game 3 and played more than 13:00 in each of the remaining four games.

The Finns had to get past Canada in the quarterfinals first, and they lost 5–4 to Canada.

The Avalanche lost their first three to the Sharks before winning Game 4 1–0 in overtime and Game 5 2–1, also in overtime. Both winning goals were scored by Joe Sakic.

The luck ran out in Game 6, which the Sharks won 3–1.

Selanne's season was over.

Together with Baizley, he tried to analyze what had gone wrong with the dream signing. The agent blamed himself for not making it appear publicly that the Avalanche general manager had had a bigger part in the signing process.

"Lacroix wanted to get credit for everything, but we had made it look like it was our great idea, which we then executed," Teemu said.

Lacroix had pulled off some great trades, for sure, such as acquiring goaltender Patrick Roy from Montreal in 1995, and defenseman Ray Bourque—both Hall of Famers—from Boston in 2000. The Avalanche won the Cup in 1996 and 2001.

Furthermore, Lacroix, as Granato's boss, may have told the coach how to use his players.

"Or maybe Granato didn't know about us signing with the team and that annoyed him. But it was an offer nobody could have refused," Teemu said.

Selanne asked for a trade midseason, but just before the trade deadline, he had a chat with Lacroix.

"He told me things would get better and that we'd drink champagne together after we'd won the Cup," Teemu said.

Sakic didn't know what to say or do.

"Joe told me that he might have demanded a trade had he been treated that way," Teemu recalled.

To make matters even more curious, Selanne and Granato were teammates at one point in San Jose. However, when the Finnish Flash joined the team, Granato, playing on the Sharks' fourth line, saw his ice time diminished to less than 5:00 a game.

"He retired that season. Maybe he just didn't like my style, but there must have been personal reasons behind it," Selanne said. "Maybe he liked players that reminded him of himself. Maybe he didn't like how I drove a Ferrari to the arena."

Whatever the reason, the lack of ice time was eating Teemu up inside. Sirpa said for the first time since they've known each other, Teemu didn't sing at home.

"It was so unlike him. The season was tough on him and it showed. We liked living in Denver, though. The kids and I went skiing often," she said.

His new friend Otto Aichinger helped Teemu get through the season.

"Otto became an important person in my life. He was my window into a world without hockey, and the worries that came with it," Selanne said.

To this day, Teemu doesn't know the reasons for Granato's behavior, and the former coach hasn't told anyone, either.

"My friends have tried to find out why, but he can't explain it. He had told Joe [Sakic] that he made a mistake with me but even then, he hadn't elaborated on it."

Kariya feels both he and Selanne learned a lot from their short time in Colorado.

"There is nobody in the world who does not have ups and downs, and I have never been afraid of them or afraid of failure. I think Teemu was the same way. Through the highs and lows of our career we have always bounced back, and things have turned out well for us," said Kariya.

A simple explanation would be that Teemu got the ice time he deserved, that his left knee was in such a bad shape that he couldn't play better.

But Selanne was still producing; he was a goal-scoring force, especially on the power play. He had worked hard to get his knee in the best possible shape and still thinks he could have helped the Avalanche more had he been given the chance.

"To be sure, I wasn't playing my best hockey in the last three seasons before the lockout and wasn't as good as I had been during my best years, but I certainly could have played a good season even with that knee," he said.

"It wasn't about the knee."

PART THREE

SECOND COMING

ISMO SYVAHUOKO HAD KNOWN FOR YEARS that his friend's left knee needed major reconstructive surgery, and he had been planning for it just as long. But each year the doctor and Teemu decided to postpone it, mostly because there was never a good time for Selanne to be away from hockey for the eight or nine months expected for full recovery and rehab.

There had been a window of opportunity in the spring of 2004 after the terrible season with the Avs, but Raimo Summanen, the coach of Finland's national team, had convinced Teemu to play in the World Cup to be held in September.

Finland lost 3–2 to Canada in the final of the best-on-best tournament amid controversy. Teemu's friend, former Edmonton Oiler Janne Niinimaa, left the team in the middle of the tournament after arguments with Summanen, who was fired after the competition.

"He's a good coach, but the days of management by fear are long gone. It turns into a negative force in the long run," Selanne said.

The 2004–05 NHL season was in doubt because of labor trouble between the NHL and the NHLPA, and the NHL shuttered arenas the day after the Canada-Finland final.

Given the history of animosity between the NHL and the NHLPA, Selanne took advantage of the uncertainty to finally have the surgery. On September 20, six days after the World Cup final, Syvahuoko performed the operation at a private clinic in Helsinki.

"I've had a lot of time to think about it and playing in the World Cup final was a great achievement considering our first line [Jere Lehtinen–Saku Koivu–Selanne] played through injuries. If that was my last game, Toronto was a great place to wrap up a career," said a philosophical Selanne.

Syvahuoko was slightly nervous about the procedure.

"Of course it's special. Teemu and I are great friends, but we've gone over everything. I'm in my own operating room, with the team that I always work with," he said. "Everybody here knows Teemu. Besides, he owns 10 percent of the clinic, so he's basically using the services of his own company."

It was not an easy operation. Syvahuoko had to repair six different things in one operation. He did kneecap alignment surgery, repaired a lateral meniscal tear and removed a related cyst, and repaired a medial meniscus tear. The lateral meniscus was also loose and thus was fixed. Plus, there were microfractures to the femoral trochlea.

The good news was that playing in the World Cup hadn't made matters worse.

Selanne had been plagued with problems in his left knee since he was a kid. Both legs had been troubled by Osgood-Schlatter disease, but he never had any issues with his other knee.

"At one point, we had a theory that maybe the 1989 leg injury or a wrong kind of weight training in the early 1990s were behind it, but we were able to discard that later," Syvahuoko said. "It's possible that he had a slight kneecap alignment problem as a kid, when he played soccer, and that had led to an alignment problem in his legs."

According to the doctor, a severe alignment problem would be a major obstacle for a hockey player because the legs simply couldn't withstand the wear and tear playing the game at an elite level puts on them. "Teemu's problem with the alignment isn't a severe one, if he's ever had it, but the kneecap injury and the leg injury in his first season made matters worse."

Selanne knew that his feet were not aligned properly, and he always had problems finding good skates. During the World Cup, for instance, he kept changing skates throughout the tournament.

"I felt there was a problem with the skates. Either the blade was askew or sharpened wrong," he said.

Selanne had his first knee injury in 1995 in Winnipeg. The team's surgeon, also Teemu's good friend, orthopedist Peter McDonald, gave Syvahuoko a pessimistic appraisal of the situation. "He told me Teemu's cartilage damage meant that he'd never be as fast as during his rookie season and that his NHL career would be short," Syvahuoko said.

"He was correct in that there was damage in the knee, and it wasn't going to get better, but he was wrong about the length of Teemu's career."

Selanne had three other arthroscopic operations between 1995 and 2004.

Sometimes he felt pain on the outside of the knee, sometimes just over the kneecap where the quadriceps muscle attaches to the patella. The ailing knee meant he wasn't able to push off as fast as he was used to, and it felt like he had lost power in his leg.

He'd also had dozens of injections, including cortisone, which had caused him to miss several games over the years.

The fact that he played for years "with just one leg" tells you how much Teemu loves the game. Many other players would have given up and not put themselves through the emotional and physical demands to get back playing the game they love.

But not Teemu.

"We'll make you a great new knee, sweet dreams," Syvahuoko told his friend just before Selanne was put under anesthesia.

The fact that Teemu was put under also indicated the seriousness of the surgery. In previous procedures, Teemu, who had an interest in medicine, had asked for spinal anesthesia so he could follow the operation on the monitors.

"I've learned all the medical terms in Latin, too. If I hadn't become a hockey player, I'd be a doctor," he joked. "I once got to assist Syvahuoko in a hip replacement surgery, with the patient's permission, of course. I handed instruments to him and operated the blood-cleaner."

The surgery was a success and the patient was moved to a private room at a hospital located about 10 minutes by car from the clinic where the operation was performed. Syvahuoko was cautiously optimistic but noted a long rehabilitation awaited his prized patient.

While in the hospital, Teemu received a surprising phone call from his friend, Helsinki Jokerit owner Harry Harkimo, who told him he wanted to pay a visit. While he was surely concerned with the well-being of his friend, he also had another agenda. He wanted to make sure Selanne was going play for Jokerit during the NHL lockout.

"Sure thing," Teemu told him.

"At least by January, right?" Harkimo went on.

Harkimo knew Jokerit's schedule included several home games in January. He had already used Teemu's name in his sales pitch to sponsors. A couple of days later after Harkimo's visit to the hospital, Selanne signed with Jokerit so that there wouldn't be any formal obstacles concerning a return to the Finnish league.

When it was time to check out of the hospital, Selanne returned to California to rehabilitate his knee with Joe Donohue, who had worked with top athletes in pro sports and had been the Ducks' resident physical therapist since the team joined the NHL. Donohue and Selanne worked together for two hours a day, three days a week, for three months.

"If I just get a chance to play hockey without pain, I may play many, many more years," Selanne said after the surgery.

In 2003, Teemu signed a one-year deal with the Colorado Avalanche in the hopes of winning a Stanley Cup. (AP Images)

Like father, like sons. From left: Teemu, Leevi, Eetu, and Eemil.

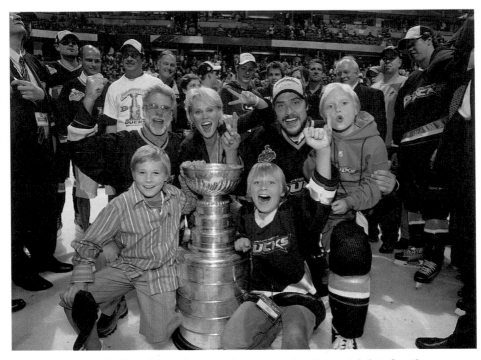

Teemu was thrilled to share the joy of winning the Cup with his family.
(Debora Robinson)

On June 6, 2007, after
14 NHL seasons,
Teemu finally hoisted
the Stanley Cup.
(Debora Robinson)

The Selanne family and their friends took full advantage of their days with the Cup in the summer of 2007.
(Top and bottom photos: Sami Mannerheimo. Middle photo: Ari Mennander.)

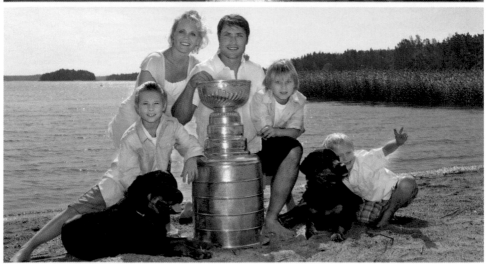

Teemu and his teammates celebrated winning bronze over
the USA at the 2014 Sochi Olympics. (Getty Images)

Teemu says the Finland team that won silver at the 2006 Torino
Olympics was the best team he ever played for. (Getty Images)

On January 11, 2015, the Ducks retired Teemu's jersey No. 8 in a touching ceremony. (Getty Images)

Teemu delivered his Hockey Hall of Fame induction speech on November 14, 2017. He was the second Finn to be inducted after Jari Kurri. (AP Images)

The Selannes were building another home in California when they found their dream house in Coto de Caza, where they still live. (Middle photo: Ari Mennander)

Anyone who knows Teemu knows
he loves his toys. He still owns his
prized 1961 Lincoln Continental.
(Top photo: Ari Mennander.
Bottom photo: Jari Tolvanen.)

Teemu's family, including his mother, Liisa, proudly supported him at his Hockey Hall of Fame induction ceremony on November 14, 2017. (Finn O'Hara/Hockey Hall of Fame)

Teemu has redefined himself as a restauranteur with Selanne Steak Tavern in Laguna Beach.

His left thigh had been much smaller prior to the surgery, and when Selanne met Donohue for the first time, the muscles were almost completely gone.

"We started from scratch. I've never seen an athlete with such a great attitude, and I've worked with some of the best in the world in football, basketball, baseball, hockey, and tennis," Donohue said. "His work ethic is unbelievable, and he's always so positive. To be one of the best in the world in what he does and be such a nice guy is an unbeatable combination."

Selanne is an avid golfer and was hoping he could rehab his knee on the course. "It was a nightmare," he said. "Can I at least chip a few balls? No. How about putting? No."

The rehab plan called for no unnecessary pressure on the knee. But it quickly yielded results, and about a month later, Selanne started to skate again, albeit lightly. Donohue also invited him to go surfing with him and Paul Kariya, also an avid surfer.

"I picked him up at 5:30 in the morning, gave him a wetsuit, and threw the board into the water. Paul and some other Ducks players were there," he said.

Selanne got on the board, bent his knees a little, and thought there was nothing to it. Donohue was shocked by how easily Selanne took to surfing.

"Even most athletes need at least an hour before they can stand on the board, but it seemed to us that he was a born surfer. We called him 'The Natural,'" Donohue said.

Besides being Selanne's personal physician, Syvahuoko served as Jokerit's doctor, which meant Harkimo and head coach Hannu Jortikka were aware of Selanne's health status. And everybody agreed Selanne should only return to Jokerit when he felt ready.

But Harkimo kept texting and calling his friend, pestering him with messages. "He was desperate to get me into uniform in January," Teemu said.

Teemu, however, wasn't ready.

"I told them that I wasn't going to take the slightest risk and that I'd play when the leg felt good. I wanted to make sure I could enjoy life even after my career, and when he still kept on texting me, I didn't reply to any of them for months."

While Harkimo and Selanne had been great friends and spent those summers riding their motorcycles around Finland in days long gone, they had drifted apart at this stage in their lives. And when Selanne noticed Harkimo didn't have time to take care of his affairs, he began to use Ari Lehto, who remains his closest advisor.

It wasn't a secret that Harkimo was a shrewd businessman. Many of the representatives of potential sponsors he met to raise money also knew the Finnish Flash, so Selanne knew what Harkimo had told his corporate partners in Finland.

"During the regular season, all revenues go to the clubs, so he got to keep all the money. He would have been happy had I played with one leg, as long as the arena was sold out," Teemu said. "And when I did get into shape, well, it wasn't as important to have me on the team since all the playoff revenues were pooled and shared with other teams in the league."

During the regular season, Harkimo did everything he could to get Teemu on the team. And when he wasn't picking up the phone, Harkimo turned to Syvahuoko.

"He could call me 10 times a day and ask me to talk Teemu into playing for Jokerit," Syvahuoko said.

Syvahuoko kept in constant touch with Teemu and even visited the Selannes in California in February. The knee was getting better, but the knee wasn't the only thing that needed to be in shape.

"Teemu had so much at stake that he had to make sure he was mentally ready as well," Syvahuoko said. "Harkimo told me that I'd better come back to Finland with Teemu. I told him I'd do my best."

The Selannes flew to Finland on March 1. Eemil and Eetu enrolled in school, played soccer with the local team KyIF, and attended the Kirkkonummi Salamat hockey school. Teemu had been involved with the creation of the hockey club (Salamat is Finnish for lightning, a reference to the Finnish Flash) and the new arena, Varuboden Arena, in the town. The team had made headlines in the winter of 2003 when it signed Canadian women's hockey star Hayley Wickenheiser to play professionally with the Salamat men's team in Finland's third-tier league, Suomi-sarja (spring 2003), and second-tier league, Mestis (autumn 2003).

"We became good friends with Hayley and our paths crossed many times after that. I saw her a lot at the Winter Olympics in 2006, 2010, and 2014," Teemu said.

Like Selanne, Wickenheiser competed in six Olympic Games, five in the hockey tournament, along with one as a member of Canada's women's softball team.

"We would not have come to Finland had I not been serious about playing with Jokerit. I worked out daily and skated every day at the local arena. I was in great shape," Teemu said. But the knee was still sore.

"Then one day I was skating, and I realized there was no pain. I almost cried. I was skating full speed. It was almost like a young horse going around and at that point I knew it would be a happy ending. I did not realize how lucky I was to be healthy and enjoy the game until this happened."

Jokerit had finished in second place in the regular season standings and advanced to the Finnish league final in the playoffs. It was at this time Syvahuoko relayed a message from the team that the welcome mat would be out if and when Selanne decided to make his return.

"While I felt I was ready, the mental pressure to resume playing got bigger by the day but I knew I had to be patient and not return unless I was ready. I followed their games and waited for the right opportunity to present itself," Teemu said. "The knee rehabilitation took a long time, and at one point I no longer believed in my chances of playing that spring, but that changed when Jokerit started to play the best-of-five finals on April 12."

Jokerit lost the first two games of the championship series to Oulu Karpat and in the third game, Jokerit beat Karpat 2–1 in Oulu, with Valtteri Filppula scoring the game-winner.

"After the game, [head coach Hannu] Jortikka asked me if I—and I quote—could make sure 'my brother' would make it to Sunday night's game in Helsinki," Syvahuoko said, referring to the close relationship he had with Selanne. "'Tell him to be at the rink tomorrow at 10.' I made sure he was serious, and that he had made sure Harkimo was okay with it, too.

"Then I called Teemu and said there was a chance to make history, that Jortikka wanted him to join the team. I asked him if he could come to Saturday's practice and Sunday's morning skate and then play the game. Teemu said he'd think about it, and I had to call him a few times about it."

Teemu thought about it and felt he was ready. "I said I'd take my equipment with me in the morning, and that I'd play if they thought I could help the team."

On Saturday morning, Selanne drove to the arena. He left his gear in the car, just in case, and went to the dressing room to say hi to the players first. "I remember that at least Glen Metropolit was there. They were wondering what I was doing there. I walked over to the bench, where I met Jortikka and Wade Immonen," Teemu recalled. (Selanne's old friend Waltteri Immonen was the assistant coach.)

"He was acting weird, and Jortikka was saying something about there not being a jersey for me, which was a crazy lie, especially since I knew they had made a jersey for me. It was the most embarrassing situation of my life. I told them it was fine with me, that I had just wanted to help."

He got in his car and drove back toward Kirkkonummi before deciding to go to the driving range to hit some golf balls. Meanwhile, Syvahuoko arrived at the arena, excited about his close friend's comeback. He bumped into Harkimo, who asked him what he was doing there.

"I told him that Teemu was going to play in Game 4 and that he was on his way to the practice. He looked at me, didn't say a word, turned around, and walked to his car," Syvahuoko said.

By sheer coincidence, Selanne called Syvahuoko and told him what had happened. An angry and frustrated Syvahuoko got in his car and started to drive toward the golf course. On his way there, he called Harkimo to tell him how disappointed and angry he was about the situation. He had finally gotten Selanne to say yes, only to hear that Jokerit had said no.

"I didn't get a good reply to that," he said.

Jortikka said Syvahuoko misunderstood him in Oulu. He said he was surprised to see Teemu at the rink that morning. Harkimo's recollection is that Syvahuoko was supposed to get him to play much sooner.

"Teemu went back and forth all season long. I think we would have welcomed him with open arms had he wanted to play the whole series," said the team owner.

Harkimo and Jortikka had concerns about a new player—even if it was Teemu Selanne—changing the chemistry of the team so late in the season.

"I told Jortikka that it was the coach's decision, but I also understand why he made it," Harkimo said.

"I was never asked to take that decision, but had I been asked, of course I would have considered putting Teemu in the lineup. Everything's allowed in love and war," said Jortikka.

Selanne and Syvahuoko are convinced it was Harkimo's decision to say no—that he wanted to get back at Teemu for not answering to his messages and not coming to Finland earlier.

Immonen was against Selanne's joining the team in Game 4 of the final. "I was, but I didn't know Jortikka had asked him to come to the rink," Immonen said. "I thought it was just Teemu not being able to make up his mind, but if they did ask him to come, it was completely wrong that he wasn't welcomed into the team."

On Sunday, Selanne watched from his box suite as Jokerit lost 0–2 Game 4. During the game, he relayed what had transpired with Harkimo to Finland general manager Jari Kurri and Finnish Ice Hockey Association president Kalervo Kummola.

"Kurri asked me to join the national team at the World Championship, but I decided against it. I could have played two games, but not a long tournament," Teemu said.

The incident put a little dent in his relationship with Immonen, but soon afterward, he and Selanne talked things through and restored their friendship.

"He was misinformed," said Teemu, who still can't understand why Harkimo did what he did. But he still has a special place for Jokerit in his heart.

"That time, they didn't need my help," he said.

THE FINNISH
FLASH IS BACK

THE NUMBER OF PEOPLE WHO BELIEVED a 35-year-old Selanne would be able to return to the top of the National Hockey League could be counted on one hand.

Teemu's agent, Don Baizley, asked Ismo Syvahuoko how long his patient was going to play with the reconstructed knee. He had gotten badly burned when he had sold the Avalanche on what ended up being a one-legged forward, and this time he wanted to be absolutely sure.

"Three years, tops," said Syvahuoko.

Selanne had other plans. He was pain-free and ecstatic. "It was an unbelievable feeling to skate without pain. It had been years."

Teemu had a hunger to resume playing and asked Baizley to find him a team.

Baizley checked with the Ducks first, but the team's new general manager, Brian Burke, said they didn't have room in the budget to add him to the roster.

"'Okay,' I said. 'Let's wait.' Then I said, 'Call San Jose,'" said Teemu. "I had a good time there and they knew me." But general manager Doug Wilson said a lot of people were pissed off that Teemu had left the team once before and signed with Colorado."

"I have to think about this," Wilson had said. "I have to talk to the owners."

The next call was to Dave Taylor, general manager of the Los Angeles Kings.

"They called back and said, 'Okay, we can pay you $1.6 million on a one-year deal,' and I said I would take it," said Selanne. "Then they called to say they wanted to make one more phone call and then we will finish this. I didn't hear from them and then I read the news that the Kings had signed Valeri Bure, and I knew it was over."

The wait was on again.

Maybe he had played his last game in the NHL.

"Then Burke called Don and told him he had $1 million in his budget," Teemu said. "Don asked me, very carefully, what I thought about that, and he was really surprised when I told him to make the deal, for sure. I didn't care about the money at that point. I wanted to go back, and I knew it would be unbelievable."

"I talked to [Ducks head coach and former teammate] Randy Carlyle and told him I am better than ever. I am stronger, and I had so much hunger to play again. I could not wait for the season to start. I told him if you give me a chance, you will not be disappointed."

Burke, who now works as a television analyst on hockey broadcasts in Canada, had some concerns about whether Selanne's knee would withstand the rigors of a punishing NHL season.

"We were really concerned about his knee and he gave us all his medical information and testimonials that it was all good," Burke said. "And Don, I think he sent us video of Teemu skating. We said we believe because we have absolute faith in Don Baizley. It is a functioning knee and is fine. But what if he hurts it again? This is an older player, so we would only agree to go to $1 million. But he just came in and lit it up and played great."

Selanne was back with a team he felt at home with, but it appeared obvious many people in the organization never thought this day would come. His No. 8 was being worn by Latvian defenseman Sandis Ozolinsh, and so Teemu began his second NHL career—his post-knee surgery career—wearing the same number as when he first came into the league: 13.

The deal was great for the Ducks, who got back a fan favorite, and according to Ducks television analyst Brian Hayward, even if Teemu only scored 15 goals a season, he was worth his $1 million salary.

One thing had changed in Anaheim. Disney had sold the team to Henry and Susan Samueli, who had hired Burke to build them a championship team. The head coach was Carlyle, Teemu's old teammate from the Jets.

"I wasn't sure how he would react to having me on the team, or if he held a grudge from our time in Winnipeg, but there was none of that. He knew what I could do," Teemu said.

The Ducks had also signed free agent Scott Niedermayer, the reigning winner of the Norris Trophy (2003–04) as the NHL's best defenseman, who wanted to win the Stanley Cup with his brother, Rob.

The lockout season had saved Selanne's knee and career, but the new collective bargaining agreement had also made life easier for players. Sometimes it's the little things that make a big difference.

"One good thing was, for example, that veteran players didn't have to share a hotel room on road trips. If I couldn't fall asleep, I could watch TV, make phone calls, and then try to fall asleep again," Teemu said.

The NHL was looking for ways to bring excitement back into the games after canceling the 2004–05 season because of labor issues. The league decided to tackle obstruction and crack down on interference, hooking, holding, and other acts that stymied scoring chances. With zero tolerance on interference in place, hockey types thought the game would become faster and more entertaining.

There were few players faster or more entertaining than Selanne. Few, if any, defensemen could stop him when he came flying down his wing.

The Ducks were a better hockey team than the one he had left in 2001. Disney had finally invested money in the team before it sold it and Bryan Murray, who was head coach in 2001–02 and general manager from 2002 to 04, had built the team piece by piece.

The most important piece was brilliant goaltender Jean-Sebastien Giguere, who was key to Anaheim's run to the Stanley Cup Final in the 2002–03 season. Samuel Pahlsson, a Swede, was a solid center worthy of consideration for the Selke Trophy, and Rob Niedermayer was a classic power forward.

Anaheim had also drafted well, especially in 2003 when they chose Ryan Getzlaf (No. 19 overall) and Corey Perry (No. 28 overall). The Ducks had also signed three top college players as free agents: Andy McDonald in 2000, Chris Kunitz in 2003, and Dustin Penner in 2004.

The captain was Scott Niedermayer, winner of three Stanley Cups and a Norris Trophy with the Devils. Teemu, who represented experience and offensive power, was an alternate captain.

"I knew we could go really far. I knew that day when I was skating I was back. I was smiling and said, 'This will be fun.' We had a great team," Teemu said.

Selanne played 80 of 82 regular season games, putting an end to the discussion about how his knee would hold up. He led the Mighty Ducks in scoring with 40 goals and 90 points and finished 13th in league scoring. Teemu also led the Mighty Ducks in playoff scoring, with 14 points in 16 games.

But there was more to his contribution to a successful team than goals and assists. Burke feels Selanne's outgoing, always positive personality was as important to Anaheim's success as much as his scoring touch.

"There is another thing that people forget, and it is not acknowledged enough, is what Teemu brings to a team; forget the goals and all the rest of it, he is always in a good mood and that is a valuable asset for a team," Burke said. "Hockey is a business filled with grumpy guys who come in in the morning and the coffee is no good and the traffic was bad and it is not sunny enough. They come into a room where there are a lot of negative guys and a lot of them bitch about everything: the butter is not soft enough on the bagels, and on and on. And in comes this guy, beaming, grinning; 'Hey boys, yes we lost 9–2 last night but we won 9–2 the other night.'

"That positivity and positive outlook is one of the assets we looked at as valuable. A player who brings a positive attitude to the room is an asset. Teemu was a great player for us, but he also brought positivity. He was not just a star on ice for us. He was an important influence in the room. He never has a bad day, and that is an asset. On that Cup team was Chris Pronger and he never has a good day, and then you have Scott Niedermayer, and your worst nightmare would be to go fishing with him because he never said a word. Then you put Teemu in the mix and he talks to everyone and he smiles at everyone, trainers, doctors, and secretaries. He has got the same politeness and same sunny smile for everybody."

"Every day, Teemu finds something to be happy about," longtime teammate Paul Kariya said. "[He] gets as mad as anyone else when we lose, but I think he forgets it quickly. Teemu keeps everybody on an even keel. When things are going poorly, he's upbeat and he keeps everybody loose. When things are going well, he's the same, so we always know what to expect from him. Guys get down, but he's there picking us up."

At the end of the season, Selanne's historic return to the game was recognized by members of the Professional Hockey Writers Association when they awarded him the Bill Masterton Memorial Trophy,

given to the player "who best exemplifies the qualities of persever-
ance, sportsmanship, and dedication to hockey." Masterton is the only
player in NHL history to die of injuries suffered in a game.

Selanne played most of the season with McDonald and Kunitz,
both of whom had already been dismissed as lost prospects, and they
became the Mighty Ducks' de facto first line.

"McDonald had the talent to go far, but his confidence was gone
and if the coach yelled at him, he froze. Carlyle and I agreed that I'd
be McDonald's mentor," Teemu recalls. "Kunitz had gone back and
forth between the NHL and the AHL, but we found a great chemistry."

McDonald's single-season point record prior to playing with
Teemu was 30. In 2005–06, he scored 34 goals and amassed 85 points.
Kunitz was put on the waivers list early in the season, and he spent
two weeks as an Atlanta Thrasher before returning to Anaheim, which
actually claimed him off waivers. He scored 19 goals and got 41 points
in 67 games and got his NHL career on track.

Niedermayer was another key player, and Selanne finally had a
defenseman who could get the puck to him when he was at full speed.

In the playoffs, Anaheim won its first-round series against Calgary
in seven games. Teemu scored the first goal of the game in Game 7.
It turned out to be the game-winner, as Anaheim won 3–0.

"I remember the game when [Ducks defenseman Francois]
Beauchemin fought [Calgary star forward Jarome] Iginla and that
was the turning point in the series. Beauch put Iginla down and we
knew on the bench it was big," Teemu recalled.

In the conference semifinal, the Mighty Ducks swept the Colorado
Avalanche, which helped Teemu get rid of some of the ghosts he still
carried with him from his season in Denver. "Tony Granato was still
there, but he had been demoted to an assistant coach's position behind
Joel Quenneville. I was so happy when we swept them," Teemu said.

He scored three points in the opening game of the series, a 5–0
win that set the stage for a sweep of the best-of-seven series.

The Edmonton Oilers turned out to be too much for the Ducks, winning the conference final 4–1. But getting to the semifinals gave the Mighty Ducks more confidence. Selanne was in heaven.

"I got peace of mind," he said.

It wasn't just the Mighty Ducks' long playoff run that had made him happy. Selanne played almost 100 games that season and proved that he still belonged among the game's elite. And once again, Finland had been an important part of it.

In 2002, the Salt Lake City Olympics had been his lifeline when things didn't work the way he wanted in the NHL. Twelve years later, he had the Sochi Olympics to look forward to when life in Anaheim had gotten tougher.

In 2005–06, Selanne was on top of his game and had re-established himself as an important player. He was happy in Anaheim and he looked forward to playing for Finland at the 2006 Torino Winter Olympics. And as things turned out, Selanne found himself in the gold-medal final.

"The whole team came together right away. It was like going home again. Coach Erkka Westerlund put in place a great defensive system and let us players work on the offensive side of the game.

"That was our moment, the pinnacle of the golden generation of Finnish hockey. I think we were the best team in the tournament, but we couldn't play our best game when it mattered," Teemu said.

Finland lost the Olympic final to Sweden, but Selanne led the tournament in goals and scoring and was named to the tournament All-Star Team. He had six goals and 11 points in eight games, playing again on a line with Saku Koivu and Jere Lehtinen.

"The Torino Olympics team was the best team I've ever played on, and the semifinal against Russia, which we won 4–0, the best hockey game I was involved with during my career. The whole team played a perfect game. Russia had all their superstars, but we dominated the game."

———————

In the off-season, the Anaheim Mighty Ducks changed their name to the Anaheim Ducks and Burke went to work finding the missing pieces for a championship team. Burke had told Teemu that after a season like that, he naturally earned a raise from his $1 million salary.

"I also told him that it meant that we couldn't add many more players, due to the salary cap restrictions," Burke said. "He told me he'd settle for a smaller salary if I promised to use the difference to improve the team."

Added Teemu, "He said, 'I know how much I should pay you, but if you take $3.75 million I have enough to sign a superstar here, and I promise that every penny will go to a good player.' I said, 'Okay, I will take it, because I want to win.'"

Selanne took what in hockey circles is known as a hometown discount. He took less than market value for a player of his stature to free up money for Burke to add a missing link to a winning team.

After agreeing to the contract, Selanne went back to Finland for the summer and while he was there, he received the best possible birthday present from Anaheim. On his birthday, Alex Gilchrist—who worked in the Ducks' PR office—called to say, "Teemu, we got Pronger."

"I said, 'Sean?'" Teemu recalled. "'No, Chris,' Alex said. What the fuck! We just played Edmonton, and he was there. I said, 'Are you fucking around?' and he said, 'No, we got Chris Pronger.' I said, 'Say it one more time.' We just traded for Chris Pronger. I knew right away we were going to win. As good a team as we had, adding Prongs, it was our year for sure if everything goes right.

"Pronger was the only guy I hated out there. He was so evil to play against, and I had a big smile when I saw him for the first time in the locker room because we always had tough times. We were yapping at each other and it was always personal, and we ended up becoming good friends."

Burke related a theory about how to build a team and how it applies to making a trade for an impact player like Pronger, the missing piece to what he thought would be a Stanley Cup champion.

"I believe there are four stages to a team: they crawl, they run, they walk, and they sprint. If you are a walking team: and you can make a deal for a third-round pick and get into the playoffs, great. Then it might be, can this get us over the hump, the Chris Pronger trade. You make that deal and you are all in at that point—either you are going to win it or you just made a horrible mistake."

Teemu detected a change in the way the Ducks carried themselves in training camp. "It was all business right away, and we started so good," he recalled.

"There were so many guys who had a mission and Scotty, even though he had won three Stanley Cups, he really wanted to win one with his brother."

Teemu credits Burke for following through with his promise to add a superstar on the blue line in Pronger.

"He built a team that was tough and dirty. We were the most-penalized team in the league and we still won. We were super tough in every category. He said we do not take shit from anyone and I always thought we can't take penalties but our penalty killers were so good. We had such great leadership. It was so unique."

"I knew we'd win the Stanley Cup. Pronger was exactly the piece we had been missing."

Pronger had won the Norris Trophy and the Hart as the league MVP in 2000 with the St. Louis Blues. With Canada, he had won the 1997 World Championship in Helsinki and Olympic gold at the 2002 Salt Lake City Winter Games. He was respected and a bit feared around the league. Now the Ducks had two of the top five defensemen in the league, with Pronger and captain Scott Niedermayer.

Pronger was the second overall pick in the 1993 NHL draft behind Alexander Daigle, who fizzled out as an NHL player. Ironically, it was Daigle who said, "Who remembers who gets picked second?" and those words definitely came back to haunt him. It is also worth mentioning that Selanne's on-ice soulmate, Paul Kariya, was the fourth overall pick in 1993.

The Ducks jumped off to a fabulous start as the team went on a 16-game points streak to start the season, an NHL record that was broken in 2012 by the Chicago Blackhawks.

Teemu's second season since the knee operation was one for the ages.

The Finnish Flash led the Ducks in points and goals and finished 11th in the league scoring race and third in goal scoring with his 48 goals and 94 points in 82 games. It was his biggest points total since 1999, and the best goals total since 1998. It also marked the fourth time in his career he didn't miss any games during the season.

He scored his 500th NHL goal in November, against the Colorado Avalanche, and played in his 1,000th regular season game in December against the Minnesota Wild.

He played in his 10th All-Star Game and became the oldest player to score more than 45 goals in a season and the first 35-year-old to score 40 goals in two consecutive seasons.

The Ducks won their division for the first time in club history and made it to the Stanley Cup Final for the second time.

And this time, they would go all the way.

In the playoffs, Teemu scored five goals and posted 15 points in 21 games. He considers one of those five goals the most important of his career.

The Ducks had beaten the Minnesota Wild in five games in the first round and the Vancouver Canucks in five games in the second round. The conference final against the Detroit Red Wings was tied at two games each.

In Game 5 in Detroit, the Red Wings scored first when Andreas Lilja beat goaltender Jean-Sebastien Giguere with a slap shot from the point.

The Ducks tied the game in the third period when Scott Nieder-mayer rushed toward the net from the point, received a pass from Teemu, and scored. Chris Pronger picked up the other assist on the goal.

In overtime, Andy McDonald and Teemu forechecked against Lilja, who turned the puck over to Selanne. He deked to his backhand and lifted the puck over Red Wings goaltender Dominik Hasek, end-ing the game.

Two nights later in Anaheim, the Ducks advanced to the Final with a 4–3 victory.

The game-winner against Detroit would be Teemu's last goal in the 2007 playoffs, but he picked up three assists in the five games in the final against the Ottawa Senators.

"I remember seeing the water bottle in the air," he said about his overtime goal, which hit the top of the net. "Who knows what might have happened had we lost that game? We had lost to the Red Wings so many times in the past."

But the Ducks did not lose; in fact, they lost only one more game on the way to their dream season, winning the Stanley Cup.

There is no shortage of people in the hockey universe who were thrilled for Selanne to achieve a lifelong dream, and one of the hap-piest was Paul Kariya.

"I was ecstatic for Teemu. Throughout his career, and going through that Colorado experience, it was, 'Is he going to win? Does he have anything left?' When he came back to the Ducks, I thought his play was unbelievable."

"And when you look at the longevity of the second part of his career, the numbers he put up were unbelievable."

Brian Hayward said Teemu became a smarter player after his knee surgery.

"Before that, he could always rely on his speed. He was still fast and strong, but not quite as fast as before the surgery, so when he returned to Anaheim, he had to be a more complete player, which also made him a better team player," he said. "He had to find the areas where he hadn't had to go when he was younger. He played two-way hockey, took hits, and battled in the corners. He saw the whole rink better."

Ironically, Ottawa Senators coach Bryan Murray was able to witness up close how the team he had helped to build as the Ducks' general manager celebrated the Stanley Cup victory.

"Selanne's return was the key for Anaheim's success," he said.

Burke added that Teemu's decision to take less money so the Ducks could add Pronger to the mix was key to winning the Cup.

"I don't know too many players who take less to win. Teemu did the right thing. When I explained it to Teemu and Don Baizley, Teemu made it clear he was all about trying to win. And that is why I was so happy with [the Washington Capitals' Alexander] Ovechkin's 2018 spring [when he hoisted the Stanley Cup when Washington beat Vegas].

"Teemu is Alexander Ovechkin, and their careers are so similar. They both had great careers and no team success, and people started to question Selanne. Last year people questioned Ovechkin for not winning and I said, 'How is it his fault?' I said look at Teemu. He had almost the same stats and he never went past the first round until he won. Of all the guys who carried the Cup around, the guy I was happiest for was Teemu.

"He and Paul chased it, and at least they tried to win. They went to Colorado to try to win, so they chased it and I respect that. I tell you what, Teemu would be a Hall of Famer without his Cup, but I don't think he would have been satisfied about his career if he had not won the Cup. He was the guy I was happiest for."

While much of the attention was focused on Selanne, he feels credit should go to Getzlaf and Perry, two young players who were Anaheim's top two scorers in the playoffs ahead of him.

"We had two unbelievable young players, and they were a big factor in the successful run to the Stanley Cup championship. I knew these two guys would be franchise players for the Ducks organization for a long time."

The next time the Stanley Cup champions played a game that counted was in London, England, at the end of September 2007. In an effort to market the NHL in Europe, the league scheduled overseas games, and the Anaheim Ducks opened the 2007–08 season against the Los Angeles Kings. But the defending Stanley Cup champions were without both Selanne and Scott Niedermayer, who were considering retirement.

Burke was patient with the veterans. "He told us we had all the time in the world. I was positive that I was going to retire. I had accomplished everything I had wanted to accomplish," Teemu said.

Sirpa, who was expecting their daughter, had always worried about the day Teemu would retire. "I wasn't sure how it was going to go, or whether he'd want to hang out with the family, but it went well. He spent a lot of time at home. I was exhausted. After all, I was 38 and pregnant," she said.

Their daughter, Veera, was born a month early on December 5, 2007. She was tiny, but she was healthy.

"Everything was perfect. I had my Cup and we had our daughter, Veera," said Teemu.

Teemu was happy with his life without hockey, and he never thought about a possible return. He had worked out in the summer, but when players reported to training camp, Teemu hit the links.

Then, in December, Niedermayer called to say he was going to resume his NHL career and invited Teemu to join him for a skating session. "It would have been at 11 at night and I couldn't find my gear, so I said no," Teemu said.

Niedermayer's return did make Teemu reconsider his career decision: To play or not to play?

"I rented some ice time at the Anaheim Ice arena where the Ducks practice because I wanted to see if skating was still fun. I was there on my own and told people after the first time that I had nothing more to give to the game. I probably would have retired had I not been asked to play with a bunch of my friends. When I played with others, hockey became fun again."

One day, Teemu took his children to a Ducks game, and watching from the stands proved to be too much for him. He got the itch to return. "I wanted to be on the ice and help the team. I called Burke and told him I was coming back."

The day after Teemu made that call, Burke traded Andy McDonald, Selanne's linemate in the run to the Cup, to the St. Louis Blues for Doug Weight. The move was made to free up cap space for the returning Niedermayer, and Teemu was furious about Burke's decision.

Again, the business side of hockey reared its ugly head.

"I almost called to say I wasn't coming back. I said, 'Why?' Had I known, I would have done everything in my power to stop it. Was that the thanks Andy got for scoring five goals in the Stanley Cup Final?"

But that didn't stop Teemu from practicing another month on his own before he felt he was ready to play again. "I missed Andy and I told the general manager many times that I wished he'd get him back. He was the best center I played with at the end of my career."

McDonald played five and a half seasons with the Blues before concussions forced him to retire in 2013.

Teemu returned to the Ducks on February 5, 2008, when they beat the New York Islanders 3–0 on Long Island. The day after the game, it was time for the traditional Stanley Cup champions' visit to the White House. The Ducks gave President George W. Bush a jersey with his name on it before the president gave a speech.

"Welcome to the White House. We're glad you're here. Like, have you noticed a lot of security around here? It's because the vice president heard there were some Ducks around," the president said, referring to Vice President Dick Cheney's recent embarrassing incident in which he shot a fellow hunter while hunting for quail.

"This Cup has been to some odd places. The Cup has been to countless bars and nightclubs across the world, and I'm sure some of the players are pleased the Cup can't talk," Bush continued.

Being at the White House was one of the highlights of Teemu's year. "It was a great experience. It's not every day you get to visit the White House."

Anaheim had lost six straight games when Teemu joined the team in New York, but the Ducks found their stride with him in the line-up again. The Ducks won five straight and lost just six of their last 26 games. Teemu scored 12 goals and had 23 points in 26 regular season games and two goals and had four points in six playoff games, but the Ducks lost to the Dallas Stars in the first round. They weren't the first Stanley Cup champion to fail to defend their title.

"That's what often happens to the reigning champs. We weren't hungry enough," Teemu said.

The World Championships were being held in Quebec City and Halifax. It was the International Ice Hockey Federation's centennial, and the world governing body wanted to have the tournament take place in the country where hockey was first played.

Canadian Doug Shedden was coaching Finland, and he really wanted to add a fresh Selanne to his roster. Finland general manager Jari Kurri called Selanne a few times about joining the team but, unsurprisingly, hadn't got a straight answer from him.

"I had heard that Teemu liked to go back and forth before making up his mind but that he couldn't say no if you spoke to him face to face. So, I told Jari that he should fly to Anaheim and pick Teemu up," Shedden said with a laugh.

Kurri wasn't laughing. "We had just arrived in Halifax, but I did book a coast-to-coast flight to Los Angeles and back."

Teemu was playing golf when his phone rang. Kurri was on the other end. "I asked him where he was, and he said, 'In Boston, on my way to California.' Then he asked me to meet him at the airport. I knew what was up. And I knew I had no alternative," Teemu recalled. "The guy whose poster I had had on my wall was on his way to pick me up for the World Championship."

Selanne met Kurri at the airport and they made some small talk, but neither one brought up the tournament. "We drove to our house, played some golf the next day, and went to the gym. Then Jari said that there was a tournament in Halifax in a couple of days and he asked me whether I'd like to play there. He had booked the flights and everything. I joined the team on April 30, three days before the first game."

Finland finished third in the tournament. Teemu scored three goals and got seven points in nine games. After his final game of the championship, Teemu announced this World Championship would be his last.

TWO MORE YEARS

SELANNE SPENT MOST OF THE SUMMER of 2008 mulling over his decision to keep playing, and he ended up signing a two-year deal with the Ducks worth $5.25 million. He still enjoyed playing and saw no reason to sign for less than two years. "The Ducks had to create some space under their salary cap, but I only wanted to play there. We still had a chance to win."

Burke stepped down as general manager in November, and a few weeks later was introduced as the general manager of the Toronto Maple Leafs. Bob Murray, who is no relation to former Ducks coach and general manager Bryan Murray, succeeded him.

The two-year deal meant Teemu might play in the 2010 Winter Olympics in Vancouver. Another motivating factor was he was just 49 goals behind Jari Kurri on the NHL's all-time goal scoring list, and two seasons would surely provide enough time for him to take over the top spot as the leading Finnish-born goal scorer in NHL history.

Selanne scored 14 goals in his first 33 games in 2008–09 but suffered an injury in December, when his left thigh was lacerated by his own skate in a game against Edmonton. After Edmonton's

Denis Grebeshkov hit him, Selanne fell and then saw blood pooling under him. "The skate was sharp as a knife, and the cut was a few millimeters from an artery, which would have been truly serious. I was told that the doctors would have had seven minutes to stop the bleeding."

He missed 17 games but finished the season with 27 goals in 65 games, leaving him 22 goals shy of Kurri's total.

The Ducks made the playoffs and beat the Sharks in the first round but lost their conference semifinal to the Detroit Red Wings. Detroit won Game 7 at home 4–3. Teemu scored two goals and added an assist.

Going into the second and last year of his deal, Selanne was bullish on the 2009–10 season. He was playing well, and he was within reach of Kurri's record for most goals by a player from Finland. Moreover, the 2010 Vancouver Olympic Games were on the horizon.

"This is certainly my last season and my last chance to win something with Team Finland. I'm going all in. An Olympic gold medal would be a nice way to cap off the career," he said.

Teemu received another motivational boost when the Ducks signed fellow Finn Saku Koivu, who was an unrestricted free agent. The two had played together on the Finnish national team and had also become close friends. Koivu was leaving the storied Montreal Canadiens, whom he had captained for a decade, for sunny California.

"I was looking for a team that has a legitimate chance to compete for the Stanley Cup. I'm also looking forward to a full season with Teemu Selanne as a teammate. We've had a lot of success, and I know the chemistry is there," Koivu said at the time.

The chemistry certainly had been there when they played for Finland. Together they won Olympic bronze in 1998 and 2010, Olympic silver in 2006, World Championship silver in 1999 and bronze in 2008, and World Cup silver in 2004.

"What made Teemu exceptional was obviously his speed, but also his perfect timing to get to the right area at the right time," Koivu said. "Playing with Teemu, I had to read the plays much faster than with others, which was challenging and rewarding. You either missed him completely—or created a wonderful scoring chance."

But you can't create chemistry by yourself. It takes two to tango, and Selanne was pumped. "He could really see the ice so well and dished such great passes that my game got elevated to another level. It's a lot more fun to search for the opening when you know you'll get the puck when you need it and where you want it," said Selanne.

Koivu's addition gave Anaheim the second line it hadn't had since McDonald was traded. Ryan Getzlaf and Corey Perry were two-thirds of a great first line, but now Selanne and Koivu would give the team even more offense. And when Scott Niedermayer re-signed, as well, expectations were sky-high.

"I hadn't found same kind of a chemistry with any other center since McDonald got traded. When GM Bob Murray asked me for my ideas, Saku was at the top of my list. I had never seen Saku as excited about anything. He had never gotten past the second round in the playoffs," Selanne said.

Things, however, did not work out as Teemu had hoped.

Not only did the Ducks not win the Stanley Cup, they didn't even make the playoffs. That was probably the best indication of the new parity in the league. The salary cap, together with the draft system, had made the league competitively even.

Puck possession had become the norm in the league, and it is a style of play with heavy emphasis on skating and skill.

There were coaches who didn't grasp the benefits of going easy on players over a grinding 82-game schedule, and Ducks coach Randy Carlyle was a card-carrying member of the old school of thinking. He didn't believe in giving players time off or going easy in practice to help players rest and recover.

"Why would I give players days off when Selanne goes playing golf and young players go drinking in bars?" Carlyle said.

The results speak for themselves.

The Ducks lost 19 of their first 30 games, and Teemu points to an exhausting training camp as one of the reasons behind the disappointing start. "Our training camp was, once again, too tough. We were beat up in the fall and lost unnecessary points in the standings. Teams that moved the puck and had fresh legs made the playoffs and went deep. We were bag-skated when we should have rested."

"But on the other hand, it sounded a little bit stupid to criticize Carlyle after he took us to the conference finals in 2006 and Stanley Cup in 2007."

Once again, injuries took a toll on the Finnish Flash. In early December, luck was not on Teemu's side when he broke his hand blocking a shot and he missed 17 games. "The puck hit me right in the middle knuckle, where the protection was poor," he said.

He returned to action in early January and was just getting into the stride of being back in the lineup when he was the victim of bad luck again. A point shot by teammate Ryan Whitney deflected off the stick of Boston forward Miroslav Satan, and the puck slammed into Selanne's face in his third game back from the hand injury.

"I just remember losing sight of the puck and then it hit me. I had three fractures in my jaw. The pain was hell, not even morphine helped. Of all the injuries I have had in my career, this was by far the most painful. The problem was that they couldn't operate until the next day because my stomach was full. After the surgery, the pain was gone, the jaw was whole again, and I didn't even need painkillers."

He missed eight games and lost 13 pounds. "The first couple of weeks I ate with a straw."

Teemu was back on the ice 10 days after the injury but quickly noticed that he had lost a step. "I was completely out of shape. I could skate two laps around the rink before having to rest."

With the Winter Olympics on the horizon, Teemu was in a hurry to get back so that he'd be able to compete in the pressure-packed best-on-best tournament. "It was the dream come true, having the Winter Olympics in Vancouver, which is one of my favorite cities. I couldn't miss it!" Teemu said.

Selanne had his helmet outfitted with a special face shield to protect his jaw. He wore it for the seven games leading up to the Vancouver Games, as well as in all of Finland's games at the Winter Olympics, although he says the face shield made it "hard to see the puck when it was in my feet."

The Vancouver Games were not the career highlight Selanne had hoped they would be. Finland's new coach, Jukka Jalonen, did not give his first line a lot of ice time, and the coach and the players weren't on the same page like Westerlund had been with his team four years earlier.

"Erkka trusted his veteran players, unlike Jukka, who wanted to make us play his European style without understanding how you play in a smaller North American rink. Erkka had the players participate in the planning both in Torino in 2006 and in Sochi in 2014," Teemu said. "Jalonen was charismatic, for sure, and he had a good coaching style. He just could have listened to the players more."

Finland advanced out of the preliminary round and beat the Czech Republic 2–0 in the quarterfinals. But it met a hungry USA in the first game of the medal round. The Americans came out strong, chasing Miikka Kiprusoff out of the net halfway through the first period when they took a 4–0 lead. They scored two more goals in the first period and won easily 6–1.

"I can't explain it. It was a shock, but not like in 2003, because they just steamrolled us from the first minute and we couldn't do anything right," Teemu said. "On the other hand, we were down 3–1 against Slovakia in the bronze-medal game and rallied back to win it 5–3."

That was the last tournament for the Selanne-Koivu-Lehtinen line on Finland's national team.

While players love playing for their flag, the Olympic tournament is an exhausting and intense two-week competition that tests physical and mental strength for anyone wearing his country's colors.

There is nothing quite like best-on-best hockey, where one minute a team can be on the attack and in an instant the players are scrambling to get back on defense. The action is fast-paced and not for the faint of heart.

Selanne felt zapped after the Vancouver Games, saying the intense competition came at the wrong time for key players on NHL clubs. "It was really hard to get mentally ready for the NHL after the Olympic tournament. We had seven guys from the Ducks in the tournament and the coaching staff didn't think about recovery at all."

When the NHL resumed play, Carlyle stayed true to his unrelenting coaching philosophy. One of his traits was how he liked to match up his lines, and that meant that the trios kept changing. That kept Saku and Selanne apart more than they would have liked.

Teemu resumed the chase of Kurri's record of 601 NHL goals, the most for a Finnish player in NHL history. He scored his 598th goal in his first game back, then went three long games without scoring, and then netted No. 599 at home against the Sharks on March 14.

Getting the milestone 600th goal turned out to be difficult.

"It was as if the nets were cursed. Teemu had lots of scoring chances, but the puck just wouldn't find the back of the net. It was crazy," Koivu recalled with a laugh.

The Ducks were in the middle of a seven-game homestand, and the Selanne house was full of Teemu's Finnish friends who had arrived in California to witness hockey history.

The chase was taking a toll on the usually calm Finnish Flash.

"It started to get to me. I knew some of the guys would have to go back home after the [March 19 game against the New York] Islanders, and we spent the night before watching VHS tapes with highlights from my career. I was trying to find patterns I could use in the game."

The Ducks beat the Islanders in overtime. Selanne didn't find the back of the net. Anaheim's next opponent was the Colorado Avalanche, and he managed to finally shake the proverbial monkey off his back. Niedermayer and Perry got the puck to Selanne, who was in his favorite spot by the side of the net early in the second period. Teemu didn't blink when he buried the milestone 600th goal.

The Honda Center crowd—including one of his Finnish friends still in Anaheim—gave their favorite player a standing ovation, and the entire team rushed onto the ice to congratulate him.

With one milestone reached, Selanne went another four games without scoring a goal.

"I thought there would not be any pressure about milestones, but for some reason breaking Jari's record took a little while. So maybe I was thinking about it because usually I don't feel any pressure. It was a big honor," Teemu said.

The Ducks decided to recognize Selanne's historic 600th goal in the game against the Dallas Stars on March 29. The team invited Kurri to Anaheim for the celebration.

"Teemu didn't want to make me feel bad and pass me when I was in the house. I remember how hard getting the 600th goal had been for me," Kurri said.

A few nights later, Selanne registered career goal No. 601 and added Nos. 602 and 603 the night after that, passing Kurri with three regular season games to spare.

"It is not something I ever thought about, scoring more goals than my childhood idol. He was such a big hero and role model for me," said Selanne.

They say records are made to be broken, but it will be hard, if not impossible, for another Finn to knock Selanne off his perch as the country's all-time NHL points leader, although Teemu refuses to admit his title is safe.

"I didn't think anybody would break Jari's, and then I came along. It is possible because there are a lot of young players now, but you need a nice, long career without injuries and stuff. It is not easy, but it is doable."

Teemu finished the injury-plagued season with 27 goals and had 48 points in 54 games. Koivu had 52 points in 71 games.

Teemu missed three games at the end of the season after he hit his head and shoulder. He had already decided that he'd call it a career after the 2009–10 season, and now it seemed even more likely. In an interview with Finnish sports newspaper *Veikkaaja*, he said he was going to retire.

He was worn out. His body was telling him his time was up.

"This is it. We have to freeze my shoulder for every game, and I haven't been able to shoot even at practices. The hockey gods didn't seem to be just hinting anymore," he recalled feeling at the time.

ONE MORE YEAR(S)

N THE SUMMER OF 2010, Teemu faced the old dilemma: to retire or not to retire?

Scott Niedermayer had retired after the 2009–10 season, but there were some people who thought Selanne had more to give, that he still had what it takes to thrive in the NHL.

"Teemu's acceleration and speed still put many younger players to shame," said Columbus Blue Jackets general manager Jarmo Kekalainen.

Teemu had played two 80-game seasons after his knee surgery, but injuries and his decision not to return to camp after the Stanley Cup victory meant he had only played 145 regular season games in the subsequent three seasons.

He could look back, see what he had achieved, and walk away satisfied. He was the highest-scoring Finn in NHL history and he also had a Stanley Cup championship ring on his finger.

What else was there for him to accomplish?

One big draw would be an Olympic gold medal, but the 2014 Sochi Winter Games were four years away.

Decisions, decisions, decisions.

One of the hardest things for a professional athlete or a top musician or any star, for that matter, is to know when to walk away. Especially if they started chasing their dream early and still loved what they do.

It wasn't a shock when Teemu decided he wasn't ready to hang up the skates for good, so he signed for another year.

"I thought it was going to be easy to retire. But when you think you can play and you can still play at a high level and you enjoy it, I don't see any reason why anybody would think that is when you should retire," Teemu told the *Los Angeles Times*.

The Ducks were happy to get the franchise's all-time leading scorer back for a base salary of $3.25 million plus bonuses. The *Times* called it "a bargain for a player of his skill and experience."

"He's still got it. He still can fly," Ducks general manager Bob Murray said.

And he was right.

Selanne, now past his 40th birthday, finished the 2010–11 season with 31 goals and 80 points in 73 games, enough for eighth place in the league scoring race. It was the first time in 11 seasons he was in the overall top 10 in scoring. Only two players had scored more points in a single season after their 40th birthday: Gordie Howe and Johnny Bucyk.

The Ducks were eliminated by the Nashville Predators in the first round of the playoffs. Teemu scored six goals in six games. But there was one memorable event from the season: Teemu got into his third fight in the NHL.

With 3:00 left in Anaheim's last game of the regular season, Jack Johnson of the Los Angeles Kings cross-checked Teemu into the boards, and Brad Richardson followed up with a hard elbow a few seconds after.

Several fights broke out on the ice, including one between Selanne and Richardson. Ducks teammate Ryan Getzlaf tried to go between them, but the usually passive Selanne had decided to go for it.

"Had the ref called [a penalty on the cross-check], there wouldn't have been a fight at all. I got in a few good punches, and I realized afterward that I could have broken my hand. I just wanted to send a message to the other teams," Teemu said.

Richardson pulled Teemu's jersey over his head and the linesmen separated the players.

"My teammates were more excited about my fight than they would be for a hat trick."

There was a method to Teemu's madness—while sending a message to the other teams, he also wanted to send a message to his own team and get his teammates fired up for the postseason. And he was tired of being abused because he was a star player.

"That would never have happened in the old days. If some Mickey Mouse tried to get rough with me in Winnipeg, Tie Domi made sure he paid a price for it. That kept the game clean. The league's decision to give longer suspensions to instigators [of fights] was a stupid decision because it handed the game over to the rats," he said.

The NHL has since made significant strides to eliminate fighting. Players still drop their gloves, but the number of fights has decreased dramatically.

"I've always been against violence, but self-defense in the rink is part of the game. I've been around for a long time and I know the difference between tough play and trying to hurt others. I didn't have a choice in L.A.," Selanne said at the time.

"The referees could put a stop to rats if they wanted to."

He was criticized for his comments, especially one about how his sons enjoyed the fight. Since his two other fights were from his rookie season—against Tyler Wright and Chris Chelios—his children had never witnessed their father in one.

"They've told me several times that I should have at least one fight so they can see it. Now they were behind the net and saw it all. I'm sure they were excited," Selanne told Finnish newspaper *Ilta-Sanomat*.

What about him? Did he enjoy it?

One hint: a photo of the fight is still the background image on his laptop.

After the season, Teemu was back in familiar territory: whether to keep playing or hang it up for good.

In early June, he decided to hit the tennis courts in Southern California to get ready for an annual celebrity Bermuda Cup tournament in Helsinki. His good friend Ismo Syvahuoko—the doctor who operated on his knees and knew Teemu's medical history better than anyone—warned him about playing tennis on hard courts, but Teemu didn't listen. He figured with the knee having been in great shape for years, he'd be fine.

Guess again.

"I thought it was weird that I couldn't straighten my leg afterward. And then the pain came," Selanne said about his hard court workout.

Ducks team physician Orr Limpisvasti examined the knee and concluded the pain was caused by cartilage wear in the reconstructed left knee. By coincidence, Syvahuoko was in California on vacation and got the chance to have a look at the scans. He didn't share Dr. Limpisvasti's opinion.

"I met with Limpisvasti at his clinic and we discussed possible treatments. I suggested we do an arthroscopy, but he didn't think it would help because you can't treat wear. I was certain Teemu had had a meniscal tear in his knee because the pain had come so suddenly, and it was different from the wear pain. When Teemu came to Finland, I had him have an arthroscopy."

After the medical procedure, Teemu was concerned. "The doctor told me the knee was basically done and that I couldn't play hockey with it. When Immu agreed with him, I was sure my career was over. But, fortunately, I didn't say anything to the Ducks."

He couldn't defend his tennis tournament title, but Selanne did make an appearance. It took him 20 minutes to walk the 150 feet from his car to the clubhouse because he was signing autographs. After that, he gave interviews for two hours and noted it would have been an easier day had he just been able to play tennis.

He kept on working out lightly and soon noticed the knee was responding well. The pain was there, but it wasn't intolerable. After a few weeks on the ice, Selanne opened the door for contract negotiations with the Ducks and signed for another year, his 19th NHL season—20th if you count the lockout season—in mid-September.

"I never thought I'd be playing this long, but why should I retire when I still love the game, and have been healthy enough? It all comes down to the same thing it's always come down to—passion for the game," Teemu said. "You either have it or you don't."

Anaheim offered Teemu $4 million for the season, which was his highest salary since 2004. While he probably could have gotten more elsewhere, the Ducks were the only choice for him.

According to Syvahuoko, it's a miracle his friend could play not just one, but three more seasons with that knee. He believed Selanne would need major surgery after retirement to have his leg aligned or have a knee replacement.

"Before the major 2004 surgery, my left knee was at 40 percent of what it could be, and between 2005 and 2011 at 100 percent. After that, maybe 85 percent. My right knee's always been at 100 percent," Teemu said.

His 20th season became another memorable one.

A week before he re-signed with the Ducks, Teemu woke up to the news of a Kontinental Hockey League (KHL) team's plane having crashed in Russia. He turned on his phone and his worst fears were confirmed. The plane that carried Lokomotiv Yaroslavl to its regular season opener had crashed, claiming the entire team. His phone was flooded with messages from all over the world, and he went through the names in his head.

"I remembered right away that Ruslan Salei had signed with them, but I also heard that he had traveled to Minsk early to meet with his parents. Unfortunately, that wasn't true," he said.

The Belarusian defenseman had been a Duck for a decade and was a good friend. He had a house in Anaheim and had been skating with the Ducks that fall. "He told me he'd play one more season in the KHL and then settle in California."

Two other friends also lost their lives. Forward Igor Korolev was a teammate in Winnipeg in 1995, and Latvian defenseman Karlis Skrastins was with Teemu on the Avalanche in 2003–04. "I couldn't believe it. I was in a state of shock for days," Teemu said.

A week after he agreed to terms with the Ducks, the team traveled to Finland for part of its training camp, an exhibition game against Jokerit, and its regular season opener against the Buffalo Sabres as part of the NHL Premiere 2011 event.

Again, Selanne was a great ambassador. "It was a great week. I took the guys boating and to the smoke saunas."

While that part of the visit to Finland was enjoyable, what wasn't fun was dealing with coach Randy Carlyle, who put his players through an intense training camp once again.

"We lost our legs again. I still don't understand why he had to drive the players to the ground during training camp. I'm sure that was why we didn't make the playoffs," said Selanne.

The Ducks beat Jokerit in a sold-out arena and fans gave their hero a standing ovation. Anaheim opened the season in Helsinki against Buffalo and lost 4–1. Then the Ducks were off to Stockholm and beat the New York Rangers 2–1 in a shootout.

The Ducks didn't find their legs during the fall and Carlyle, the coach who had won the team's Stanley Cup, was fired on November 30.

Bruce Boudreau, who had been fired by the Washington Capitals at the end of the previous season, replaced him.

Teemu's season had the makings of a mediocre and forgettable tour of duty had there not been a few highlights along the way.

In March, Teemu picked up two assists in a game against the Colorado Avalanche and passed Jari Kurri on the NHL's all-time scoring list, becoming the top-scoring Finn ever with 1,399 regular season points.

Selanne was also named to the All-Star Game, but he declined. Corey Perry represented the Ducks instead.

The biggest highlight was his return to Winnipeg, the place where his NHL career started.

The Atlanta Thrashers, an expansion team that had begun play in 1999, had made the playoffs just once in their 11 years in Georgia, and the franchise was losing money. In January 2011, court documents revealed the team had lost $130 million since 2005, and the owners were looking to sell the team.

In May, it was announced the team had been sold to True North Sports and Entertainment and that the Thrashers would be relocated to Winnipeg. The new team got the old name, which somewhat muddied the waters because the original Jets had moved and become the Phoenix (now Arizona) Coyotes.

Teemu's first game in Winnipeg in mid-December was the hottest ticket in the city, as everyone was excited about their favorite star's return to Manitoba.

Selanne, too, was pumped: "The feeling was mutual. My whole family, including my mother, flew to Winnipeg ahead of me. We had a game in Chicago the night before."

Sirpa and the kids enjoyed every second of their visit. They stayed at the Leipsics' while Teemu's mother, Liisa, spent the night with her friend Liisa Nygard Johnson, the sister of Finnish-born fashion mogul Peter Nygard.

The Ducks arrived in Winnipeg in the middle of the night and hundreds of fans met them at the airport.

Selanne's visit in Winnipeg was short but sweet.

"We got to the hotel at three in the morning, and it was really cold, but the fans had stayed there waiting for me. I bet they woke up everybody in the hotel when they yelled my name," he said.

It was the first time Selanne had been in Winnipeg since November 2004, when he had been in town to say goodbye to the Winnipeg Arena, in a special ceremony that featured an AHL game between the Manitoba Moose and the Utah Grizzlies.

"That was emotional, too. After all, I played the first four seasons of my NHL career there."

Selanne was celebrated with six standing ovations: during the pre-game skate, a pregame video greeting with Teemu's record-breaking 54th goal on the Jumbotron; his first shift; during the first commercial break when they showed another highlight reel on the videoboard; postgame when Teemu stayed on the ice by himself; and when he was named the first star of the game.

"Every time I touched the puck, the crowd cheered. When another Duck had the puck, they booed him. I felt everybody's eyes on me already when we had the pregame skate," he said with a chuckle.

The Jets won the game 5–3, and Teemu had two assists.

"It was such an emotional night. I was in tears when Teemu took the ice. The Jets made it such a great event," Sirpa said. "And it was wonderful to have our kids see how the fans loved their father there. We also were able to show them our old house in Winnipeg."

Sirpa wasn't the only one wiping tears off her cheeks.

Teemu's mother, Liisa, had spent a lot of time in town early on when Sirpa was at school in Finland and Teemu was alone in Winnipeg. "Winnipeg's such an important place for me that I was crying all the time. I have so many friends there," she said.

As for the kids, the fact they had the chance to play hockey outside made it even more special.

"We played hockey on an outdoor rink every day, and even after the game we played some more on the pond behind the Leipsic house," Eemil said.

His knee problems in check, Selanne played all 82 regular season games and scored 26 goals and had 66 points to lead the team in scoring for the first time in five years.

The Ducks missed the playoffs again, and the retirement watch was back in full swing. Even if Teemu wanted to take some time to think about whether to keep playing, there were constant reminders. Some started before the season ended and others picked up when it was over.

Selanne chuckles now when he thinks about how much fuss was made about whether he was done once and for all.

"After every year I tried to retire, but the thing for me it was almost a joke, one more year and one more year. I always would say, 'This is my last year,' or 'I think this is my last year,' but for me that is how it felt," he said.

"In the summertime I was so committed and I knew I would do everything, there would be no shortcuts and then I would be done. And then after the season, I would take a month off and see how I feel. Then after a month I started feeling I wasn't ready. That is how I was motivated and for seven years it worked great.

"That is why I say the guys who sign seven-year deals, they start to feel comfortable. They can't push the way they should, the mind automatically switches. If the guys made one year at a time they would be so much better. But I understand they all want the security."

Members of the media, and diehard fans, started to follow him to make sure they'd be there if he let it slip his career was over.

"I remember how other players asked Teemu for sticks and he'd always sign them personally to us. I have at least five 'last-game sticks' from Teemu," Ryan Getzlaf said with a laugh.

When Selanne played his last regular season game, cameras followed him from the moment he left home to drive to the game until the moment he left his stall in the dressing room to go back home.

Fans held signs that read ONE MORE YEAR in the stands, leaving a few people wondering whether they were made the year before, or the year before that.

But he wasn't done. He signed the biggest contract of his "second" NHL career, a one-year deal worth $4.5 million, in July 2012.

"While I'm still amazed by his speed and skill level, it's Teemu's love for the game and his teammates that makes him so special," said general manager Bob Murray. "Anaheim is where he belongs."

"Age is a funny thing," Selanne said at a news conference to announce the signing. "A lot of times, I don't really feel 42. It all depends how good you feel, how healthy you are, and how much passion you have for the game. That is why I still enjoy the game. It's fun to go to the rink every morning. It sounds pretty old, but mentally, I am still the same level as Getzlaf and those other guys."

He said he wasn't thinking about his stats, but you can be sure he was aware of how his 663 goals were just two behind Czech star Jaromir Jagr, the all-time leading European goal scorer in the NHL.

But it wasn't all sunny days.

The dark cloud over what most expected would be his last season—it was definitely going to be his last—was the collective bargaining talks between the NHL and the Players' Association.

"Had the entire season gotten canceled like in 2004–05, my career would have been over," Teemu said.

Once again, management locked out the players and once again, there was speculation, especially in Finland, whether Teemu would return home and play for Jokerit. Selanne however, stayed in California.

"It's possible that I would have signed with Jokerit if the NHL season had been wiped out. Maybe this time they would have liked to have me," he said, recalling the fiasco from years previous.

Selanne and Saku Koivu stayed in the US, and the Finns worked out on their own. The NHL teams forbade their coaches and trainers from assisting locked-out players.

"It was pretty frustrating. There were times when Saku and I were the only ones on the ice. It reminded me how things were at the beginning of my career, when I had to buy and take care of the gear myself. Having wet hockey equipment on the floor for four months made me appreciate the equipment managers' work even more."

NHL players were deeply bitter toward league commissioner Gary Bettman, and they thought he was about to destroy yet another season. Revenue sharing was the NHL's main objective in contract talks, and the players didn't think it was a big enough reason not to play.

"We were ready to play under the old CBA rules while they negotiated the new one. That would have been fair to the fans. It seemed to me the owners wanted to destroy the game," said Teemu.

With no hockey, he had more time to think about what was going on in the world. In 2012, he wasn't as active on social media as he is today. Well, not officially, anyway.

"He was there in a way, always making comments on what happens on my Facebook page," Sirpa said with a laugh.

He often asked his buddies to tweet something, and then loved seeing Twitter's reactions. There certainly were reactions when, for example, he told his friend to start a rumor about Teemu signing with the Jets.

Other than that, all he could do was wait.

In early November, the NHL canceled the Winter Classic, its marquee event scheduled for New Year's Day with more than 100,000 people expected to watch the Red Wings and the Maple Leafs play outdoors at Michigan Stadium in Ann Arbor.

Clearly, the entire season was in danger.

Later that month, the All-Star Game, scheduled for late January in Columbus, Ohio, was canceled. On December 20, the league canceled games through January 14, which became the final deadline for there to be time for a shortened but meaningful regular season.

The negotiations picked up speed right after New Year's Day, and on January 6, Bettman and NHLPA executive director Donald Fehr announced they had a tentative agreement. The NHL Board of Governors ratified the agreement three days later.

GAME ON

———

THE PUCK DROPPED ON THE SHORTENED NHL SEASON on January 19, 2013, giving players a few days to report to a seven-day training camp. The regular season schedule was shortened to 48 games. The Ducks played their 48 games in 99 days and had nine back-to-back games.

"It was the toughest spring of my career. Compared to a regular 82-game schedule, there was no time for recovery," said Selanne.

He jumped off to a great start, scoring twice and adding four assists, in the Ducks' first game, a 7–3 triumph over the Vancouver Canucks. The oldest player in the league still had it, and his advanced hockey age came up regularly, even when Selanne least expected it. One time Cam Fowler, the Ducks' 20-year-old defenseman, introduced Teemu to his parents.

"Cam said, 'Here's my mother, she's the same age as you.' We laughed," Teemu said.

He also recalled the funniest yell during the lockout-shortened season. "A middle-aged man yelled, 'Hey, Selanne, let the kids play!'"

Despite the grueling schedule, Teemu was determined to make the most of it. His new pregame music was Dire Straits' "Sultans of Swing," which he played while driving to the Honda Center.

Teemu wasn't the only busy hockey player in the Selanne household that year. Eemil and Eetu were playing high school hockey and their cousin, Sirpa's nephew Tatu Hiltunen, who lived with the Selannes, played on the same school team. Eetu and Leevi also played with the junior Ducks. Veera's sports were tennis, gymnastics, and horseback riding.

"The highlight of the year was when the boys' school team, the Santa Margarita Eagles, won the national high school title in the final tournament in Florida," said the proud father. Leevi won the same title with Eagles in the 2018 tournament.

Selanne had another four-point night in St. Louis in Anaheim's 11th game of the season and became the oldest player in NHL history to have two four-point games in one season. But the points didn't come like they used to, and Selanne found himself in a position he had never been before.

"I was prepared to see my ice time shrink. It was natural with the tough schedule. But I didn't expect to be pulled out of the first power play unit," he said.

Teemu had always been Anaheim's key player on the power play, and he'd been sent over the boards to play 4-on-4 in the final minutes of the game and in overtime.

"Now, I was on the bench. I did get power play minutes with our second unit, but it wasn't the same."

Teemu had amassed 455 points in 462 games since 2005, and, according to several analysts, he was one of the greatest power play specialists in the history of the game.

Even if he had lost a step—which at 42 was certainly possible— surely the Ducks could have used his experience on the power play. When Selanne was on the first unit, the Ducks' power play had been among the best in the league. After coach Bruce Boudreau pulled Teemu, it was among the weakest.

Saku Koivu, who was having a great season, grabbed a spot in the top unit.

"Saku deserved his spot there, but we both should have been in the first unit," Selanne said.

Coach Boudreau didn't explain his logic, and Teemu didn't ask, but the move seemed strange. And when Boudreau wouldn't use him even when the Ducks had a two-man advantage, Selanne had had enough.

"People were saying that the team had to get ready for life after me, and let young players take some responsibility, but the NHL is not social work. I'm sure I could have helped the team. It was pointless to keep me on the bench," he said.

"I had heard stories that on his other teams, Boudreau wanted older players to play support roles rather than play to their strengths. I started feel the same way after a while."

"I was the leading scorer on the team, and after 20 games, all of a sudden my ice time dropped to 12, 13 minutes from 17, 20, for no reason. If I was playing bad I would understand, but I was the leading scorer on the team. But we were winning."

The Ducks made the playoffs in 2013, but were eliminated in the first round by Detroit. They took the Red Wings to Game 7 but lost 3–2. Teemu played fewer than 13:00 a game.

"After the Detroit series, Boudreau apologized to me for not giving me top-unit power play time. He said he had planned to use me in the second round. Unbelievable," Teemu said.

He scored 12 goals and had 24 points in 46 regular season games, and added three points in seven playoff games, to climb on the all-time scoring list. He also became the Finn with the most NHL regular season games played, passing Teppo Numminen.

Teemu was upset, but he thought things would get better.

He was wrong.

Originally, the 2012–13 season was supposed to have been his last. His decision to play "one more year" surprised everybody, even people in his closest circles.

"I wasn't sure about it myself, but I kept on working out like I had in the past and skated several times a week. What made it more fun was that Eetu, who was 15, worked out with me," he said.

The death of his longtime agent, Don Baizley, clouded his summer. Baizley died on June 27, of nonsmokers' lung cancer at home in Winnipeg. He was 71.

"Don was much more than an agent for me, he was a great friend and a very special person. He supported me like my American dad, a mentor and supporter whom I could trust with everything," Selanne said.

Baizley was the pro's pro of player agents. He was powerful; influential; and immensely well liked by players, agents, and general managers, and he never tooted his own horn. When he died following a 14-month illness, people paid tribute by saying there was not a better man in the great game of hockey.

Baizley represented a who's who of clients, including Selanne, Joe Sakic, Jari Kurri, Peter Forsberg, Paul Kariya, Teppo Numminen, Theo Fleury, Saku Koivu, Anders Hedberg, and Ulf Nilsson. At one point in the 1990s, he represented almost all the Finns and Swedes in the NHL.

When Kariya was asked why he hired Baizley as his agent when he was a youngster leaving the University of Maine for the NHL and being pursued by an army of guys who wanted to do his bidding, Kariya said it was because "every agent said if you don't want me, then you should get Don Baizley. So I did."

"The most important thing is to make the players trust you," Baizley said before he passed in 2013. "If you lose that trust, everybody will know it and you lose your credibility.

"In the early days, the clubs did not want to pay anything and the player asked for millions. That was the starting point for negotiations.

When player salaries were published for everyone to see in the early 1990s, that made my job much easier.

"In the 1970s, club owners hated agents. They thought that we were destroying hockey."

They were wrong.

Baizley knew when he first met Selanne that he was a special player who would have a massive impact in the NHL.

"Teemu was a very positive, easygoing guy. He is upbeat and I don't think I have ever seen him being sad," Baizley said. "He has a special gift."

"The fact he came back after the season he had in Colorado and came back at the top of his sport, that is a story nobody could believe. It was unbelievable."

Baizley's funeral was held at Winnipeg's MTS Centre, and approximately 1,000 people from all corners of the hockey map came to pay their respects.

There was a moment during the service that speaks volumes about how hockey fans in Winnipeg loved the Jets and the impact Baizley had on the team, and the city itself, by being at the forefront of bringing Europeans to the NHL.

Selanne and Kurri were walking back to their hotel after the funeral, sharing memories of their friend, when a family stopped its car at a red light at an intersection, got out, ran over to them, and asked them to take a photo of the family. Within seconds, about 50 people surrounded Selanne and Kurri, wanting a selfie with them and telling them how proud of Baizley they were and how thankful they were he brought stars like the Finns to the NHL.

"This is a very special example of how Winnipeggers are. They are just great people and great hockey fans," said Selanne.

Selanne had been Baizley's client longer than any other player, but now he had to negotiate his last contract on his own.

The desire to play was still there. The itch needed scratching.

He even attended Finland's summer meeting for Olympic candidates—"just in case. Better safe than sorry."

He had a lot on his mind.

When he thought about which teams he would like to play for, the Jets were part of the group. He remembered how the fans greeted him when he returned to the city in 2011 and how much he enjoyed playing there when he joined the NHL.

"Somehow I felt that finishing my career where I started sounded so uniquely possible, especially given how my role on Boudreau's team didn't feel fair," Teemu said.

"I was still motivated to play. I also wanted to play in the Olympics and in the outdoor game against the Kings at Dodger Stadium," he said, referring the NHL's newly established Stadium Series.

Ducks general manager Bob Murray had implied Selanne would always have a place on the team for as long as he wanted. Teemu decided to make up his mind after meeting with Boudreau.

"I said that I'd only come back if I felt I was going to get a fair chance. That I'd get the ice time I'd deserve. Boudreau promised me that I'd get power play minutes, first or second unit, and that I'd average about 15 minutes a game. He even told me he'd like to see me score my 700th goal."

The Selannes flew back to California from Finland in August, as usual. On August 30, he signed a one-year deal with the Ducks worth $2 million, and he and the team decided to have some fun with the official announcement.

The Ducks and Selanne uploaded a video to YouTube that shows a relaxed Selanne teeing off for a round of golf. He grows frustrated as he flubs one shot after another. In the last minute of the video, Teemu has a short chip to the green, but his shot ends up in the water. He tosses the club in the water and then the golf bag, only to realize he left his phone and keys in the bag.

He jumps in, wades to the bag, retrieves the phone, and places a call. "Hi, Bob [Murray, Ducks general manager], it's Teemu. Yeah, I'm coming back. . .but this is it. This is my final one," he says.

The video went viral and has been viewed more than 3 million times. The news of Teemu's comeback echoed around the league, and it was obvious that the 2013–14 season was going to be a farewell tour.

As is customary for Teemu, he got off to a good start, getting four points in his first five games, and his ice time was above the 15:00 Boudreau had promised. Then, in his fifth game, it dropped to 11:58. And that's how it went all season.

In March, there was a five-game stretch during which his ice time was never under 15:00, but there were also games in which he played less than 11:00.

It seemed that the longer the season went, the less ice time he saw, and in the end he averaged 14:00 a game.

To save on the wear and tear of his 43-year-old body, Boudreau suggested Teemu not play back-to-back games. Teemu was in agreement, but with one suggestion: "The plan sounded good but not if I play less than 13:00 a game," he said.

"I sat down with Bruce before I signed and I said, 'Bruce, I will come back only if you promise me if I am better than the young guys, you play me more,' and he said okay. And the same thing happened. First game, I get four points and things are going well. Then he takes me off the first power play, and I am like, this is not fair. It was the same as I felt in Colorado. Inside, it really hurt me."

All that brought with it the longest goalless streak in his career. Early in the season Teemu went 19 games—more than a month and a half—without scoring and picked up just one assist in that time. His pointless streak was 16 games.

And if that wasn't enough, Philadelphia Flyers defenseman Luke Schenn's stick hit Selanne in the mouth in late October, forcing him to miss three games. He lost a denture and received 40 stitches.

"The mouth guard saved me from getting a fracture, and I was lucky not to get hit in the lower jaw, where I had three metal plates due to an old injury," he added.

During the fall, Selanne vented his frustration to his closest friends via texts that aren't suitable for print. By the end of November, Syvahuoko started to get really worried.

"Teemu sent me the angriest text message I'd ever seen," he said.

The fans couldn't have known about any of this because, in front of the media, Teemu was the same old positive fellow he had always been, talking about the team—not himself.

"We keep winning, that's the most important thing. Sure, I haven't got as many points as I'd like but I have nothing to complain about," he told Finnish public broadcasting company Yle.

The reality gap couldn't have been wider.

But there was light at the end of the tunnel. Or, a tiny match. Well. . .there was hope.

"I met with Team Finland head coach Erkka Westerlund in Florida in mid-November and he told me I'd be on the Olympic team if I just wanted to play in one more tournament," Teemu said.

Keijo Sailynoja, one of Teemu's oldest friends, had never visited him in California, but in late November—after Syvahuoko had gotten the angry text—he joined Syvahuoko and his daughters on a week-long trip to Coto de Caza.

"I had never seen Teemu as deflated and hopeless as he was then. He was angry and disappointed and he thought it was the coach's fault. When I saw what was going on there, I understood him," Sailynoja said.

"I'm proud of the way he kept his inner feelings from the fans, the reporters, and his teammates."

In January, Selanne had the chance to play in the Stadium Series outdoor game at Dodger Stadium in front of 54,099 spectators in mild weather. The temperature was that of a nice spring day in Finland, 17°C (62°F). He picked up an assist.

The Ducks' power play continued to be among the worst in the league, but Boudreau refused to give Selanne, who was one of the top power play specialists in NHL history, a chance on the top unit. "This really frustrated me," Teemu said.

"The Ducks had always been one of the best power play teams, and we have had a lot of pride to keep it that way. I was hoping that Getzlaf would go to bat and help me force Boudreau to keep me on the first unit. Our first unit had been so solid, with great chemistry, and it sounded almost crazy to break up that unit," Selanne said.

Getzlaf was not thrilled when he was told Teemu thought he didn't do enough to help him get more ice time.

"Teemu doesn't know everything that goes on. He doesn't know how many times I had conversations about him in the last two years, to help him, to try and get him to where he wanted to be," he said in 2014.

"As a captain, it's my job to weed through things that I can go to the coach with, and things that I can't. Teemu doesn't know all the discussions that I've had about him, and there's been many times when I've went to bat for him, and there are some times when I have to step away and just let the coach and GM make their decision."

"Power play is not science, it is an art," Teemu said. "You trust your instincts, rely on your creativity. Maybe Boudreau thought I was too inexperienced. Maybe he had checked the stats and noted that I had scored 25 power play goals in my career. . .only he had dropped a zero at the end." (Teemu scored 255 power play goals in his NHL career.)

Just before leaving for the Olympics, Selanne sat down with Boudreau again for a one-on-one meeting.

"He told me that I should make harder passes. I dropped my jaw. That was the end of the meeting."

The prospect of his final Olympic tournament brightened his outlook. "The Sochi tournament was my way out. Had there not been the Olympic tournament, I would have thrown in the towel midseason.

"My last year was so tough. I played on the third line, and then luckily there was the Sochi Olympics and that kept my mind fresh. Westerlund said, 'You will be on the first line in the Olympics,' and that is what I wanted to hear. I started doing extra things, and then in Sochi we played unbelievable."

Finland wasn't a favorite going into the tournament, especially when it lost both Koivu brothers—Mikko was injured and Saku declined an invitation—and Valtteri Filppula before the tournament. The Finnish offense wasn't considered the team's strength, at least on paper.

"The upside for me was that I got a bigger role. I got to play big power play minutes, and the rest is history," he said.

Westerlund made Selanne captain of the team that brought together three generations of Finnish players, and once again Finland surprised the experts by finishing third behind Canada and Sweden.

Westerlund had told him early on that he'd be a big part of the team.

"My original idea for our first line was Filppula–Mikko Koivu–Teemu," he said.

With both Filppula and Koivu out due to injuries, Westerlund put Selanne on the same line with 18-year-old Aleksander Barkov and 21-year-old Mikael Granlund. Just as Teemu had read Jari Kurri's book when he was a boy, Mikael Granlund's most cherished book was the book Teemu's father Ilmari had written about Selanne in the early 1990s.

"I must have read it 10 times," Granlund said. "I get chills when I think about the tournament. It was my first Olympic tournament and I got to play with my biggest idol."

Barkov was injured in the tournament's second game, but the Granlund-Selanne connection worked wonders.

Finland beat Russia in the quarterfinal 3–1. Selanne scored the game-winner, assisted by Granlund, while Granlund scored the final goal, assisted by Selanne.

In the semifinal, the Swedes squeezed out a 2–1 win and went on to the final against Canada, which Canada won.

Finland took on the USA in the bronze-medal game and, as team captain, Selanne whipped his team into shape to win his last game in the Finnish national team jersey.

It worked.

Tuukka Rask recorded a shutout and Selanne scored twice as Finland beat the USA 5–0.

"The guys really did everything to get me the hat trick in the third period," he said.

Granlund picked up assists to Selanne's goals and led Finland in scoring. He finished third in tournament scoring with three goals and seven points in six games. Selanne had scored six points in six games and was voted to the First All-Star Team and named tournament MVP.

"I'm proud of the fact that Erkka had faith in me. I've had a Lion's heart for 26 years," Teemu said.

After his Stanley Cup championship, Teemu ranks the Olympic medals highest in his collection. Those medals and a small version of the Stanley Cup are the only ones visible at his Selanne Steak Tavern in California.

"When I was a kid and watched the Olympics, I always loved seeing somebody win a medal. Didn't matter what kind of a medal or in which sport. I just thought he or she had made it big. It was fantastic," Selanne said.

Just months before his retirement, Selanne had proved he could still play at the highest level of international hockey.

Back in Anaheim, things stayed the same and, if anything, his life became more miserable. He played in the first power play unit in his first game back, but after that, his ice time diminished again.

"I wanted to show the Ducks and Boudreau what I can do if you give me a chance. Then I come back and I play less. We won lots of games and then we lost three games, and I went to Boudreau and said 'Bruce, I don't feel this is fair. Give me a chance.'"

When Boudreau was asked about his veteran forward being the Olympic MVP, he said Selanne was the media's favorite, probably forgetting that the Hart Trophy, for example, is also voted for by representatives of the media.

"I really wanted to give him a piece of my mind, but didn't," Teemu said.

In March, Teemu went to Boudreau and asked for one last chance to play with Getzlaf and Perry on the first line. Boudreau was having a difficult time to find someone to play with them, and Selanne was confident he could keep pace.

"I asked Boudreau to give me three games to play with Getzlaf and Perry, and if I can't produce and I don't play well, you can give up on me," Teemu said.

In the first two games with Getzlaf and Perry, Selanne scored two goals and had four points, but it didn't matter. He soon found himself down the lineup again.

"The third game, after the first shift, I found myself back in the third line. I was like, 'Fuck this shit,' and that is how it was the rest of the year."

Toward the end of the season, each road game was another stop on Selanne's farewell tour.

In the 81st game of the regular season, the Los Angeles Kings organized one of the finest celebrations of Teemu and gave him a personalized surfboard as a present. But because of Boudreau's plan not to play Selanne in back-to-back games, he wasn't in the lineup against the Kings. The Ducks were going to close out the season at home against the Colorado Avalanche the next night.

Ryan Getzlaf didn't play in the last game, nursing injuries and resting before the playoffs, so Teemu captained the Ducks in the last regular season game of his storied career.

"It was a great honor and felt really good," he said.

The Ducks beat the Avalanche 3–2 in overtime and the crowd couldn't get enough of Teemu, who played more than 18:00.

After the game, Teemu stayed on the ice, and skated around to say goodbye and thank you to the fans. "These Ducks fans have been so special and so kind for me. I have always had so special relationship with our fans, and it feels so good to share all the great moments with them.

"And then I saw [Avalanche goalie and former teammate Jean-Sebastien Giguere] Jiggy on the Avs bench, and I grabbed him and we did couple of laps together and celebrated also his career, which was ending after the season as well. Jiggy has been huge part of Ducks organization and has been very important player for the fans. And for me truly a friend and teammate with whom I had great years together. And of course, he was the Stanley Cup–winning goalie for us."

The fans appreciated seeing their favorite NHL superstars, and the crowd went wild.

Selanne's last game even managed to get Paul Kariya, who retired in 2010, to make a rare public appearance. Kariya came to the Honda Center to watch his hockey soulmate play his last regular season game.

"I invited him to the game and he watched it from my suite together with another great friend, Joe Sakic. It meant a lot to me that these two guys were there," Teemu said.

Anaheim's regular season record was the best in franchise history. The Ducks won 54 games, won their division and the Western Conference, and finished second overall in the league, behind the Boston Bruins.

But Boudreau failed to guide the team past the second round. His Washington Capitals advanced to the second round twice in his four years as coach, and the Ducks had now gotten to the second round just once.

They won their first two home games in the first-round series against the Dallas Stars but lost Game 3 in Dallas 3–0. The next day

Teemu woke up to receive the biggest humiliation of his career when Bruce Boudreau made him a healthy scratch in Game 4. He had been a healthy scratch once before, in a playoff game in Colorado, but this was worse. He was in Anaheim, his happy place. His home.

According to Boudreau, the team needed more physicality, and Emerson Etem filled the Teemu-sized hole. The 22-year-old had played 29 regular season games for the Ducks and had 11 points.

Selanne was shocked but not completely surprised, since he had been benched for long stretches during Game 3, getting only 10:00 on the ice. Boudreau had told him about the change the day before Game 4.

Throughout his career, the even-mannered Selanne had never criticized a coach or even raised his voice, let alone screamed at one, but there is always a first time for everything.

He waited until the other players had left the ice and skated to where Boudreau was standing.

"And then I let it go. I told him exactly how I had been feeling, and I wanted to get answers why this has happened. He was trying to explain something but actually it didn't make sense to me at all.

"Bruce is a super-nice guy but there was something weird. There was something that he didn't tell me. I told him that if he wanted to win something, he needed me. Nobody else wanted to win as much as I did. Then I dissed him. I got two years' worth of frustration out of my system. I didn't feel good to say these things, but I felt I had to," Teemu said.

A few years later, Boudreau and Selanne sat down over a beer to see whether they could patch things up.

"I asked him to tell me what really happened. He said, 'Teemu, the only thing I could say is it wasn't all my decision.' He mentioned something that the scouts and GM were part of decision-making."

Boudreau later tried to lessen the tension with Teemu.

"Nobody likes hearing anything negative about themselves, so in that sense I'm a little disappointed," Boudreau told the media. "But I understand the frustration."

"I'm sure I'm going to see him again. And listen, he was one of my favorite guys. I've always liked him and admired him. I don't think anyone here has ever heard me say a bad word about him, ever. And that will continue."

The Stars won Game 4 in Dallas 4–2 and Teemu returned to the lineup for Game 5. The Ducks advanced to the second round against the Los Angeles Kings, but not much had changed in the coach's mind.

The Kings took away the Ducks' home-ice advantage by winning the first two games in Anaheim, but Teemu still didn't get more ice time.

Eemil Selanne, then 18, took to Twitter to support his father.

During the Stars series, he tweeted: "ROSTER MOVE: Bruce Boudreau has been reassigned to Norfolk Admirals (AHL)." He later deleted the tweet, but the message was already out there. The Selannes were on the warpath.

Sirpa was just as upset on social media, telling her Facebook friends the Ducks were going to be in big trouble.

The Ducks won three straight games against the Kings, first 3–2 with Selanne scoring what would be the last goal of his career, and then 2–0 and 4–3.

The Ducks had a chance to clinch the series, but the Kings won Game 6 at home 2–1.

Game 7 was either going to be a great triumph for the Ducks or the last game of Teemu's career. He didn't give any interviews the day before the game because he didn't want to distract the team.

"I didn't want anybody starting to think too much about some player's maybe last game or stuff. It's not about that, you know. It's all distractions. The focus should be this game, and only this game," he said after the morning skate.

The game turned out to be Teemu's last. . .and the furthest thing from a Ducks triumph. The Kings scored three unanswered goals in the first period. Teemu texted Sirpa, Syvahuoko, and his friend Mike Pagano during the first intermission: "[F-----g] joke."

Los Angeles won 6–2, sending Selanne into retirement bitter and frustrated.

He did get the farewell he deserved, though, as he was on the ice for the last 1:00 of play and the entire crowd, both Kings and Ducks fans, gave him a standing ovation. Both teams stayed on the ice after the game to pay their respects to the 43-year-old legend.

"I always remember the Kings players staying on the ice and clapping. It was so classy from their side. It was emotional and it was not the way I was thinking of going out. It was an emotional and melancholic moment. The Kings players were classy, every single one of them came to congratulate me on a great career," Teemu recalled.

He kept it together on the ice, but as he stepped off it and high-fived fans on his way to the tunnel, he saw his son Leevi in the crowd and burst into tears.

"I realized it was truly the end. I had to calm myself down for a while before going into the dressing room," he said.

Afterward, he spoke with the media patiently, but he kept his emotions to himself.

"It's been a fantastic journey and I could never have imagined, not even in my wildest fantasies, that I'd get to have a career like this. It's hard to understand that something I've done since I was a kid has now come to a sudden stop.

"There's nothing wrong in the relationship between Bruce Boudreau and me. We just have a difference of opinion on what kind of a player I am. I know I could still be a first-line player, but this is the right time to retire."

While Selanne was answering reporters' questions, his family and friends were waiting for him at the Jack Daniel's Old No. 7 restaurant at the Honda Center, and they were joined by Ducks player Saku Koivu and Francois Beauchemin.

And when Teemu joined them, he quickly summed up his feelings.

"This team deserved so much better. It was so disappointing to finish my career this way. I really believed that this team had all the tools to win the Stanley Cup," he said.

A couple days later, many of the players were surprised that the usual end-of-season exit meetings between individual players and the coach were off.

"It was the first time in my career that I didn't have an exit inter-view with a coach," Teemu said.

The Ducks at that time were built around Getzlaf and Perry, who had signed eight-year extensions in March 2013, and were the obvi-ous leaders of the team.

The Kings went on to win their second Stanley Cup in three years. California teams had won three Stanley Cups in eight years. Hockey's rise in California had begun with the trade that brought Wayne Gretzky to Los Angeles in 1988, but Teemu also played a significant role in making hockey a more popular sport in the region.

The architects of the Kings' Stanley Cup championship teams were, coincidentally, the same men who had traded for Teemu in San Jose in 2001: general manager Dean Lombardi and head coach Darryl Sutter.

Sutter, like Detroit Red Wings coach Mike Babcock the year ear-lier, was pleased when playing the Ducks that Selanne stayed on the bench. Hockey insiders compared Teemu to Jaromir Jagr, who's two years younger than Teemu and always got top power play minutes on the clubs he played for.

In his final season, Selanne scored nine goals and had 27 points in 64 games, and he added six points in 12 playoff games. His ice time in all 12 playoff games was under 15:00—under 11:00 in four of the games.

In 21 NHL seasons, he scored 684 goals and had 773 assists for 1,457 points in 1,451 regular season games. He played 130 playoff games and scored 44 goals and had 88 points.

In 2014, Teemu summed up his last season like this: "You're as good as your coach wants you to be. If we had any other coach, I'd still be playing. But I always look at the big picture and thank God there was Sochi. That saved my last season."

––––––––––––

On January 11, 2015, Selanne became the first player in Anaheim Ducks history to have his jersey retired. A touching presentation at the Honda Center in Anaheim showcased the genuineness of the Finnish Flash before his No. 8 jersey was raised to the rafters.

"I was waiting for this for a long time, and I knew it would be a very special and important night. I invited 60 friends from Finland and many more from North America to celebrate this special weekend with me. I have always said that this would not been possible without so many people's support, help, and love. And I was so happy to share this weekend with all of them.

"I didn't cry, but it was close," he said afterward. "The toughest part for my emotions was when I was walking down the stairs onstage. I think the whole thing just hit so hard. Plus, I had to concentrate so that I didn't fall down. But what a night. I never stop wondering at the impact with the people. It's all around me. It's very special.

"It was so special for my family, and a lot of other people too. It was a proud moment. I did not realize how big it was. They did it like nobody has done it before, and they really paid attention to details, every little detail. It was a special and memorable moment."

Perhaps the most poignant moment came when Selanne thanked his wife, Sirpa, who shed tears. Selanne then recognized his seven-year-old daughter, Veera, as "my princess" and said of his family, including sons Eemil, 18, Eetu, 17, and Leevi, 14, "You guys are my life."

He also talked about what the Orange County community has meant to him since he arrived in Anaheim following the trade from the Winnipeg Jets in February 1996 and what it meant for him and the Ducks to change the sports landscape there.

"People ask me, 'Was the 2007 Stanley Cup the biggest thing in my career?'" Selanne said. "I say, 'Yeah, but the biggest thing is we won it right here.' Thank you so much. This night is so special for me. I'm never going to forget this."

The honors kept coming.

The Finnish Ice Hockey Association retired his number from international competition in a memorable and emotional ceremony at the Hartwall Arena in Helsinki, the home arena of the Finnish Lions, on December 30, 2015, prior to a World Junior Championship game between Finland and Slovakia.

"It's been a wonderful year. First, the Anaheim Ducks retired my number in January, and now the Finnish federation did the same. I'm very grateful for that," Teemu said.

In January 2017, the NHL was in the midst of celebrating its centennial and, as part of the festivities, issued a list of the 100 greatest players ever to play. It was no shock to see Selanne named to its elite club. In describing Teemu's style of play, the NHL said the Finnish Flash was "a man who was a Ferrari on skates, a right wing with a stride as smooth and fluid as hot syrup; who moved so fast he would've left rubber if it were possible to do such a thing on a sheet of ice."

No kidding.

On May 21, 2017, Teemu was inducted into the International Ice Hockey Federation's Hall of Fame, and the recognition was also fitting. Teemu played in a record six Winter Olympics (1992, 1998, 2002, 2006, 2010, and 2014), winning three bronze medals and the 2006 silver medal. He was named Best Forward in Torino in 2006 and tournament MVP in Sochi in 2014. The fleet-footed right winger also owns a 1999 IIHF Ice Hockey World Championship silver medal and a 2008 bronze.

On November 12, 2017, Selanne received the ultimate individual honor when he took his place in the Hockey Hall of Fame in Toronto along with former Ducks linemate Paul Kariya and Dave Andreychuk, Danielle Goyette, and Mark Recchi. Selanne joined Jari Kurri as the only players from Finland in the hall.

"When I was a little boy growing up in Finland, if someone would have told me what kind of career I would have it would be hard to believe. All I wanted to do was play sports and especially hockey," he said in his acceptance speech.

Selanne was particularly pleased to go into the hall with Kariya. After all, the duo dazzled in 308 career games together with the Mighty Ducks, accounting for 35 percent of the team's goals from 1995–96 to 2000–01. "They were good individually," said fellow inductee Mark Recci, a contemporary. "But they were so, so good together."

The two direct opposites in personality became both close friends and superstars in the NHL.

"As big an honor as it is, it is even bigger going in with Paul. My goal was to play on the top league in Finland and my dream was to play on the national team and my fantasy was the NHL. The NHL felt like it was too far."

"The chemistry that we had, it was magical every night," Teemu said.

Added Kariya: "If I didn't get the opportunity to play with him, I wouldn't be in the Hall of Fame, so I'm very thankful."

On the day the hall announced its new members, Kariya was surfing, and when he checked his phone when he returned home, there were 20 messages.

"The first one was from Teemu. I checked his call and in the highest-pitched voice I have ever heard, it was like screaming, 'We are going into the hall together.' He was in Finland and I was like, what is he saying? What is going on? Then it was, 'Oh my God.'"

"We will always be brothers," Kariya said during his acceptance speech. "In this life and the next."

"For me, by far the best player I ever played [with]," Selanne said of Kariya. "I have learned so much from you. You and I always joked that half my [time] I played hockey and half I tried to make you into a normal person."

Kariya then told a funny story about planning a celebration with his girlfriend along with Teemu and Sirpa to show how similar the two are.

"We were discussing a party we were going to have here. Teemu was arguing with Sirpa about decorations and stuff, and when Teemu would answer Sirpa, my girlfriend would look over at me and say, this is exactly you. She said, you and Teemu think identically. So, when people say we are opposite personalities, he is very open and I am quieter, but we think about life the same, and not just about hockey.

"We think about life exactly the same. It is how we got about our lives is totally different but our views on life are identical. It is probably how our parents raised us. If you talk about something politically or something away from hockey, I can guarantee we think the same way."

The funny thing is, when Selanne was sent to Anaheim, the skeptics said it would never work out with Kariya because they were so different. Yet it did, gloriously. The two direct opposites in personality became both close friends and NHL superstars.

"I played with a lot of players, but I learned the most from Paul and Joe Sakic. I showed up at the rink and I did everything the right way, but I did not know how to live as an athlete until I met those two guys," Teemu said. "Paul's commitment to hockey off the ice was, well, I told him he takes it way too seriously. I learned so much from him, and he made me focus and do so much more extra.

"We were like a team. We watched tapes together. After every shift we talked and sometimes we were yelling at each other. We were like brothers."

In his Hall of Fame speech, Selanne said this of Kariya: "Everything you have done for me I'm so proud. Thank you so much."

———————

NHL players may not work eight hours a day, but they work 28 days out of 30 in each month for most of the year. They compete every day, and they push themselves to the edge of their limits while traveling 100 days a year, through jet lag and injuries.

It takes mental toughness to do that.

And to do it for 20 years?

Columbus Blue Jackets general manager Jarmo Kekalainen knows exactly what it takes. "The difference between a good player and a great player is that a great player stays loose and relaxed even under the most stressful situations. They can handle failure better and they know how to bounce back.

"Besides his natural physical attributes, Teemu's biggest strength was his ability to instinctively enjoy playing the game. He had the same passion, and looseness, whether he was playing road hockey or in the Stanley Cup Final or the Olympic Final."

There's one trait that made Selanne truly special. He said he remembers every single goal he's scored.

"I simply went through every game in my mind before I went to bed and rescored all the goals in my head. I also went through the chances that I had missed and thought about what I should have done instead. That's why they stick to my mind," he said.

"I'm sure it helped me with scoring. All those chances and replayed chances stayed in my mind, and I've always said that when you get the chance, you have to react instinctively, and not think at all. So, I study the game."

And as a goal scorer, he encourages young players to focus on scoring.

"Pure goal scorers are often considered selfish players and I wish they'd be cherished a little more. They have a huge responsibility for a team's success, but I feel that it's often considered underrated. Sometimes I think people look down on players who think of goals first.

"I don't even know if goal scoring was taught anywhere before I set up my goal-scoring academy, Selanne Academy. Even in the NHL, I thought we should have had goal-scoring drills once a week. You don't get many chances to score in a game but when you do, you have to be ready," Teemu said.

The Selanne Academy has developed an excellent reception in Finland, where all the best U16 national team forwards have been guided by their idol since 2016. The first Selanne Academy students, born in 2001, included Kaapo Kakko, who became an instant hero in his homeland when he scored the winning goal in Finland's 3–2 victory over the United States at the 2019 U20 World Championship Final.

It was the third gold medal in six years and fifth in tournament history for Finland, one more than the Americans. The Finns previously triumphed in 1987, 1998, 2014, and 2016. Winning is becoming a habit now.

"There are very good young goal scorers and players from Finland coming. I am very proud of them," Teemu said.

As a player, Teemu worked on his scoring touch, even if it meant he had to have his business manager on the ice, passing him pucks, in the summer.

Raimo Summanen, former NHL player and former Team Finland head coach, is amazed at what Selanne accomplished. "Scoring goals is the biggest challenge in hockey, and if you can be a great scorer for 10 years, it's a bigger feat than being a playmaker for 10 years."

Summanen notes that it wasn't just Teemu's willingness to work on his scoring that made him a special player.

"He worked on his flexibility by stretching and working out like crazy. He was like a Cheshire cat, always smiling, but ready to jump at any second. He looks like a careless, happy-go-lucky guy but underneath the surface, he's a tough athlete," he said.

Teemu has always stretched and made sure his body was in the best possible shape, but as he grew older, he had to take new constraints into consideration.

"I learned to listen to my body. I made up my mind about the day's workout in the morning. Getting enough recovery time is the key," he said.

His friends still wonder about his flexibility, which is a result of that daily stretching. When he was rooming with Teppo Numminen in Winnipeg, he tried to get his fellow Jet to stretch every evening with him.

"I did it one night and was minus-3 in the next game. That was the end of my stretching," Numminen said with a smile.

Stretching wasn't the only thing that kept Teemu's legs in shape.

He also started using active release technique therapy, which eases soft tissue injuries, in 2006, and deep tissue manipulation that uses massage, trigger point, electrical modalities, and ultrasound to treat soft tissue problems. They became a part of his weekly routine.

His teammates couldn't believe how he could watch TV just minutes before the game, only to turn into a tough competitor for the opening faceoff.

"While the others were focusing on the game with towels over their heads, I was watching *Baywatch*. My full focus was on when the puck dropped," he said. "Had it been up to me, I would have gone to the arena only 30 minutes before the warm-up. I hate having nothing to do. I'm sure I was the fastest player to put on the equipment in the entire league," he said.

Teemu captained the Mighty Ducks for a while and was the Team Finland captain in the Salt Lake City and Sochi Olympics, but he wasn't the ideal captain. He was the ideal alternate captain, though, and an important part of any team's leadership group.

"Teemu is more of a prankster than a team captain," said his old junior coach Leo Aikas.

Former Finland head coach Hannu Aravirta feels a team's leading goal scorer isn't always the best choice for captain, anyway.

"A pure goal scorer has so much going on inside his own head, especially if the pucks aren't going in," he said.

Then again, Selanne did wear the "C" on Finland's national team.

"When Teemu opened his mouth, everybody listened. He matured into an excellent captain toward the end of his career," said Erkka Westerlund, Finland's head coach in Sochi.

Talking to people about Selanne, one phrase often comes up again and again: "He's a great player, but an even better human being." It's hard to imagine getting higher praise. Both fans and media have voted Teemu "the most fan-friendly player in NHL history."

"If an ad agency had to come up with the perfect athlete, they'd present Teemu Selanne. He's the ultimate pro: well-behaved, handles everybody respectfully, and has the movie-star good looks," said Brian Hayward.

Hayward said the locals didn't understand how Teemu and Sirpa could have a big sign saying SELANNE outside their house. After all, he was a celebrity.

"We were used to pro athletes hiding and keeping a low profile, and here was this Finnish superstar who played road hockey with the kids on his street," he said.

"I don't know anybody else who loves life as much as Teemu does," added Kariya.

Selanne was a goal scorer who could play tough, but he would not play dirty. That's why he was the finalist for the Lady Byng Trophy (for sportsmanship and gentlemanly play) five times, finishing third three times and as runner-up twice.

"Fortunately, I didn't win it. The award's description is a disgrace to the game. Several GMs told me that whoever wins the Lady Byng gets traded immediately," Teemu said with a laugh.

Alpo Suhonen, the first European head coach in the NHL, likens his countryman to Peter Pan, the boy who refuses to grow up. The NHL was his Neverland.

"Teemu had an unbelievable talent with an unbelievable capacity to work. He's also an unbelievable social talent who has an endless need to be accepted, together with an eternal longing to be loved," Suhonen said.

"He's a narcissist, in a good way, because his positive sides are more dominant than the negative sides. He has the rare ability to turn his narcissistic energy into something good, which is also a form of talent," he added.

Teemu wanted to be in the spotlight, he wanted to perform, he wanted to be admired by the fans, and he wanted to score. He wanted to be popular.

"The same happened outside the arena, where each fan got his full attention, while other stars drove behind them in their fancy cars," Suhonen said.

"Teemu is a combination of the lightness of being. The ability to not recognize his mortality or any other limitations is highlighted in him. He thinks everything is possible."

Suhonen said Selanne is unique in that sense, and not only among hockey players.

"I think you'd have to look for them in the entertainment business, in rock 'n roll, or in the movies to find anything similar. Then again, sport is really close to performance culture, even if sports people often don't want to see it that way," Suhonen said.

PART FOUR

FATHER, HUSBAND, BROTHER, BUDDY, BUSINESSMAN, RETIREE

WHEN TEEMU SELANNE THINKS BACK TO HIS CHILDHOOD, he remembers playing outdoors, freedom, and the feeling of brotherhood. As an adult, he holds on to similar feelings. Thanks to hockey, he's a wealthy man and enjoys a wonderful lifestyle.

But his logic of life is still the same. The more friends he has and the more things are happening around him, the better.

"I don't like being alone. I've always liked being a part of a herd," he said.

The doors to the Selanne home have always been and will always be open to friends, year-round, both in Finland and in California—just like they were open in his childhood home in Espoo. Sirpa has had to learn to deal with an ongoing carousel of visitors.

"Sometimes I feel like I'm running an inn. During the summers in Finland, we don't have a lot of time to spend just among the family.

Teemu just can't say no when he's asked to do something, and yet, that time is always away from me and the kids," she said.

Now, it's not like his friends are always asking him to do things. He asks his friends. Selanne likes to know that somebody is always ready to go golfing or boating with him or can come to their house to sit in the sauna—on short notice, when he calls.

Selanne's posse has had a different lineup depending on where they have been in their lives. Those whose spouses have wanted to spend more time together have dropped out. Those who don't mind planning their summers according to his schedule are still there.

"Sometimes I think Teemu wants to spend more time with his friends than his family—he's always had a court of his own around him," said his mother, Liisa.

"During the season I don't have much time for my friends. Between season ending and season starting is the only time that I can spend with my friends," Teemu said.

Everything around him is like a rite, a holy ceremony in which everybody tries to please the master to the best of his or her ability. If Teemu likes a certain artist, they all like the same artist. If Teemu wakes up in the middle of the night and wants to play golf, that's exactly what everybody else wants to do, too. He'll never get enough of being the center of attention.

In short: Teemu does what he wants to do, and others do what he wants to do.

There's no point in asking him to visit your summer cottage, because he hates being at the cottage. So Sirpa and the kids visit her parents' place without him.

"I've always chosen carefully what to put my energy in. If I'm not into something, no money in the world can make me do it. But if my four-wheeler runs out of gas in the middle of the night, I'll be happy to walk 10 miles to get some," Teemu said.

Teemu lives his life to the max and he loves every second of it. He's a free spirit who navigates through life trusting his instincts. He's never used a calendar to plan his time.

"At best, I've had a piece of paper with the week's practice times in my pocket," he said.

It's always here and now that matters. He's never even booked a time for a haircut.

"If I think I need a haircut, I hop in my car and go to the first available barber shop."

Simple as that.

Or is it?

"Teemu's a really good guy, a free spirit, and a wild kid," said Juha Ikonen, his junior teammate from EJK Espoo. "Like he's always been. Now he's got people sucking up to him, but every time we meet, it's like nothing's changed."

But those closest to him see also another Selanne.

Few people know him as well as twin brother Paavo and fewer have the guts to speak of him as frankly as he does. And nobody talks to him like Paavo.

"I call Teemu sometimes a little despot," he laughs.

"If things don't go the way he wants them to go, the troublemakers will get shut out, and that includes his friends' wives and girlfriends. If he doesn't like them, both will have to go," said Paavo. "He's never had to take care of anything since Sirpa has done it all. If Teemu wants to go golfing, that's what he'll do."

"There are so many things that I cannot do during the season. Normal people have no idea how disciplined a life professional athletes have to live. If I have chance to play golf, I will go," Teemu said.

His childhood friend Harri Ylonen is more sympathetic.

"If you get used to being in the middle of the hype and you see everybody always doing things for you, of course you change. That's human," he said.

His mother, Liisa, is proud of the positive side of her son's character.

"He's open, optimistic, positive, and he's got a child's faith in a better future. That's what has made the fruitful ground from which his success as a hockey player and a human being has grown," she said.

Not that Mom thinks he's perfect. "He cannot make decisions. He drives everybody crazy. He'd rather go underground for six months than say no."

Nobody knows Selanne's selfishness as well as his family.

"For example, he never told us that they were going to make a documentary film about him," said Paavo. "The camera crew just showed up one day. I suppose most people would have asked us if it was okay that we were going to be interviewed."

The younger twin was in good company in being in the dark, though. Sirpa didn't know about the film, either.

"We were flying to Finland for the summer when Teemu told us about 30 minutes before landing that a camera crew was going to meet us at the airport. It would have been nice to be a little better prepared," Sirpa said, with a laugh.

According to Waltteri Immonen, selfishness is not a trait that fits only Teemu. He is a friend of leading Formula One driver Kimi Raikkonen, and he sees similarities in both friends.

"The best top athletes have to be selfish. They would never have made it otherwise. People around them have accepted their selfishness, maybe even encouraged it. It's not a great trait in a human being but they're so focused on their sport that they don't even see it themselves," he said.

Selanne doesn't like to get deep or talk about his personal problems or issues with anybody but Sirpa. On the other hand, he also has the ability to get over negative things and move forward quickly. He's always looking forward, never back.

It's not easy for him to take criticism. He also doesn't like authority, which is why the only authority now in his life is assigned to him.

"I don't think he thanks people enough, but he does show his gratitude in other ways," said Paavo.

Over the years, Selanne has bought thousands of tickets to his games and has never made a big deal out of it. Even if a friend of a friend of a friend—often a Finnish celebrity—has needed a ticket to a game, Selanne has fixed one up for him. Players only get two complimentary tickets per game.

"Everything that's mine belongs to my friends, too," he once said.

"When I barbecue steaks and one of them isn't as good as the others, I'll eat that one myself. My friends' well-being has always been important to me."

And surely it's good to be his friend.

"He never chooses favorites between friends," said longtime friend Kari Kotivirta. "Once we were on an island to celebrate the Finnish midsummer and on our way back, Teemu wanted everybody to board his small, seven-person boat, even those who hadn't come to the island with him.

"He wanted everybody to go home together, instead of some having to take a regular ferry back, even if it meant that his boat was barely floating anymore."

The Selannes are in Finland seven weeks each summer, but they used to spend more of their summers there when the children didn't go to school. Their—or his, really—summer begins with his hockey school, where he and his Finnish Flash hockey school friends have a hotel booked.

Most of his posse follows him to Vuokatti, where the hockey school is, but for Selanne, the key is to kick off the summer with Sailynoja, Immonen, Markus Ketterer, and Syvahuoko, the same four buddies who were there the first time in 1995.

That takes 10 days out of the summer. After that comes the Bermuda Cup celebrity tennis tournament, followed by a party in Helsinki and the postparty party on Selanne's boat. He spends the tournament day with his tennis buddies, but some of the other friends and Sirpa's friends join them afterward in a Helsinki nightclub.

A third tradition is a vacation trip with another family.

During his career, he skated about three times a week in the offseason and played golf almost every day.

These days, it's easier for him to find time for riding his jet ski, playing tennis, going to the gym, swimming, hanging out, and cycling. And there are two important golf tournaments, the Children's Hospital's tournament and the Finnish Flash charity golf tournament.

Oh, and there's one more must-do: a boat trip to Kotka, Finland, to visit the annual Kotka Maritime Festival, with 200,000 other people looking to have fun.

When Teemu's there, he'll join his gang of buddies, which includes childhood friends, their partners, and friends he's made along the years. In addition to Sailynoja, Immonen, Ketterer, and Syvahuoko, only one friend has made it from his teenage years to today: Mikko Vaahtoranta.

Regardless of the lineup, one thing's for sure. Traveling with Selanne and his buddies won't be boring. In 2004, when Team Finland's chartered plane was ready to take off for a tournament in Toronto, two of his friends were missing.

"I was wondering where they were, and I called one of them," Teemu said. "He told me he was about to hit the shower. I told him it was a great joke, but that the plane was taking off in 45 minutes. I told them to get to the airport immediately.

"Finnish Ice Hockey Association president Kalervo Kummola and the players were annoyed, and the airport CEO came down to tell us to leave. Fortunately, he was a huge hockey fan, and I could play for some time and the guys made it there in time."

It wasn't just a matter of it being an annoyance to other players and the management; having a chartered plane stay grounded past its time is expensive.

"Waiting for passengers for almost an hour probably wouldn't have been possible anywhere else but in Canada, where hockey is like religion," said Selanne.

And when he walked on board with his buddies, everybody applauded, thinking he was late again.

During the summer, his boat becomes one of Helsinki's hot spots.

"One time, we were on the boat watching the Formula One Grand Prix in Hungary on TV. Right after the race, Kimi Raikkonen called me to ask me if the party was still going on," Selanne said. "I told him we were about to drive from Kotka to Helsinki. He told me he'd take the private plane to Helsinki.

"When we got back to the pier in Helsinki, the guys couldn't believe their eyes. Kimi was there and soon sitting next to them."

Selanne is also good friends with other Finnish sports stars. Tennis player Jarkko Nieminen used to visit the Selannes during the Indian Wells Masters played near Palm Springs, California, in March.

"I played tennis with him for a couple of hours once. I'll admit that I didn't have my legs in the Ducks game the next day," Teemu recalls.

Selanne is a trusting person by nature. Naturally, he's been disappointed with some friends, even close ones, but the biggest shock for him came when he moved to Winnipeg.

"I had come up through the Finnish system in which your teammates are like one big family. It was shocking to realize that I was playing with others who wanted me to fail. In the NHL, you're on your own," he said.

His image is squeaky-clean, and it's not far off the mark. He hardly ever gets very drunk, and he didn't even drink coffee until he came to Colorado in 2003.

"I sat so much on the bench and yawned that I started to drink coffee to keep awake. These days, I drink two cups in the morning and one during the day," he said.

He truly is the happy-go-lucky guy everybody talks about. He's always joking around—for example, he'll lift his T-shirt, show off his abs, and comment, "Not a bad body after four kids, right?"

He has a big presence and he rarely misses a chance to take shots at his friends.

"He's a great guy, but he also loves to fire zingers at others. He always has his eyes on somebody who becomes the target of his one-liners, but he doesn't take them out on somebody who can't handle it. Like me, I'm not much of a talker," said Harri Ylonen.

Once again, nobody knows that side of Teemu better than his twin brother.

"That's one thing that has changed," said Paavo. "I used to be the butt of all his jokes. For example, he'd give me some clothes he'd gotten from sponsors, and the next time we saw each other, he'd grab my shirt and tell that I was wearing one of his shirts. What's changed is that now he can do that to anybody in his group of friends."

Maybe the reason that has changed is that—as everybody in the group knows—Paavo is the bigger and stronger of the two. The brotherly love hasn't always been smooth sailing, and they have had their physical fights, even as adults.

"I remember one time he, once again, said something to a friend of his, and I thought he was getting too personal and out of line, so I told him that," Paavo said. "One thing led to another, we started to wrestle, and I threw him in the sea. He got angry and tried to punch me. I think he missed, but still."

Even today, if things don't go his way, he may shove Paavo. That's when the rest of the buddies go between them and hold back Paavo.

It's not easy to live a more relaxed life than he does, though. He doesn't even know the meaning of the word "stress."

"I've never been stressed out about anything. Well, in summer 1993, when I ran from event to event, I had some stomach pain," Teemu said.

———————

A man who lives in the moment, and who doesn't use a calendar, always reserves the right to change his mind. And that's why, even after he's agreed to do something the next day, he'll end the discussion with "All right, let's talk. Be in touch tomorrow."

That usually means things can change.

The friends also know something else about Selanne. "He would have been completely lost without Sirpa," said Vaahtoranta.

Sirpa and Teemu are a tight team—Teemu calls Sirpa "Sippe," Teemu is just Teemu—and they celebrated their 20th wedding anniversary in the summer of 2016. Teemu posted beautiful photos on social media, with the caption, "20 years with this amazing lady, love you! I feel very lucky. . ."

At least he knows it and recognizes his luck.

"We had our biggest crisis when I left for the NHL. It wasn't easy to be apart for so long when she was in school. Sirpa gets angry quickly, but she also cools down just as quickly. Our fights, if we have them, are always short ones," he said.

They still cuddle and kiss each other like they did when they first met.

"We both think touching each other makes us feel closer to each other. I think you have to show your emotions, both your love and your jealousy, not that the latter has been a big problem lately, although it raised its ugly head in 2014 when Teemu suddenly got hot again," Sirpa said.

"The Sochi tournament made Teemu more popular than ever. I don't think he's ever had as many people, especially women and girls, follow him around as he did then," she added.

Sirpa has taken care of Teemu and their children as she has grown from an insecure teenage girl into an independent woman, a mother, and a wife. She's been her husband's confidant, assistant, and driver. She also leads her own life, which lacks the glamor many people imagine her having. Her feet are firmly on the ground.

"Of course we have a lot more money than many other people, but we try to be sensible about it and we try to teach our kids that you have to work for it," she said.

"Sirpa, Veera, and I travel in business class, but the boys are in economy," he added.

On the other hand, during the last half of his career, Selanne put more emphasis on his chances to win the Cup and being happy in California than chasing the biggest paycheck.

"I didn't care about the money during my last nine seasons," he said.

Money doesn't bring happiness, but it does make some things easier.

"I've always wanted to spread happiness around me, and my family gets to enjoy my wealth. My parents always flew in business class, and they could use credit cards I got them. And all my charity work is a way for me to give back and show my gratitude," he said.

The boys—Eemil, Eetu, and Leevi—are now responsible young men.

"They respect Teemu and they understand why he's been away so much," Sirpa said. "To Veera, Teemu is the most important man in the world. She helps me rein him in when needed."

"Our children mean the world to me, and we're so lucky to have them," Selanne said. "It's been interesting to see how different they are, and yet, they're all such great people in their own ways. They have made our lives richer more than anything else."

Eemil Jalo Ilmari was named after Teemu's maternal grandfather. Jalo is a name they liked and Ilmari, obviously, is Teemu's father's name.

Eetu Nikodemus "looked like an Eetu when he was born." Teemu is a diminutive of Nikodemus.

For Leevi Samuel, Leevi was Sirpa's favorite uncle's name and Samuel a name she liked.

Teemu and Sirpa liked the way the name Veera looks, and Johanna is Sirpa's middle name.

Both Sirpa's and Teemu's parents and siblings have been a big part of their lives, and Sirpa and her mother-in-law, Liisa, had a close relationship.

Kirsi, Ilmari's wife, has also been an important person in Teemu's and Sirpa's lives, even if Teemu is still upset with how Kirsi was pushed away early on.

"She had nothing to do with the divorce," he said.

Selanne, in turn, got to know Sirpa's parents well when the young couple lived in their house early on, and now the extended family from that side includes Sirpa's two sisters' six children.

Liisa and Terttu, the grandmothers, were best friends.

"We're like sisters, and Sirpa is like my own daughter. I've noticed that it's not always like that," Liisa said back in 2014.

And then there was their dog, Theodor von Flaschenburg, or Teddy, who joined Selanne and Sirpa in Winnipeg in 1993, having traveled from Finland to Canada with Sirpa's father, Erkki. Theodor stayed with Teemu and Erkki for a couple months before Sirpa arrived with her mother, Terttu.

When Selanne picked them up at the airport, he told Sirpa they could take Terttu back to their place so she could be with her husband while Sirpa and Teemu would stay at a hotel for the night.

"I thought it was wonderful that he wanted to spend the night alone with me. In the morning, when we woke up, Teemu told me he was going to pick up the paper from the lobby. That sounded odd to me. I mean, he never reads the paper," Sirpa said.

When the door opened again, in came Theodor, a rottweiler puppy with a red ribbon around his neck, wondering where he was.

The name, Teddy, had strong echoes of the English translation of his rally car–driving pseudonym, Teddy Flash.

Selanne has always had a soft spot for animals.

The next year, Teddy got company in Thunder von Domi, or just Domi, named after Jets tough guy and Selanne buddy Tie Domi, of course.

"I had a hard time coming up with a good name but when I picked him up, he threw up, pooped, and peed in the car, and since I thought his head was quite large, I realized he was just like Domi," Teemu said with a chuckle.

When Tie Domi heard about his namesake, he drove over to Selanne's place to have a look.

"He was furious, and I had to lie to him and tell him that in Finland it's a huge honor to have a friend name his dog after you. That calmed him down," Selanne said.

The dogs, Teddy and Domi, died a year apart, in 2005 and 2006, respectively. The Selannes are dog people, and in the fall of 2006, they welcomed their new rottweilers, Rocky and Roxy, to the family. Four years later, Veera got her Tibetan Spaniel, Niki.

Rocky died in 2017 and Roxy in 2018. Teemu and Sirpa added a new rottweiler, Stella, and later Simba, a mix of Seefer and Boucheron, joined the family.

They have also had numerous horses and cats. The first horse was Enzo, who died in 2011. They bought Rambo when they moved to Coto de Caza in 2000. They also have two of their friends' horses at their stables to keep Rambo company.

"We also had the world's most expensive cat, Angel," Teemu said.

In June 2007, when the Selannes were celebrating the Ducks' Stanley Cup win, the gates at their home were open all night. In the morning, they found Angel's bloody body in Roxy's bed in the garage. Their first instinct was to think the dogs had injured the cat, but Teemu didn't believe they could have done it. He just hurried to take Angel to the vet.

"The doctor said right away that it looked like a coyote bite. Apparently, they go for the hind legs first. Our dogs had chased the coyotes away but a little too late. And then Roxy had carried Angel into his bed in the garage," he said.

Meanwhile, Sirpa had already given the boys a speech about the circle of life and how dogs and cats aren't always friends. Then Selanne called her and told her it had been a coyote and that the dogs had most likely saved Angel's life.

The boys, then 11, 9, and 7, asked their father if he could play one more year so that they could afford the operation that would save Angel.

They could afford two operations.

"It cost us $15,000," he said.

Angel survived and returned to Coto de Caza, but she died six months later.

The Selannes have also had two other cats, Charlie and Tiger, but both of them have disappeared mysteriously.

"Probably the coyotes have taken them," Teemu said sadly.

Aside from animals, tennis and golf are Teemu's passions. And golf is something he can do with the whole family.

"The first time I played golf was in Winnipeg. They asked me if I shot from left or right. I didn't know. Probably right, I said. I had never held a club in my hand before," he said.

He took with him two clubs and followed the group to the course.

"They asked me where my bag was. I told them I didn't need one since I had the two clubs with me. Everybody laughed."

Ilmari brought him a golf bag from Africa and even bought him a full set of clubs, but he didn't bite.

"Tennis was everything to me. I told Jari Kurri that I'd pick up golf the day when I couldn't hit a moving ball anymore. He just told me to wait."

Kurri was right. Selanne took to golf and became an avid player. He even caddied for Finnish pro Mikko Ilonen during the Par 3 Contest prior to the start of the Masters at Augusta National Golf Club in April 8, 2015. "I was very honored to caddie my good friend Mikko. I had always wanted to go there. And what a year it was. That was just a taste of Augusta."

Two weeks later he was back at Augusta, which is one of the most famous golf courses in the world. Playing the famed course fulfilled a dream for Teemu.

"Henry and Susan Samueli, the owners of the Anaheim Ducks, were wondering what to give me as a gift when my number was retired. Ryan Getzlaf had suggested a trip to Augusta. And yes, it was an incredibly wonderful gift and experience. It was a dream come true," Teemu said.

Augusta is golfer's paradise where it's almost impossible to get to play. You cannot apply to join Augusta National; you can only be invited to join, and the Samuelis were able to give Teemu what you could call the perfect retirement gift.

Teemu was allowed to invite two friends to join him. "The first choice was easy. Mike Pagano is like a brother to me. In addition, I called Rick Booth, one of my best golfing friends. We were there three days and it was amazing," Teemu said.

Pagano is a former US Marine pilot who flew the F/A-18 Hornet fighter jet for 20 years. "We became good friends right in 1996 when I came to Anaheim to play. I got to fly to the Hornet simulator, and Mike, who is from Buffalo, was the leader of the simulator. We both like golf and speed. Mike lives in San Diego, and we and our families spend a lot of time together."

Selanne's passion for golf was the impetus for him to open a golf academy in Finland, along with Finnish pro Mika Piltz. The Selanne & Piltz Golf Academy opened in 2015, one year before the hockey-focused Selanne Academy.

"I want to do everything where my passions are. I encourage young people to follow the career of a top athlete. I mentor them; I help them build the confidence that can carry them to the top. When I am at the camps in the summer when I am back in Finland, I don't sit in the stands and watch the kids. I play with the students and explain what it takes to play sports at a high level. One of the most important things they need to know is how to deal with bad days when things don't go the way you want," Teemu said.

"Golf is such a challenging sport. You hit one shot right down the middle of the fairway, and then you flub the next shot. You can hit 73 today and 89 tomorrow. There are so many things to consider. I don't know of any other sport as challenging.

"My dream is to play all the top 100 courses in America. I also want to see all the major Grand Slam tournaments in golf and tennis. Up to now, I have seen the Masters in golf one time and I have been to Wimbledon for tennis twice," Teemu said.

Selanne also enjoys his car collection and has plans to build a garage for 20 cars. He's always had a passion for driving cars, as well as buying and selling cars, ever since that yellow 1976 Ford Escort he had when he was a teenager.

"A mark of a great car is that you can feel every single stone on the road in your buttocks," Teemu said.

His second car was a big American car, the red 1961 Lincoln Continental he used to pick up Sirpa (and for the Jokerit championship parade), and his third car a white 1979 Ford Escort RS 2000—in which Sirpa backed into his boat that was sitting on their yard in Espoo.

"She's the only person I know who's had a car accident with a boat," he said with a laugh.

Since then, he has collected dozens of cars, from Ferraris to Mercedes-Benzes, most of which he's found with the help of a California-based fellow Finn, Simo Veharanta. And, of course, he still has that Lincoln.

"I remember early on, we were in a burger place after a Jets-Kings game, and before anyone had had time to order food, Teppo Numminen had ordered a Mercedes from me. Jari Kurri did the same right after, and then Teemu said he wanted a 1964 Mercedes convertible and a 1968 Corvette. Then we ordered burgers," Veharanta said with a smile.

In the 1980s, when Selanne was still living in Finland, he was a regular sight at car cruising events and attended drag races. And of course, he drove in rallies himself, with Kai Eklund as his copilot. Eklund's first race was in 1986, and Teemu raced his first in 1993, an unofficial race in Finland.

Selanne graduated to bigger races and in 1995 he drove the pace car at one Finnish rally, and ended up in a ditch.

A month later, he raced in the Jyvaskyla World Cup rally, with Pekka Huolman as his copilot.

"He was very calm, and focused on my notes," said Huolman.

Their car broke down on the second day, and he had to drop out.

In 1996, the World Cup of Hockey kept him from returning to Jyvaskyla but in 1997 he was back. "Teddy Flash" and Pekka Huolman finished in 33rd place and 12th in Group N, reserved for standard production vehicles.

In 1998, he had the chance to drive a real cannon of a car when Marcus Gronholm, a Finnish two-time world champion, arranged for him to use the Spanish world champion Carlos Sainz's car, which Sainz had driven in a race just a few months earlier.

"It was my first world rally specification car. It was wild. I just wanted to drive more and more," Selanne said.

And he drove well, on par with the best of the young drivers in his class. On the 16th leg, the longest and most difficult one, he finished 29th and made a record-long 52-meter jump.

"It was a mistake but fortunately, we landed safely."

He finished 24th, an incredible feat considering he was an amateur. And while he could have put the pedal to the metal and driven a lot faster, he didn't. He did not take any big risks, and the experts later wondered how he would have done had he given the rally a chance.

The year after that, he had that big accident in Tampere, which also ended his rally career. Not that it had been the first accident for him.

He had his first one right after he received his driver's license when he and a couple of friends wanted to get something to eat late at night. He drove fast—too fast—because he was running out of gas and he wanted to get the speed up so he could then just cruise to the gas station in neutral. But when he switched to neutral, he somehow put it into reverse instead.

"The wheels jammed, and the car flipped over four times, ending up in the ditch. Something was wrong with the gearbox, you shouldn't even be able to do that. Had we had seatbelts on, we would have died. Now we all ended up on the car's floor, and that saved us since the car was completely flattened."

Selanne was fined and one of the buddies had to get physical therapy for his back problems, but other than that, they got off with only a scare.

The third big accident made the biggest headlines, and he wasn't even involved in it.

In 2006, he and his friends had been at a beer festival in Tallinn, Estonia, and the Hanko regatta in Finland. On their way back to Helsinki, he stopped at their house, while the rest of the 23-man-strong posse continued their journey toward Helsinki.

Around midnight, the boat ran aground outside Helsinki. The guy driving the boat focused on making sure everybody was safe, and he navigated to another pier with the help of the bow thrusters. But the 17-meter boat took in so much water that it sank just feet from the pier.

Selanne was questioned for turning the boat over to an unqualified captain, and after a couple of years in the Finnish court system, both he and his friend were found not guilty of negligence. However, they had already been convicted in the court of public opinion.

"It was one of the cases that made me lose faith in Finnish media. The way the accident was handled in the papers was unfair and sensationalist," Teemu said.

He sold the boat and the next summer bought the boat he still owns, a Sunseeker 74 Manhattan called "Lucky Eight."

Teemu was just 18 years old when he visited the Winnipeg Jets' training camp for the first time and did some charity work for the franchise.

"I realized how good it feels to help others," he said.

One of the best programs he saw there was the Jets' Goals for Kids, in which a sponsor made a donation to a children's hospital for each goal its player scored.

"It was a fantastic idea," he said.

It helps if you are a prolific goal scorer.

In 1993–94, he had a deal with Pizza Hut in which the company paid $600 for each goal he scored.

"Teemu's goal total came up to $15,000, but what did Teemu do? He matched Pizza Hut's donation because his injury kept him at 25 goals," said Lori Summers, who led the program for the Jets.

Since then, Teemu has become one of the most famous workers for charities in Finland, having founded the Association of Friends of the University Children's Hospitals. The association's teddy bear mascot is obviously named "Teemu."

Over the years, Teemu has met hundreds of sick children. He has invited them to his games, visited the Helsinki children's hospital several times every year, and made numerous donations to the kids—most of them behind the scenes.

Early on, when he scored a hat trick in the NHL, he had all the caps fans threw onto the ice sent to the patients at the children's hospital. The annual Bermuda Cup tennis tournament raises money for the children's hospital, as well.

"The best feedback is when the nurses tell me that a young boy or girl hasn't needed pain medication for a few days after my visit," he said. "One kid had told his friend about meeting me at the hospital and the friend had told him he wanted to get sick, too. I've wanted to help make the hospital a place where exciting and good things can happen, too."

He knows he is the kids' role model and his will to help is genuine.

"When I became involved with the children's hospital in the early 1990s, I thought it was just plain wrong that the hospitals didn't have the equipment they needed," he said. "Every child deserves the opportunity to lead a good life.

"Everybody should pay a visit to a children's hospital at least once to remind themselves to be happy with their lives."

He has stayed involved with the charity work even though his NHL career has ended.

"If we can save one kid, it's worth all the work," he said.

Selanne also has his own Finnish Flash charity organization, which got started when he received invitations from dozens of hockey schools to be their star instructor.

"It was really hard for me to say no to all of them and then Immonen, Sailynoja, Ketterer, and I realized that it was smarter for us to have our own hockey school. That way, we could just say that we put all our attention to that one," he said.

Immonen knew a Nokia executive who, in turn, helped find corporate partners. The core activity of the Finnish Flash organization is still the hockey school, which was held for the 25th time in 2019.

"We want to raise money for youth, female, and disabled athletes. We've organized sports marketing seminars, charity games, and Finnish Flash golf tournaments," Selanne said.

"Everything, even having fun, becomes even more fun when you add an element of charity into it."

His career earnings were $76,857,790, not including a few million he received as bonuses and a few million he made through his sponsorship deals.

Selanne's contract included bonuses for winning or being a finalist for the Hart Trophy, making the First or Second All-Star Team, and finishing in the top four in scoring. Hitting a bonus could add another $500,000 on to his salary, and the best part was the bonuses were added to his base salary for the following season. "Hitting two of the bonus thresholds would add $1 million to the salary for next season," he said. But hitting a bonus wasn't a priority for Selanne. He did not want to compete against a teammate in the scoring race. His priority was winning the Stanley Cup.

Selanne could have made even more money had he chased a bigger paycheck, but staying in Anaheim was more important to him. He was good for the Ducks both as a productive player on the ice and as a salary cap tool. Since Teemu wanted to stay and since he was over 35, the Ducks could pay him bonuses that didn't count against the salary cap.

Czech winger Jaromir Jagr is the all-time leader in NHL career earnings, with more than $130 million. Chris Pronger and Nicklas Lidstrom are currently the other two, with earnings over $100 million, but there will be others.

The Pittsburgh Penguins' Sidney Crosby and the Washington Capitals' Alexander Ovechkin are both in the middle of contracts worth more than $100 million, and when Montreal Canadiens defenseman Shea Weber's contract expires in 2026, he will have made $110 million on his last contract alone.

Teemu paid about 45 percent of his income in taxes and five percent as agent's fees.

"We got the paycheck every two weeks. I got 10 percent; the rest went directly into savings and investments," he said. "My love for cars has been the only extravagance I've really had. I'm always looking for new cars and selling my old ones."

Not even millions of dollars in taxes paid have made life in the US easy for a foreigner. "I'm supposed to get the green card automatically in the mail, but I've always had to do a lot of paperwork to get it," he said.

Selanne has settled into retirement with great ease.

Teemu and Sirpa enjoy living in Coto de Caza, which is one of Orange County's oldest and most expensive master-planned communities. Coto de Caza was the site of the riding, running, shooting, and fencing components of the modern pentathlon event at the 1984 Los Angeles Olympic Games and most recently gained fame as the site for the reality television show *The Real Housewives of Orange County*.

He and Sirpa listed their six-acre estate for sale early in 2018 and were planning to build a smaller home in the community.

Teemu plays tennis four to five times a week, with friends in tournaments and a local tennis league. When he's not on the tennis court, you can probably find him on the golf course.

"I love it when there are no commitments," he said. "From eight in the morning to about two in the afternoon, I can do whatever I want. Then, when I come home, we have things to do."

"We travel. We go see Eetu, who is playing hockey at Northeastern. We take ski trips." Life, for the most part, is good.

In May 2018, Teemu and his family met with grief.

Teemu was on a golf trip in Palm Springs with friends Joe Sakic, Mike Pagano, and Otto Aichinger when he woke up in the morning and saw that Paavo had left both a text message and a voicemail on his cell.

"I first heard a voice message," Teemu said. "Paavo wept and said he had very bad news. Mom was in the hospital and may not be able to survive. Please call."

Liisa had knee surgery and there were complications: a blood clot formed, and damage spread to the lungs, heart, and brain.

"It was the biggest shock of my life. It felt like the world stopped."

Liisa hadn't told Teemu that she was going to have knee replacement surgery. She knew Teemu and Ismo Syvahuoko, who was also a very good friend of the extended Selanne family, would have told her not to hurry, and to get another opinion about the procedure.

"However, her knees were in such poor condition that her quality of life suffered badly from them. He wanted to cut them both at one time and before the summer," Teemu said. "Unfortunately, the surgery was done at a small medical center in Porvoo, about 50 kilometers from Helsinki, where there was no support for any such unexpected situations. If the surgery had been done in Helsinki, maybe the situation wouldn't have been so bad."

Liisa's surgery had gone well, and she had already walking with the help of a stroller.

"Then, when she went to physiotherapy to get instructions for rehabilitation, she suddenly said things did not feel right. Then she collapsed on the floor."

Teemu rushed back to his home and arrangements were being made to travel to Finland when they received a message from the hospital that the situation was a little better.

"Unfortunately, this wasn't true," Teemu said.

Just as they were boarding the plane for the flight to Helsinki, Teemu received a text from Paavo: "Don't wait for miracles. Mom won't survive."

"Fortunately, we arrived in time at the hospital to say goodbye and say thanks to her and be with her in her final moments. It was the worst day of my life. It felt so wrong that such a wonderful person was taken away in this way."

No matter your age, it is never easy losing a parent. Liisa was 81.

"It is inconceivable how she always had time for others. I miss her, we all miss her very much," Teemu said. "It was a very sad day. It is still sad. I don't think you can ever recover from losing your loved one, but especially your mom.

"There has not been a single day I have not thought about her."

Teemu is a familiar face around Southern California, where he has redefined himself as a restaurateur. Selanne Steak Tavern in Laguna Beach is a popular dinner spot with a 4.5-star rating on Yelp.

He's given up on rally-car driving. "I was driving rally cars a couple years ago and decided, you know what, there is too much risk. It takes so much time to prepare. When I was young there is no fear. I had that accident, such a stupid misunderstanding and it almost cost everyone their life."

Selanne remains a force in his native Finland, where Ari Lehto has been his business manager for more than a decade. They got to know each other in 1999 through Lehto's involvement in the Finnish Flash charity work, as the representative of his employer, BMW.

"I had wanted to get into real estate and construction business. Designing houses has always been close to my heart, and Ari had good connections there. He took on the project management of our new house in Hila," Teemu said.

In 2004, they founded TS Holding Oy, and Lehto became its full-time employee and Selanne's manager.

After a few acquisitions and investments, Teemu has consolidated his businesses under TS Invest, which is owned by TS Holding. Investors include former and current NHL players Niklas Backstrom, Valtteri Filppula, Jori Lehtera, Ville Leino, Antti Miettinen, Antti Niemi, Pekka Rinne, Tuomo Ruutu, Kimmo Timonen, Olli Jokinen, Jere Lehtinen, and Ville Nieminen.

"I know how easy it is to get involved with buddies' companies without thinking too much, and we decided to give people a chance to invest in a serious real estate development company," he said.

Selanne acquired a share of a company named Ultivista, in 2007, and it has grown into a midsized company.

Then there is the Finnish Flash Foundation, which donates money to youth sports and pays for equipment for kids in need of support.

Turn the subject to hockey, and Teemu becomes animated. He may be retired, but his heart remains in the coolest game on ice.

Selanne takes great pride in having represented Finland in six Olympic Games, and he feels the National Hockey League is making a big mistake if it does not allow players to compete at the 2022 Beijing Winter Games.

"My first Olympic Games was Albertville [France, in 1992] and it was amateur-level hockey," he said. "The next one was Nagano [Japan, in 1998], when all the best players were there, and you could feel it was something really special."

Selanne represented his country at the 2002 Salt Lake Games, at which time the media wondered whether that was his Winter Olympics swan song.

"I said there was no way I was going to play in Torino in 2006 and I ended up playing in Torino, Vancouver [2010], and Sochi [2014]. It just shows how much fun it was for me."

The 2014 Sochi Winter Games was his sixth appearance at the Olympic Games, and he went out in fine style. The 43-year-old became the oldest player to win a medal in Olympic hockey when the Finns took the bronze. He was named most valuable player of the Olympic tournament as selected by the media and added six points to his Olympic record career total of 24 goals and 19 assists for 43 points in 37 games to set the Olympic record for most points.

Teemu's Olympic medal collection includes a silver medal from the 2006 Torino Winter Games, and bronze from the 1998 Games in Nagano, 2010 Games in Vancouver, and 2014 Games in Sochi.

"We all knew each other right away and we knew who is going to play with who," he said, referring to his Olympic tenure. "There is no competition about the spots. Everybody knows their role and accepts their spots and they do as best as they can."

"We knew we did not have the skill like other teams, but we knew also if we worked harder we might have a chance. We knew we can't beat every big country, but we can surprise people. That is why in Torino, we beat Canada and we beat the USA, we beat Russia, we beat the Czechs. And then our worst game was against Sweden. I think we just ran out of gas, but that tournament was the first time in my national team career we were better than everyone," Teemu said.

Finland definitely punches above its weight class on the world stage. Finland has approximately one-tenth the number of male hockey players as Canada, according to the International Ice Hockey Federation's 2018 player survey.

There were a record 43 Finns who have made NHL rosters in the 2018–19, and that marked the first time there were more Finns in the league than Russians.

Selanne and Jari Kurri were the exceptions to the rule when you look historically at the role Finns have played on NHL teams. Finns were typically grinders or third-line players—the type of players general managers love because of their tireless work ethic.

A decade ago, a majority of the Finns in the NHL were 25 years old or older, but that's since come full circle. The latest wave of Finns are Selanne-type clones—young guns who can skate and score. It is an impressive group that includes Patrik Laine of the Winnipeg Jets, Aleksander Barkov of the Florida Panthers, Colorado winger Mikko Rantanen, Carolina center Sebastian Aho, Toronto right winger Kasperi Kapanen, and Montreal center Jesperi Kotkaniemi. And while he's not a scorer, Dallas defenseman Miro Heiskanen has made people take note of his potential.

What led to the change was a 2009 hockey summit by the Finnish Ice Hockey Association during which the country's top hockey minds took a hard look at every aspect of hockey development in the country.

Teemu welcomed the new approach to player development.

"The thing is, in early 2000, Finnish hockey decided to create the same kind of player personality, and it did not work. And they did research that said they, individually, were not so good. We work hard as a team, but other teams are way ahead of us in individual skills and goal scoring. Then they started focusing on individual skills," Teemu said.

Selanne is doing his part to foster individual skills. The prime goal of the Selanne Academy is to develop scorers. Twice a year, the Selanne Academy welcomes the top forwards from Finland's national U16 team for a week-long session on scoring drills. The country's top U16 teenagers are given clinics and sit through video presentations from Finland's most prolific scorer in history.

"I try to teach them how to think in different situations. How many chances do you get in a game? If you get four, that is unbelievable, but if you don't practice, scoring comes so quickly so if it is not body memory, muscle memory, you can't do it.

"It is unbelievable in that one year how much better they have become. It is so much fun and they all want to learn to score the goals. I like to give back. That is my biggest passion," Teemu said.

Selanne makes himself available to the Ducks for promotional purposes and assisted ownership to convince his close friend Paul Kariya to have his jersey raised to the rafters alongside his.

"He did not want to do the jersey retirement. The owner called, and he said no. General manager Bob Murray called, and he said no. So, then they called me, and they said, 'Teemu, you are the only guy who he might listen to.' I called him for three months and he said no for the first two. He said, 'Stop calling me, I do not deserve this, and I said, 'Bullshit.'

"Finally, I said, 'I am not calling you anymore, but you should do this for me. Our numbers should be up there forever, and I will be a sad man if you don't do this.' He said, 'Let me think about it.'"

Teemu was on hand for the ceremony on October 21, 2018. He promised not to roast Kariya, but then joked about seeing his future teammate at an awards ceremony in 1993 for the first time and wondering, "Who is that little boy?"

The teams for which Teemu has the fondest memories of playing over his 26-year professional career are Jokerit, the Winnipeg Jets and Anaheim Ducks, and Finland's national team. All have left a big mark on his heart.

"Jokerit was like family for me. The story was perfect. The Jets brand was already important to me before my NHL career, because there had been a lot of Finnish star players during the years before my time. And the way the Ducks took care of me was a unique experience," he said.

"Playing for the national team was like being part of a big family. Kalervo Kummola, chairman of the Finnish Ice Hockey Association, was like a father for us, and it was great to be and play in 'Kummola's mafia.' I am very proud of our small nation's success. And, of course, the greatest honor for a Finn is to pull on his national team shirt," Teemu said.

"I'm really happy that I was able to start my NHL career in Winnipeg, which is a true hockey town. It was great to be involved in a city with such passion for hockey and for their Jets. After all, it's totally incomprehensible how the whole city adopted us and the team, and it was amazing the impact I had on them in my four seasons as a Jet. It was mutual love. And after 20 years, every time I go to Winnipeg, the emotions are huge, and even though the Jets' original organization moved to Phoenix, the current Jets organization has respected my work as if I were their own son. I appreciate it very much," Selanne said.

"Anaheim has become my second home. The relationship between the Ducks organization and me is really strong, and it is a two-way relationship. The mutual loyalty and respect is strong. And I was able to play for many years with Paul Kariya and finally won the Stanley Cup in Anaheim, which became the crown of my career."

Will there ever be another player like Selanne?

When he retired in 2014, he was a full-fledged pro who did everything in his power to be the best that he could be. What drove him?

"Until my major knee surgery in 2004, I had basically just been cruising. Everything came easy to me. I didn't think about nutrition or recovery times or alcohol use. That surgery marked the beginning of the last period of my career and I realized I would have to start to work, and work hard," he said.

Not that Teemu hadn't worked hard in the past; he had always taken training seriously. But he became a more complete athlete.

"Until then, I had been out partying somewhere every summer weekend. If I was hungry, I ate three burgers, and if I still was hungry, I ate three more, with fries. Later, I would still hang out with my friends, but I was more careful with nutrition, and made sure I got enough sleep.

"I've never drunk alcohol on the night before a game. For example, in Winnipeg, many of my teammates got drunk after each game, even if we played again the following night. Now, if we had a day off, I could go out. In the last nine seasons, I never got drunk during the season," he said.

What was the secret? How could he play in the NHL until he was 43?

"I knew how to live in the now. I enjoyed every moment of it."

For many fans, especially in Finland, Teemu has been the only reason to follow the NHL, or sports in general. He's always been a special case. He's one of the few athletes who is on a first-name basis with the world, like Serena or Tiger or LeBron.

Of course, fame and success have had their price. In his case, he paid with his knees.

The secret of his long career is partly genetic; he was born fast, and he's always had the endurance. But even more importantly, he's always loved to train.

He's always been ambitious, and he put in the hours to become the best.

"I've had to pay a price for my success, but I don't really think about it that way. If you can make things fun, nothing feels too hard," he said.

Selanne stayed at the top of the hockey world for more than 20 years, which is remarkable, considering that the average length of an NHL career is about four years.

When Kariya was asked about the impact Selanne had on him, he didn't pause for a second before he responded. "He has made me a better person."

Will there ever be another Teemu Selanne? Will hockey fans ever get the thrill of seeing another Ferrari on skates?

"There may be someone who passes Teemu someday, but there won't be his equal," said Brian Burke. "The Finnish Flash was truly what he was. He was worth the price of a ticket and there are not too many players you can say that about."

What does Selanne think? Will there be a second Finnish Flash?

"I think the right answer is probably no," Teemu said. "On the ice, yes. Off the ice, maybe."

"It was a unique journey, for sure."

TEEMU SELANNE CAREER STATISTICS, AWARDS, AND ACHIEVEMENTS

Career Statistics

Season	Team	League	Regular Season		
			GP	G	A
1987-88	Jokerit Helsinki	FinD1	5	1	1
1988-89	Jokerit Helsinki	FinD1	35	36	33
1989-90	Jokerit Helsinki	SM-liiga	11	4	8
1990-91	Jokerit Helsinki	SM-liiga	42	33	25
1991-92	Jokerit Helsinki	SM-liiga	44	39	23
1992-93	Winnipeg Jets	NHL	84	76	56
1993-94	Winnipeg Jets	NHL	51	25	29
1994-95	Winnipeg Jets	NHL	45	22	26
1994-95	Jokerit Helsinki	SM-liiga	20	7	12
1995-96	Winnipeg Jets	NHL	51	24	48
1995-96	Anaheim Mighty Ducks	NHL	28	16	20
1996-97	Anaheim Mighty Ducks	NHL	78	51	58
1997-98	Anaheim Mighty Ducks	NHL	73	52	34
1998-99	Anaheim Mighty Ducks	NHL	75	47	60
1999-00	Anaheim Mighty Ducks	NHL	79	33	52
2000-01	Anaheim Mighty Ducks	NHL	61	26	33
2000-01	San Jose Sharks	NHL	12	7	6
2001-02	San Jose Sharks	NHL	82	29	25
2002-03	San Jose Sharks	NHL	82	28	36
2003-04	Colorado Avalanche	NHL	78	16	16
2005-06	Anaheim Mighty Ducks	NHL	80	40	50
2006-07	Anaheim Ducks	NHL	82	48	46
2007-08	Anaheim Ducks	NHL	26	12	11
2008-09	Anaheim Ducks	NHL	65	27	27
2009-10	Anaheim Ducks	NHL	54	27	21
2010-11	Anaheim Ducks	NHL	73	31	49
2011-12	Anaheim Ducks	NHL	82	26	40
2012-13	Anaheim Ducks	NHL	46	12	12
2013-14	Anaheim Ducks	NHL	64	9	18
		NHL Totals	1451	684	773
		SM-liiga totals	117	83	68

| Pts | PIM | +/- | Playoffs | | | | |
			GP	G	A	Pts	PIM
2	0	1					
69	14	33					
12	0		--	--	--	--	--
58	12	13	--	--	--	--	--
62	20		10	10	7	17	18
132	45	8	6	4	2	6	2
54	22	-23	--	--	--	--	--
48	2	1	--	--	--	--	--
19	6	3	--	--	--	--	--
72	18	3	--	--	--	--	--
36	4	2	--	--	--	--	--
109	34	28	11	7	3	10	4
86	30	12	--	--	--	--	--
107	30	18	4	2	2	4	2
85	12	6	--	--	--	--	--
59	36	-8	--	--	--	--	--
13	0	1	6	0	2	2	2
54	40	-11	12	5	3	8	2
64	30	-6	--	--	--	--	--
32	32	2	10	0	3	3	2
90	44	28	16	6	8	14	6
94	82	26	21	5	10	15	10
23	8	5	6	2	2	4	6
54	36	-3	13	4	2	6	4
48	16	3	--	--	--	--	--
80	49	6	6	6	1	7	12
66	50	-1	--	--	--	--	--
24	28	-10	7	1	2	3	6
27	12	8	12	2	4	6	4
1457	660		130	44	44	88	62
151	38		10	10	7	17	18

Tournaments

Year	Team	Event	GP	G	A	Pts	PIM
1988	Finland	IIHF European Junior Championships	6	7	9	16	8
1989	Finland	IIHF World Junior Championships	7	5	5	10	10
1991	Finland	Ice Hockey World Championships	10	6	5	11	2
1991	Finland	Canada Cup	6	1	1	2	2
1992	Finland	Olympics	8	7	4	11	6
1996	Finland	Ice Hockey World Championships	6	5	3	8	0
1996	Finland	World Cup of Hockey	4	3	2	5	0
1998	Finland	Olympics	5	4	6	10	8
1999	Finland	Ice Hockey World Championships	11	3	8	11	2
2002	Finland	Olympics	4	3	0	3	2
2003	Finland	Ice Hockey World Championships	7	8	3	11	2
2004	Finland	World Cup of Hockey	6	1	3	4	4
2006	Finland	Olympics	8	6	5	11	4
2008	Finland	Ice Hockey World Championships	9	3	4	7	12
2010	Finland	Olympics	6	0	2	2	0
2014	Finland	Olympics	6	4	2	6	4
Senior Totals			96	54	48	102	48

Medals

Olympic Games

Silver	2006 Turin
Bronze	1998 Nagano
Bronze	2010 Vancouver
Bronze	2014 Sochi

World Championships

Silver	1999 Norway
Bronze	2008 Canada

Canada Cup / World Cup

Silver	2004 Toronto
Bronze	1991 Hamilton

IIHF European Junior Championships

Silver	1988 Czechoslovakia

Awards and Achievements

Year	League	Award
1990–91	SM-liiga	Raimo Kilpio Trophy
1990–91; 1991 –92	SM-liiga	SM-liiga All-Star Team
1991–92	SM-liiga	Aarne Honkavaara Trophy
1991–92	SM-liiga	SM-liiga Champion

Year	League	Award
1992–93	NHL	Calder Memorial Trophy
1992–93	NHL	NHL All-Rookie Team
1992–93; 1996–97	NHL	First Team All-Star
1993–94; 1996–00; 2002–03; 2007	NHL	NHL All-Star Game
1998–99	NHL	Maurice "Rocket" Richard Trophy
2005–06	NHL	Bill Masterton Memorial Trophy
2006–07	NHL	Stanley Cup Champion
2006–07	NHL	Clarence S. Campbell Bowl
2015	NHL	Anaheim Ducks No. 8 jersey retired

Year	League	Award
1988	International	EJC All-Star Team
1994–95	International	IIHF European Cup Champion (Jokerit)

Year	League	Award
1999	International	World Championship Most Valuable Player
1999	International	World Championship All-Star Team
2006	International	Best Forward of the Olympic Games
2006, 2014	International	Olympic All-Star Team
2014	International	Most Valuable Player of the Olympic Games
2017	International	IIHF's Hall of Fame
2017	International	Hockey Hall of Fame

Career Records

Record	Total
NHL record most goals by a rookie	76, 1992–93
NHL record most points by a rookie	132, 1992–93
NHL record, most goals by a Finnish-born player, career	684
WPG/ARI franchise record most goals, single season	76, 1992–93
WPG/ARI franchise record most points, single season	132, 1992–93
WPG/ARI franchise record consecutive games with a goal	9, March 15 – April 1, 1993
Anaheim franchise record most goals, career	457
Anaheim franchise record most goals, single season	52, 1997–98
Anaheim franchise record most assists, career	531
Anaheim franchise record most points, career	988
Anaheim franchise record most points, single season	109, 1996–97
Anaheim franchise record most power play goals, career	182
Anaheim franchise record most power play assists, career	224 (as of 2019–20)

Record	Total
Anaheim franchise record most power play points, career	402 (as of 2019–20)
Anaheim franchise record most games played, career	966
Anaheim franchise record most hat tricks, career	13
Anaheim franchise record consecutive games with a goal	11, October 21 – November 10, 1997
Anaheim franchise record most assists, single game	5, three times
Most points in Olympic competition, career	43